He dreams of soil carpeted
with needles of red spruce.

She's more a lichen type.
With a passion for reindeer
moss that goes kkr*iishh!*
when crushed underfoot.
Like tearing open Velcro.

They've been living forever
in a three-room, basement
flat, the walls so mouldy
they're decomposing.

Going there at night, squashed together in souped-up cars, no mufflers, extra loud, windows decorated with stickers in Gothic lettering, bodies spray-painted sooty black by mechanics in the family.

Everything in these vehicles was geared to the adrenaline rush of the guys sitting in the cockpit.

Guzzling cans of Budweiser after the usual smoke show. Listening to the kids raucously shrieking in their drunken stupor. Sensing how desire plays havoc with your whole body at the drop of a hat, every pore closing, shivering.

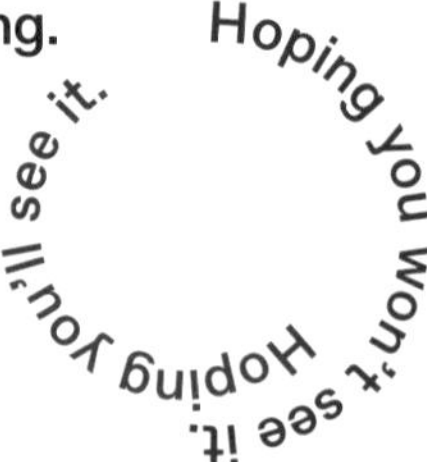

Tiny translucent squares of paper melting on your tongue. An hour spent near to bursting in tense anticipation.

Ignoring the impenetrable woods and everything beyond the headlights and the glow of the campfire. Hurling into it whatever comes your way.

One night it was a tyre;
at daybreak, everybody was blowing black snot into their handkerchiefs —sobering.

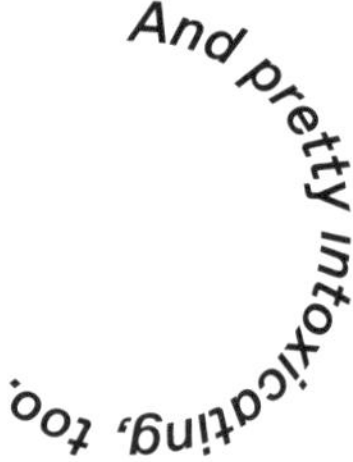

ERSCHÖPFT DURCH DIE CHRONISCHEN FLOPS

AND PRETTY INTOXICATING, TOO

EINE ZEIT FÜR ALLES
EINE BLUME IM KNOPFLOCH
SCHLAMMBAD
SAISONALE VERIRRUNGEN
SALZLAGER
UNABÄNDERLICHER TROTT
FREIER FALL
EISENBAHNBUMMELEIEN
GLÜHENDE KOHLEN
VERLORENE ELASTIZITÄT
FEUCHTES MILIEU
ALLGEMEINE PANIK

BYE BYE

L O A D S

THE LONG THIN BLADES OF GRASS FLITTING BETWEEN OUR FINGERS NON-STOP, SO BEAUTIFUL. AND SUPPLE

WO ESCH DAS WO?

IL RÊVE D'HUMUS PIQUETÉ
D'AIGUILLES DE SAPIN ROUSSES
ELLE EST DE TYPE LICHEN.
SON DADA : LES MOUSSES DE
RENNE, QUI PAR TEMPS SEC
S'ATOMISENT SOUS LE PIED
AVEC UN SCRATCH ! DE BANDES
VELCRO QU'ON SÉPARE.
ILS PARTAGENT DEPUIS BELLE
LURETTE UN TROIS-PIÈCES
EN DEMI SOUS-SOL AUX MURS
MANGÉS PAR LA MOISISSURE

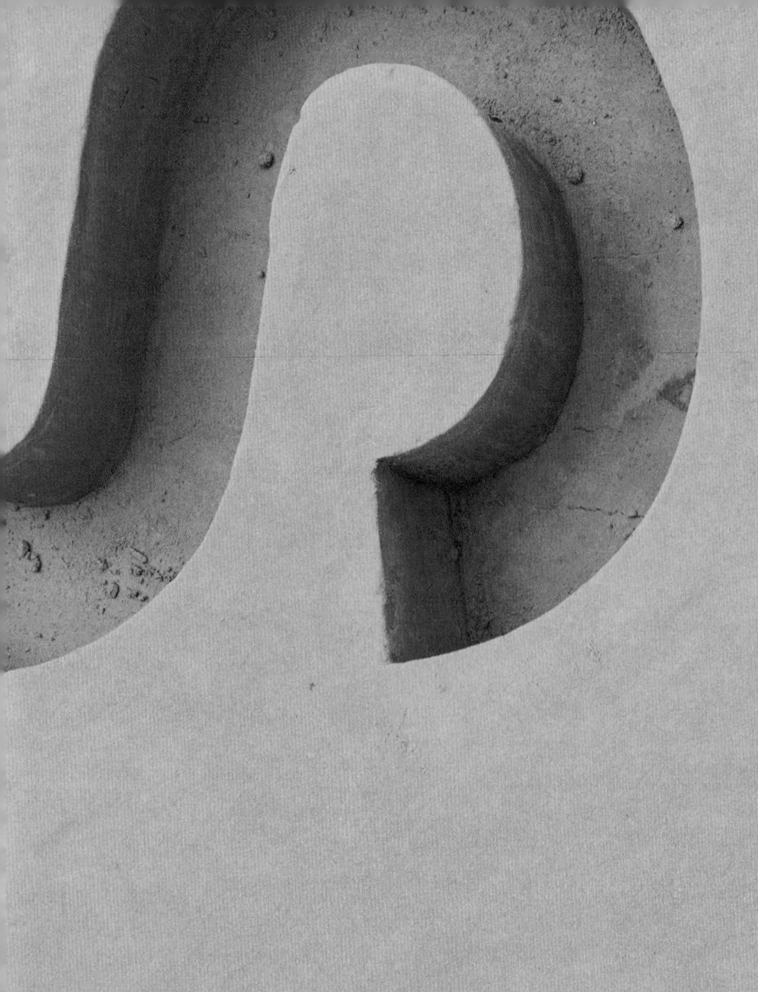

No Edit Can Fail Tint
2020
60 × 1059 × 641 cm
Earthenware, foundry sand,
gasoline, water

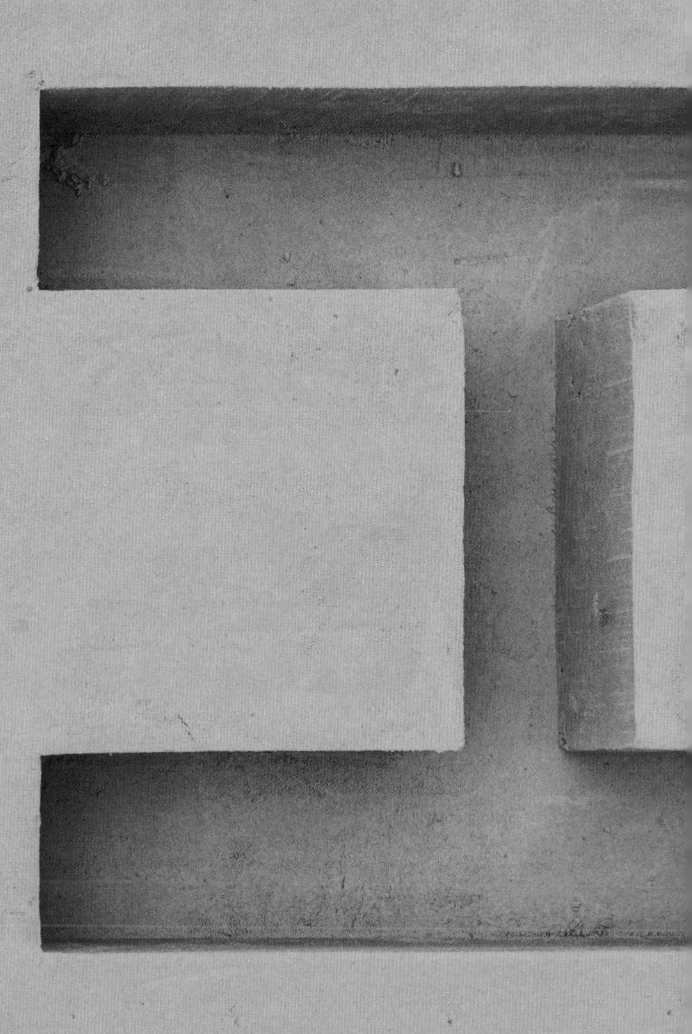

No Edit Can Fail Tint
2020
60 × 1059 × 641 cm
Earthenware, foundry sand, gasoline, water

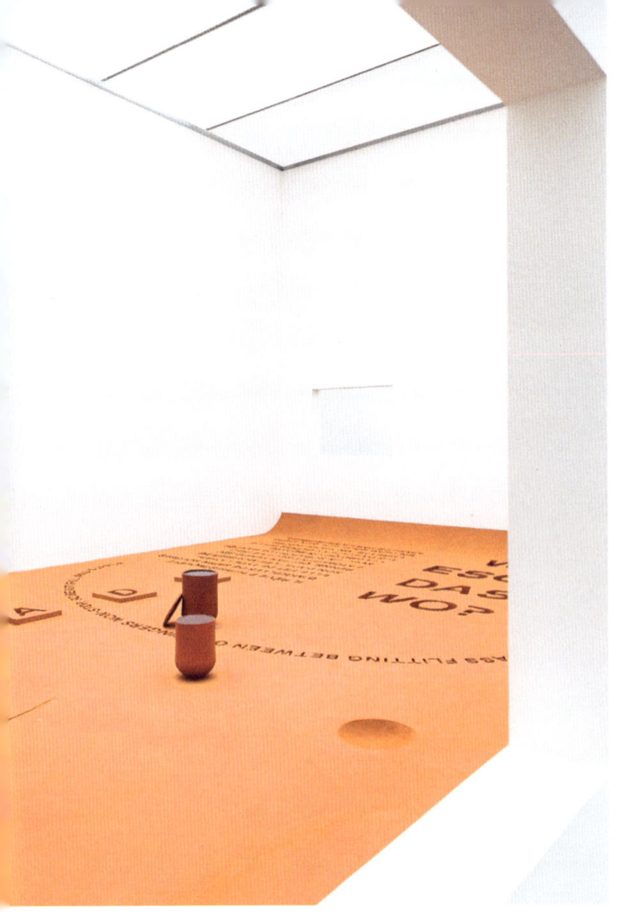

Des jets qui se croisent, bifurquent, propulsent leur minéralité dans toutes les directions, fusent en un réseau compliqué et grumeleux. Ils pourraient jaillir — via bouche et œsophage — de panses révulsées, or ils viennent d'on ne sait où et éructent en circuit fermé. À défaut d'aller quelque part, ils promènent à chacune de leurs extrémités un capuchon obtus composé de deux inséparables: un noyau de litchi passablement rabougri chevillé à une coque enduite de laque (on pense à du caramel, surtout ne pas lécher).

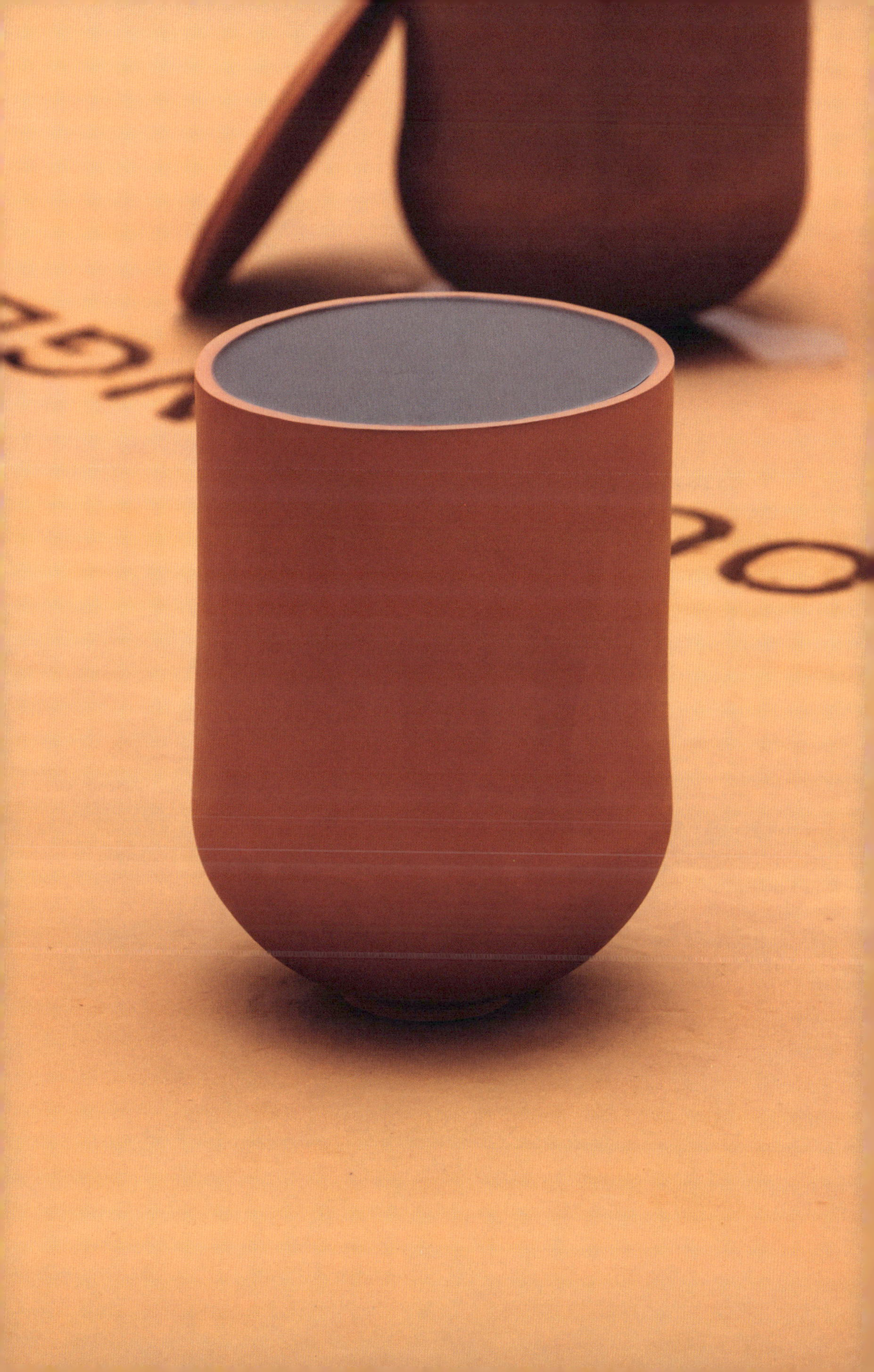

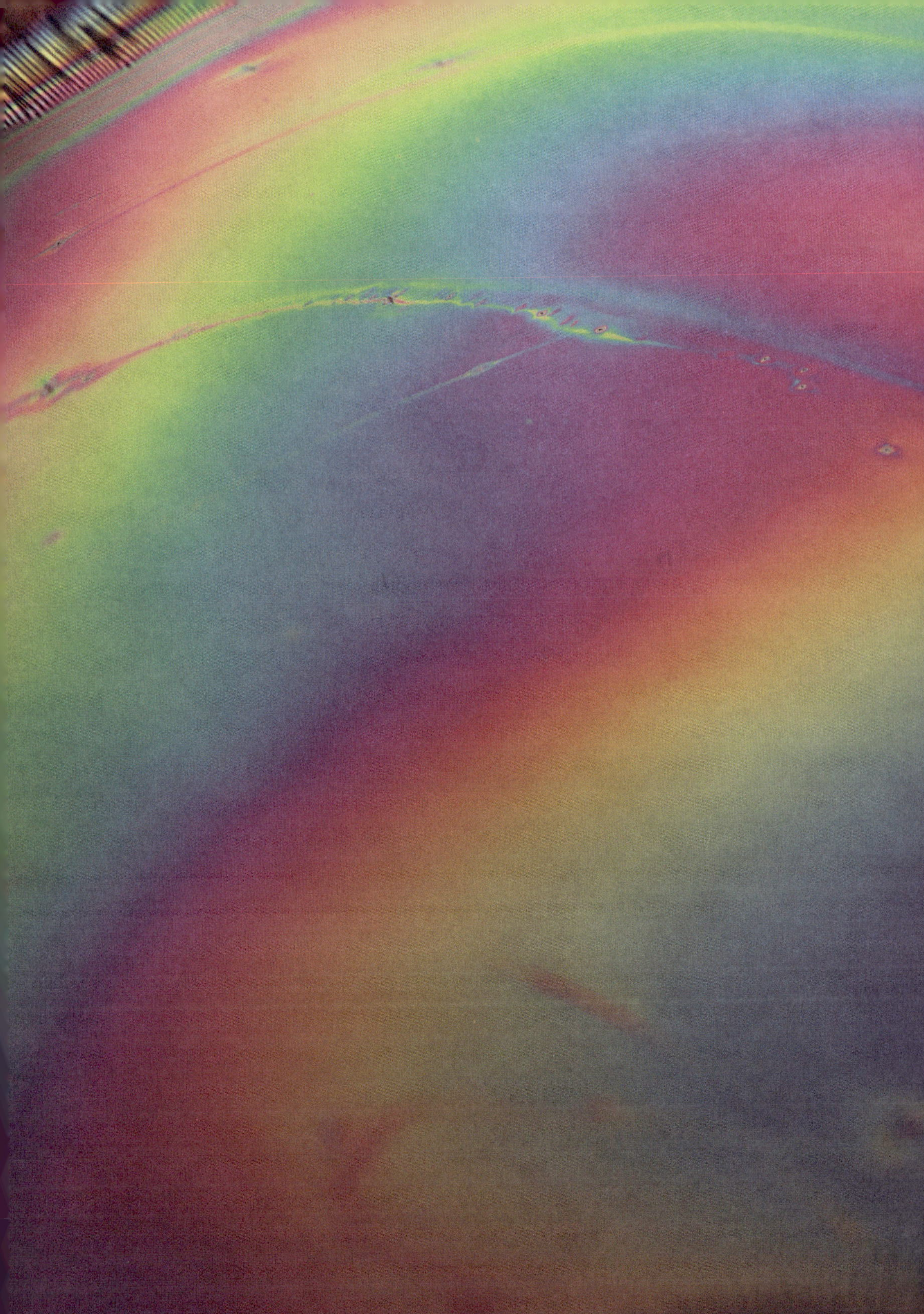

←

No Edit Can Fail Tint
2020
60 × 1059 × 641 cm
Earthenware, foundry sand,
gasoline, water

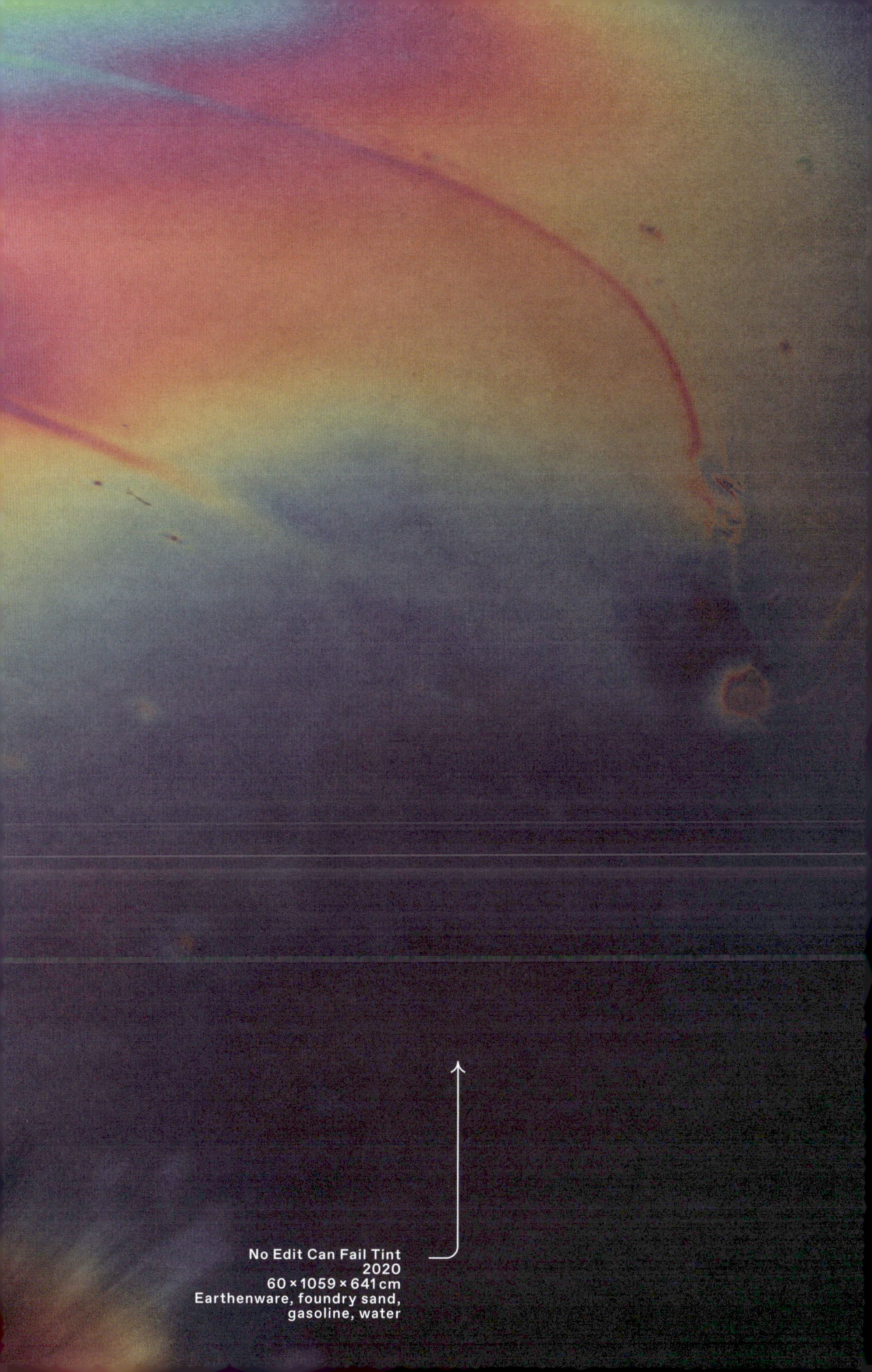

No Edit Can Fail Tint
2020
60 × 1059 × 641 cm
Earthenware, foundry sand,
gasoline, water

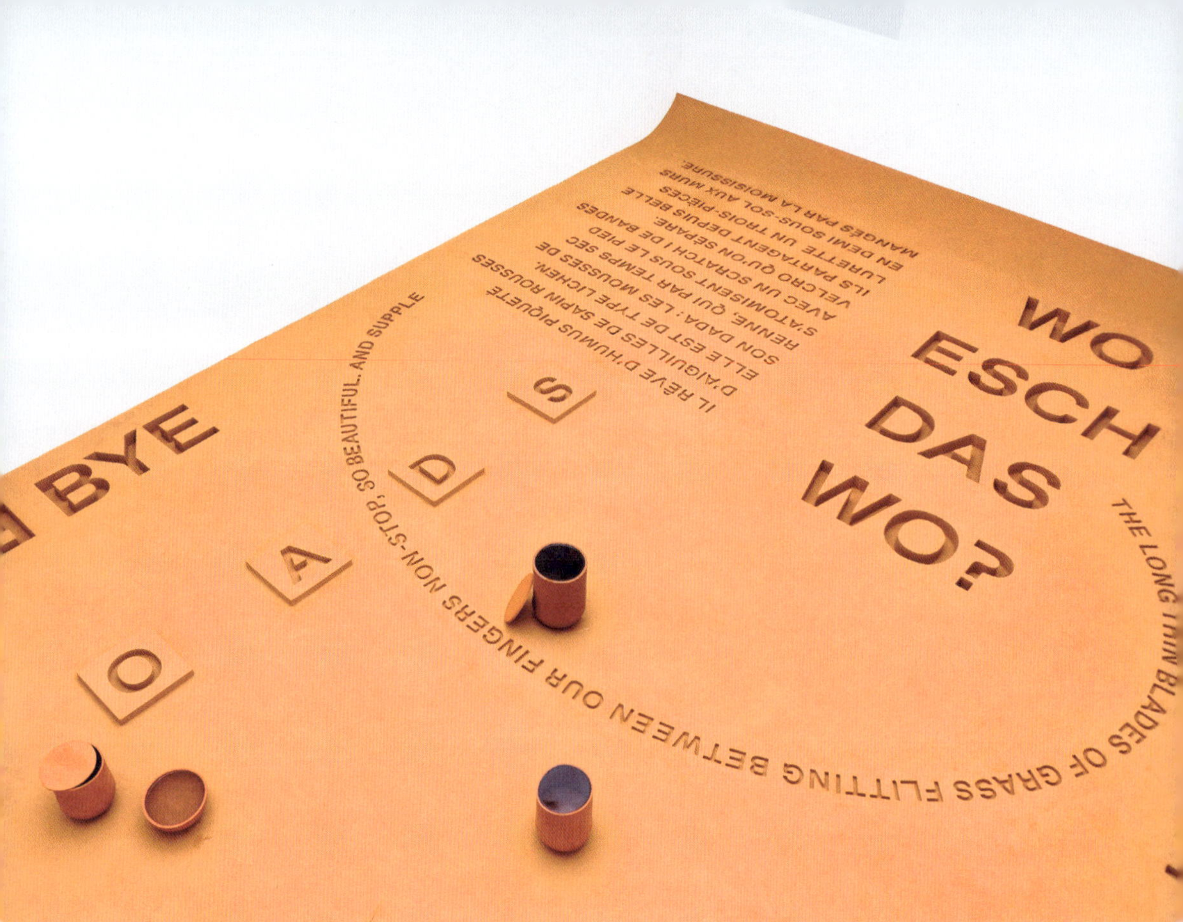

WO
ESCH
DAS
WO?
IL RÊVE D'HUMUS PIQUETÉ
D'AIGUILLES DE SAPIN ROUSSES
ELLE EST DE TYPE LICHEN,
SON DADA : LES MOUSSES DE
RENNE, QUI PAR TEMPS SEC
S'ATOMISENT SOUS LE PIED
AVEC UN SCRATCH I DE BANDES
VELCRO QU'ON SÉPARE.
ILS PARTAGENT DEPUIS BELLE
LURETTE UN TROIS-PIÈCES
EN DEMI SOUS-SOL AUX MURS
MANGÉS PAR LA MOISISSURE.
BYE
O A D S
THE LONG THIN BLADES OF GRASS FLITTING BETWEEN OUR FINGERS NON-STOP, SO BEAUTIFUL. AND SUPPLE

Von Druckverhältnissen, Wortzauber und dem (Alb-)Traum ewigen Lebens

Sprachliche und materielle Verfahren

Claire Hoffmann

Während dreier Tage schreit das neugeborene Kind und die Eltern können es mit keinen Mitteln beruhigen. Verzweifelt rufen sie den alten Appa. Der Schamane kommt und singt eine Nacht lang. Morgens fragt er die Eltern, wie sie ihr Mädchen nennen wollen: Uliana. Appa entgegnet, sie solle nicht so heissen, sondern Daria, nach ihrer Grossmutter. Sobald das kleine Mädchen den «richtigen» Namen erhält, beruhigt sie sich und schläft fortan seelenruhig. Die französische Anthropologin Nastassja Martin lebte jahrelang bei den Even in Kamtschatka. Das in der Sowjetunion von seinen Rentieren enteignete Nomadenvolk, das nun vom Jagen und Fischen lebt, hat ein animistisches Verhältnis zu Tieren und seiner Umwelt, was sich besonders in Träumen und in einer sprachlichen Spannung zwischen performativer Macht des Gesagten und Unsagbaren ausdrückt. Die alte Frau Daria, bei der die Anthropologin jahrelang lebte und zu der sie eine enge Freundschaft entwickelte, erzählte ihr diese frühe prägende Episode ihres Lebens.[1]

Wie wichtig es ist, richtige Namen zu geben, zu benützen, weiterzugeben — seien es die von Menschen oder uns umgebenden Tieren und Pflanzen —, lässt diese Geschichte aus einem mystisch-schamanischen Zusammenhang erahnen.[2] Was uns umgibt, treffend benennen zu können, ihm einen Namen zu geben heisst, es in seiner Existenz zu würdigen. Das Benannte wird dadurch auch aus einer vagen, undefinierten Umgebung herausgeholt. Durch die Benennung auf etwas aufmerksam zu werden, erlaubt in Folge auch darauf zu achten, die Vielheit der Beziehungen zu sehen, in denen das eben erst Benannte steht. Die Medien-Philosophin Jenny Odell beschreibt in ihrem Buch zur Aufmerksamkeitsökonomie genau dieses Phänomen: Als begeisterte Vogelbeobachterin verlor für sie der generische Begriff «Vogel» irgendwann jegliche Bedeutung. Er wurde ersetzt durch eine Vielzahl von Vogelarten sowie deren Beziehungen zu und Interaktionen mit anderen Spezies — vom benennenden Nomen hin zu konjugierten Verben, die ein breites, stets weiter wachsendes Netz aufspannen.[3] Etwas zu benennen, kann jedoch auch bedeuten, Macht und Anspruch auf das Benannte zu erheben, wie etliche Beispiele der kolonialen Geschichte zeigen, typischerweise etwa in den europäischen Namen von Pflanzen, die über die lokalen Namen gestülpt werden — und somit ein verankertes Wissen überschreiben, verdrängen, vergessen lassen.

Maude Léonard-Contants plastisches Werk lässt uns in diese rätselhafte Beziehung von Objekt und Sprache eintauchen. Man könnte hier einwenden, dass dies in der Linguistik und Sprachphilosophie zur Genüge seziert wurde. Mit ihrer skulpturalen Praxis lädt die Künstlerin jedoch ein, in die multiplen Beziehungen, die sich zwischen den Dingen und Wörtern entfalten, neu einzutauchen und sich von einer physischen, unmittelbaren, visuell-haptischen Syntax leiten zu lassen, die, nach Odells Vorschlag, aktiv, beschreibend, verbindend ist. Maude Léonard-Contants Arbeiten lassen uns darüber nachdenken, wie die Wörter zu den Werken kommen, die Materialien zu ihren Formen, wie geografisch versetztes Wissen sich neu verankern und Wurzeln schlagen kann — etwa wenn unmittelbare Gefühle von Zugehörigkeit und Zuhause beim Wiedererkennen einer bekannten Pflanze aufkommen: Maude Léonard-Contant verarbeitete dieses Erlebnis, als sie in der Schweiz Winterschachtelhalm entdeckte, der ihr aus ihrer Kindheit in Kanada vertraut ist und den sie als Naturheilmittel kennt. Diese Urpflanze begleitet sie fortan in diversen Werken.

In ihrer Praxis versucht Maude Léonard-Contant Ihre künstlerischen Rohstoffe — seien sie natürlich oder synthetisch oder auch sprachlich — durch konjugierende Aktivitäten in eine andere Dynamik und zueinander in Bezug zu setzen. Die in ihrer Präzision und haptischen Qualität

1 Nastassja Martin, *À l'est des rêves. Réponses Even aux crises systémiques,* Editions La découverte, Les empêcheurs de penser en rond, Paris 2022, S. 93–94.

2 Ein Beispiel der definitorischen Macht des Namens aus der europäischen Tradition ist das Märchen vom «Rumpelstilzchen», dessen Macht im Geheimnis seines Namens steckt und verloren geht, sobald sein Name bekannt wird.

3 Jenny Odell, *How to Do Nothing. Resisting the Attention Economy,* Melville House Publishing, Brooklyn, London 2019, S. 157.

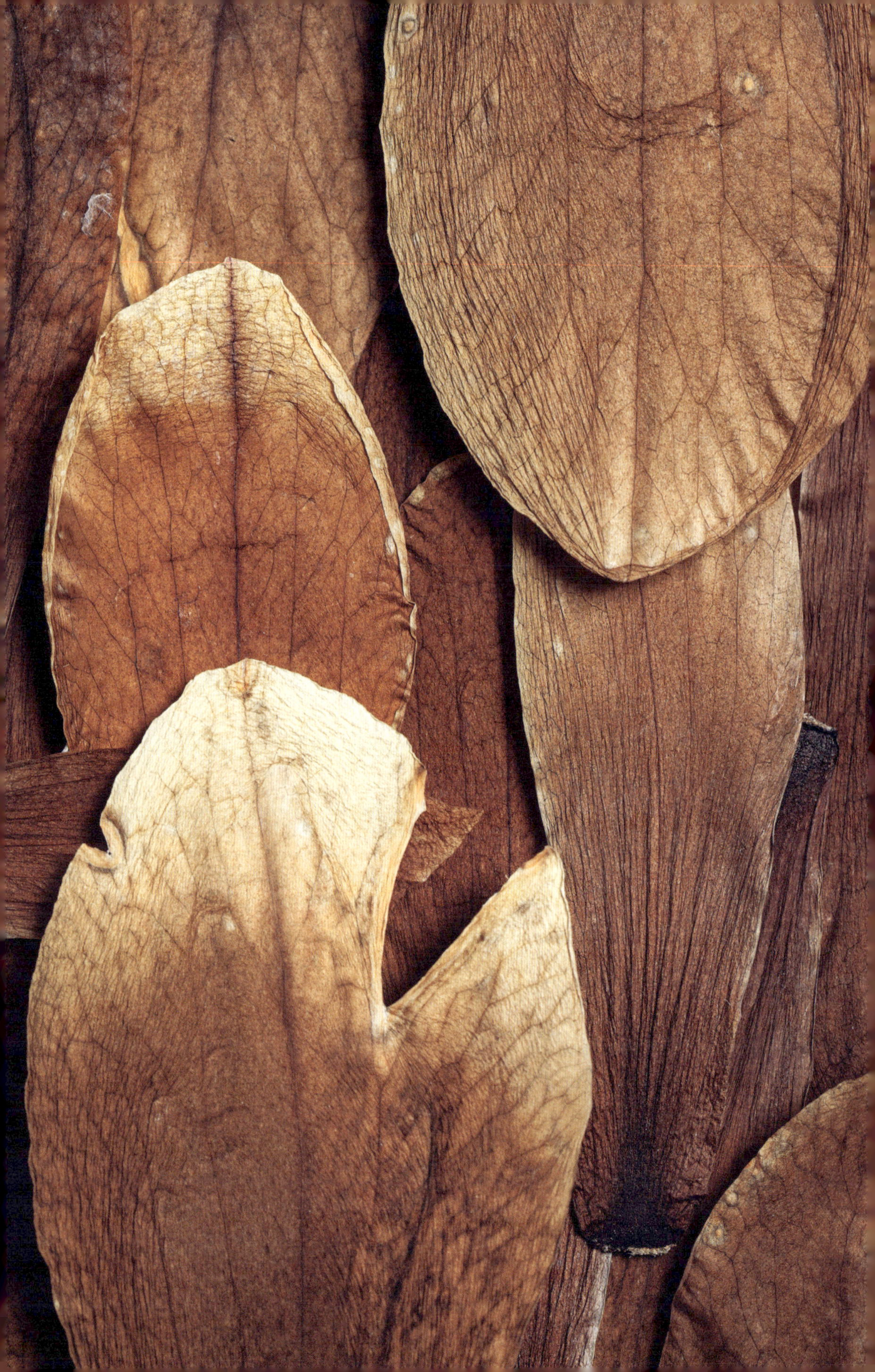

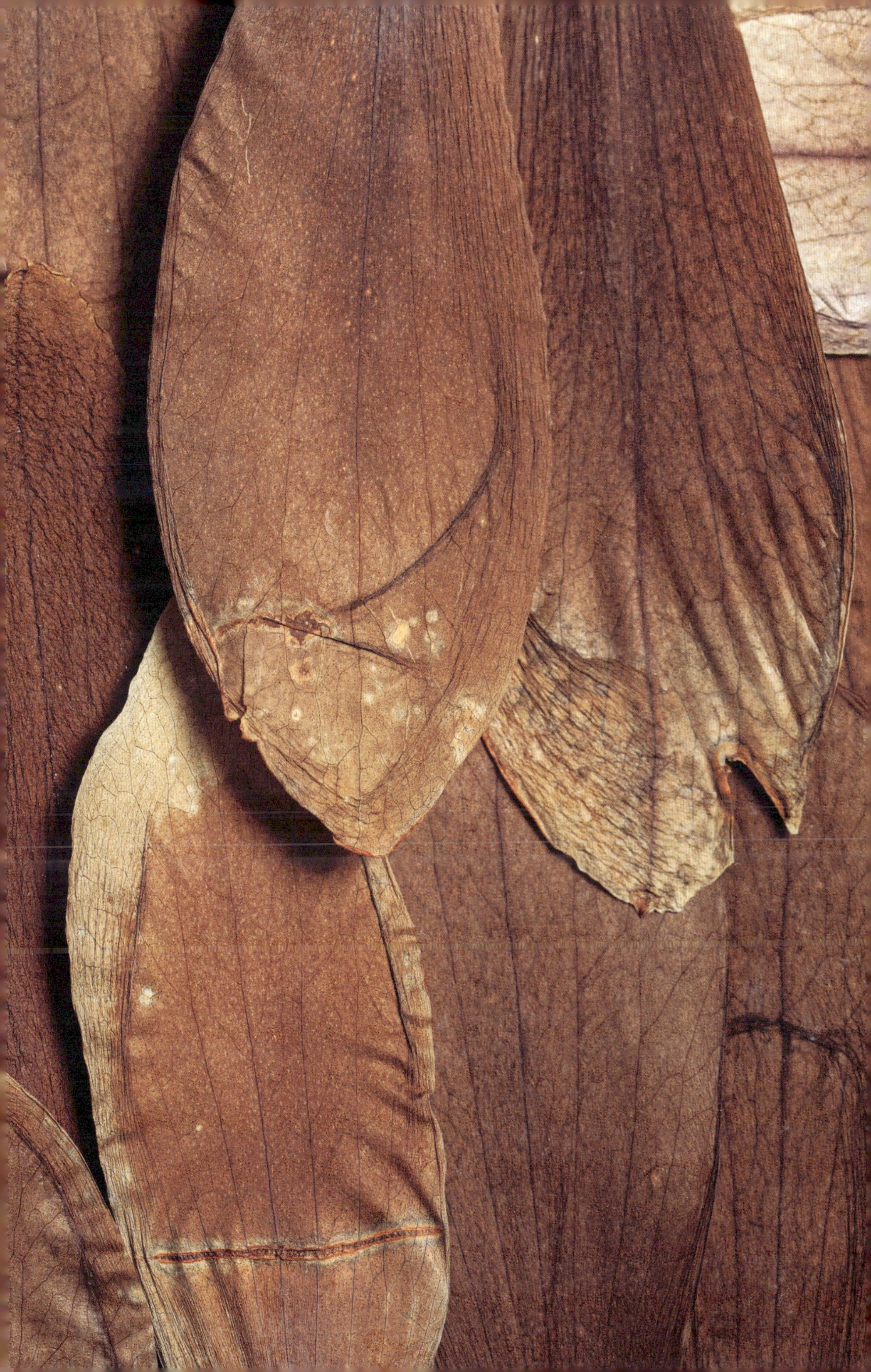

eingesetzten Materialien lenken so die Aufmerksamkeit auf die formgebenden Aktivitäten, die sich in ihnen eingeschrieben haben — biegen, schleifen, falten, giessen, pressen, (ver-)schmelzen, spannen, aushöhlen. Erstaunlicherweise passen diese urskulpturalen Vorgänge genauso zur linguistischen Ebene, wenn etwa in Maude Léonard-Contants persönlichem Parcours Basel- und Luzernerdeutsch auf Québécois, Englisch und Hochdeutsch trifft und sie poetische Register und Alltagsausdrücke zwischen Lesbarkeit und Missverständnis bis zu neuen Bedeutungen zu verweben weiss. Es bleibt ein Zwischenraum für Ungewissheiten, die sich dem Begrifflichen entziehen, die an den Rändern der Bedeutungen und des Verständlichen Ahnungen und Nuancen zulassen. Eindrückliches Beispiel hierfür sind Maude Léonard-Contants raumgreifende Installationen mit Giesssand, die sich laufend verändern können und von Sprachspielen durchdrungen sind.

Die Arbeit *No One by One (fiercely)* ist gesättigt von solchen materiell-sprachlichen Gegensätzen, die sich in der Wahl des Materials, der Farbe und von Bearbeitungsschritten bis hin zum Entstehungskontext des Werks zeigen. Die metallene Hand erinnert entfernt an einen Napf, ihre Materialität evoziert einen streng funktionalen Kontext. Die Form wurde mit Wasser ausgefräst. Anschliessend wurde sie «angelassen» — ein eigenartiges Verb, um das Industrieverfahren zu bezeichnen, bei dem Chromstahl auf hohe Temperatur erhitzt wird, um seine Stabilität zu stärken. Ein Nebeneffekt davon ist die kühle, blaue Oxidation. Das Werk vereint die gegensätzlichen Elemente Feuer und Wasser. Enthalten sind diese auch im Brennvorgang der Porzellanperlen, die sich wie eine Kette über die Hand mit oxidiert blauen Fingerspitzen schlängeln. In Maude Léonard-Contants Erzählung eingebettet, geht die Installation auf das sommerliche Blaubeerensammeln in Kanada zurück. Hier verschmelzen Kindheitserinnerungen des lustvollen Sammelns mit derselben Tätigkeit nun unter neuen Vorzeichen als Mutter, deren Kleinkind die frisch gepickten Beeren direkt aus ihren vom Beerensaft blau gefärbten Händen isst — und zwar nicht einzeln, *one by one*, sondern *fiercely*, «wie ein kleines Tier».[4] Das universale Verhältnis von Ernähren, Anleiten und Nachahmen verbindet sich hier mit einem grösseren Zyklus, in dem die Künstlerin die spärlicher werdenden Beeren beobachtet, diese mit der direkten Gefahr der hungrigen und daher näher an die Bewohnungen rückenden Bären — und indirekt mit dem grösseren Zusammenhang der klimatischen Veränderungen — verknüpft. Hier wird die Spannung deutlich zwischen den nährenden natürlichen Ressourcen[5] und der Fragilität eben dieser lebendigen Systeme. Dies schärft sich besonders in dem Aufeinandertreffen der süssen Beeren und dem im Chromstahl enthaltenen toxischen Nickel. Der Einsatz dieses für unsere Gesellschaft vitalen Metalls reicht von Batterien bis zur allgegenwärtigen Verwendung in den rostfreien Legierungen, die dem gesellschaftlichen Bedürfnis nach aseptischen, hygienischen, vor allem aber nicht alternden Dingen entspricht. Menschliche, tierische und geologische Zeiten und Erzählungen treffen aufeinander, im Werk zu erahnen als Begegnung des Weichen und Scharfen, Heissen und Kalten, Süssen und Giftigen, Vergänglichen und Permanenten. Nastassja Martin fasst dieses Paradox treffend zusammen: « Nous vivons dans un monde qui ne rouille pas, qui ne doit pas rouiller. Un monde brillant, sans taches. Nous construisons les objets de notre monde précisément pour qu'ils durent sans que le temps ne semble passer sur eux : à l'image des métaux inoxydables, nous aimerions nous croire immortels. »[6]

4 Maude Léonard-Contant in ihrer E-Mail-Korrespondenz mit der Künstlerin Marta Margnetti und der Kuratorin Eva-Maria Knüsel, in Vorbereitung für die Doppelausstellung *Knuckles Down* mit Marta Margnetti im Kunstraum Mayday in Basel (19.9.–31.10.2021).

5 Heute unter dem Wortungeheuer der «Ökosystemdienstleistung» gefasst, ein Ausdruck eines durchaus löblichen Bemühens, den monetären bis kulturellen Wert der Ökosysteme und Biodiversität für deren Erhalt zu stärken.

6 Vgl. hierzu Nastassja Martin, op. cit., S. 168 und das gesamte letzte Kapitel, « Conclusion. Ni, métal du diable », S. 263–280. Der Nickelabbau ist gerade im hohen Norden ein lauerndes ökologisches Desaster. In Kamtschatka befindet sich eine riesige, von den USA und der Schweiz betriebene Nickelmine, die einerseits den Lebensraum der Even vor anderen ökonomischen Zugriffen schützt, deren chemisch-toxische Ausflüsse jedoch die angrenzende Tundra langsam sättigt und in den nahegelegenen Fluss überzulaufen droht.

Von dieser Komplexität der Beziehungen, die einer einfachen Binarität widersteht und vielmehr die ständige Abhängigkeit in ihren Nuancen auffächert, spricht auch Maude Léonard-Contants neue Installation. Ihre schwarz-weisse Anmutung mag dazu verleiten, ein Kontrastprogramm zu erwarten, was sogleich von den spezifischen formgebenden Verfahren und der präzisen Materialwahl aufgebrochen wird. In enger Zusammenarbeit mit dem Meister-Plissier Karen Grigorian der *Maison du Pli* in Paris schafft die Künstlerin das stoffliche, bauschige Element der Installation: die Plissees. Die Seidenstoffe, fliessend und an sich formlos, kamen in handgefaltete, ausgeklügelte Pressformen, um mit Druck und Dampf in dreidimensionale, hier sich aufbäumende, dort erschlaffende Landschaften gefaltet zu werden. Die Seidenplissees sind dabei ein (vorläufiger?) Endpunkt einer bereits langen Verkettung von Transformationen, angefangen mit dem Kokon der Seidenraupen, hin zur industriellen Seidenproduktion und -verarbeitung bis zur handwerklichen Kompression und der letztendlichen künstlerischen Entfaltung im Ausstellungsraum. Hier im Ausstellungsraum begegnen die leichten Stoffe einem weiteren tierischen Material: Das glänzende dunkle Leder, das sich über die Rundungen spannt, einer geballten Faust oder einem in sich selbst eingerollten Wesen gleich, bildet als dunkles Gewicht einen Gegenpol. Eingepasst in diese beiden starken skulpturalen Formen finden sich getrocknete Blüten, Blätter, Stängel. Die gesammelten Pflanzen wurden gepresst und getrocknet, was sie fragil und zerbrechlich, zugleich länger haltbar macht, als Heilmitteln oder auch rein als Blütenschmuck. Maude Léonard-Contants Bouquet verknüpft ihr tief verankertes kanadisches Pflanzenwissen mit ihrer Wiederbegegnung mit altbekannten Pflanzen im neuen Lebensumfeld und dem neu zu gewinnenden botanischen Vokabular der europäischen Flora. Erstaunt über die hohe Anzahl lokaler toxischer Spezies — und deren Anwendung in zahlreichen Naturheilmitteln bis hin zu industriell hergestellten Pharmaka — erzählt dieses Herbarium von einem ganz persönlichen, hybriden, stets wachsenden Verhältnis zur lebenden Pflanzenwelt und vom menschlichen Zugriff darauf, von Wertschätzung bis Ausbeutung.

Nirgends versucht die Arbeit der Künstlerin diese vielen Widersprüche und inhärenten Abhängigkeiten aufzulösen. Der Druck und die Spannung, die sowohl in den konkreten technischen Verfahren wie im Einsatz der tierischen und pflanzlichen Materialien stecken, sind eingebettet in das Gesamtbild der Installation, die bestimmt wird von einer unmittelbaren Sinnlichkeit, durchdrungen von grosser Sorgfalt und ästhetischer Aufmerksamkeit. Wir bleiben mit der Künstlerin auf der Suche nach den passenden Wörtern für diese komplexe Abhängigkeit zwischen den Spezies, die von Gewalt und Fürsorge, Verletzung und Heilung, Würdigung und Schändung zu sprechen scheint, und vielleicht nur in einem erträumten Namen eine Auflösung zu finden vermag.

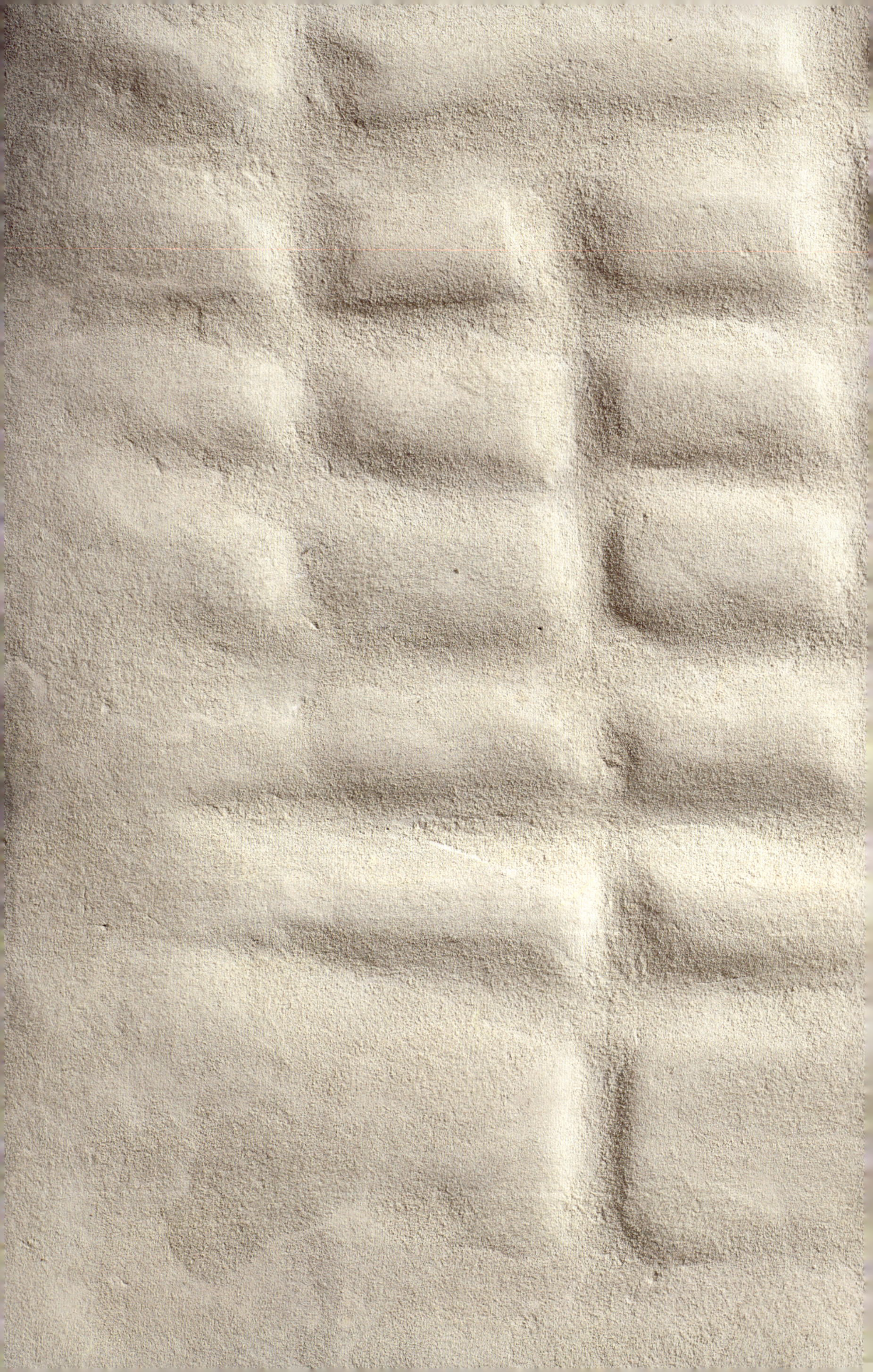

Untitled
2013
50 × 60 × 45 cm
Cork, polystyrene

Tastafel
2015
55 × 195 × 110 cm
MDF, pastel, polystyrene, wood paste

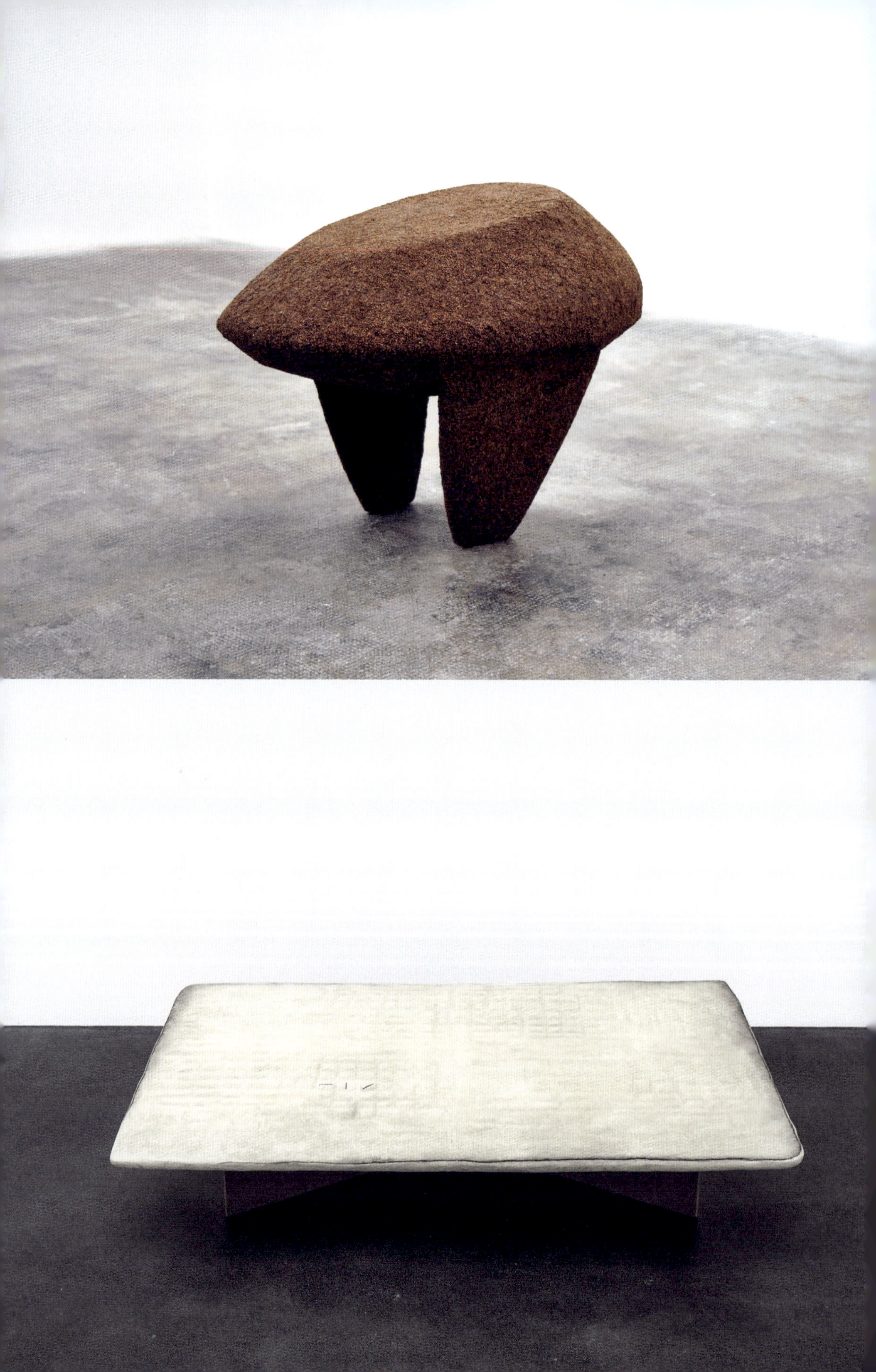

Am frühen Morgen treiben Sch a u m p a k e t e

auf dem noch gl a t t e n S e e .

Darunter auch prallvolle

und eher f l o c k i g e .

Manche bestehen aus einem kompakten,

fast beigefarbenen Sch a u m ,

andere, lichtdurchlässige,

strecken ihre Trauben

aus laschen Blasen sch m a c h t e n d a u s .

Auf Zehenspitzen wage ich mich unter sie

und weiss nicht,

soll ich sie fürchten oder b e w u n d e r n .

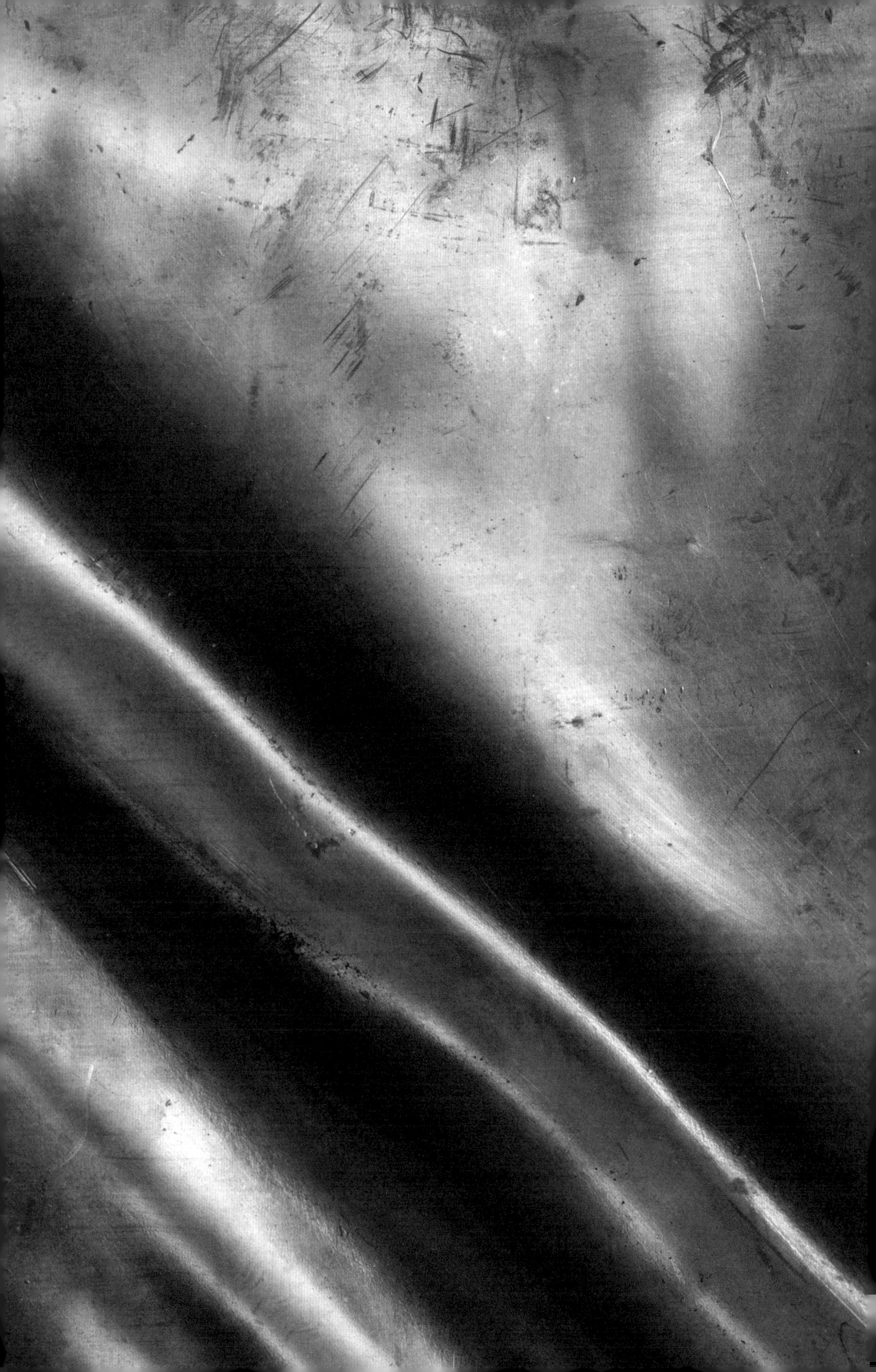

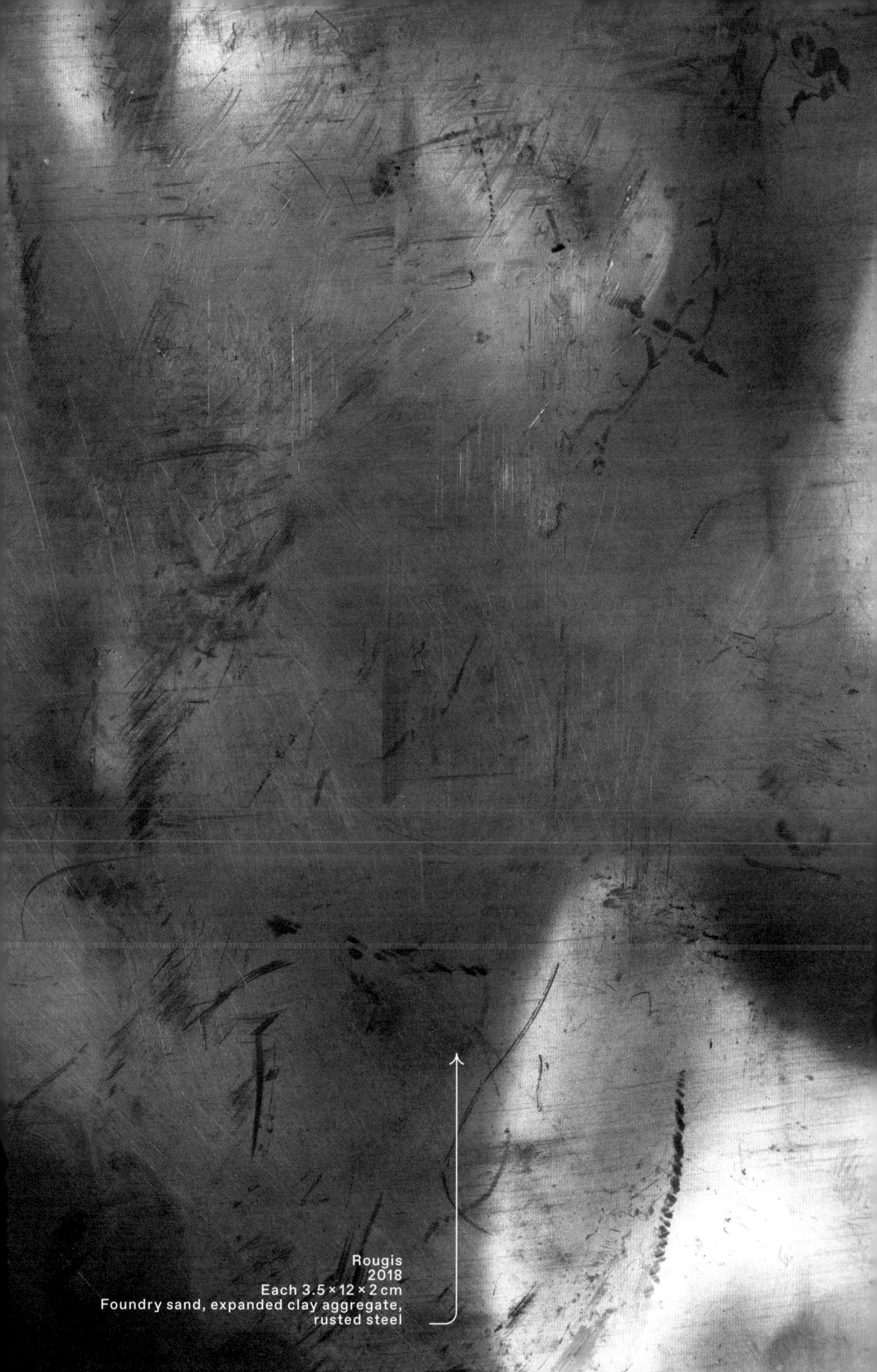

Rougis
2018
Each 3.5 × 12 × 2 cm
Foundry sand, expanded clay aggregate, rusted steel

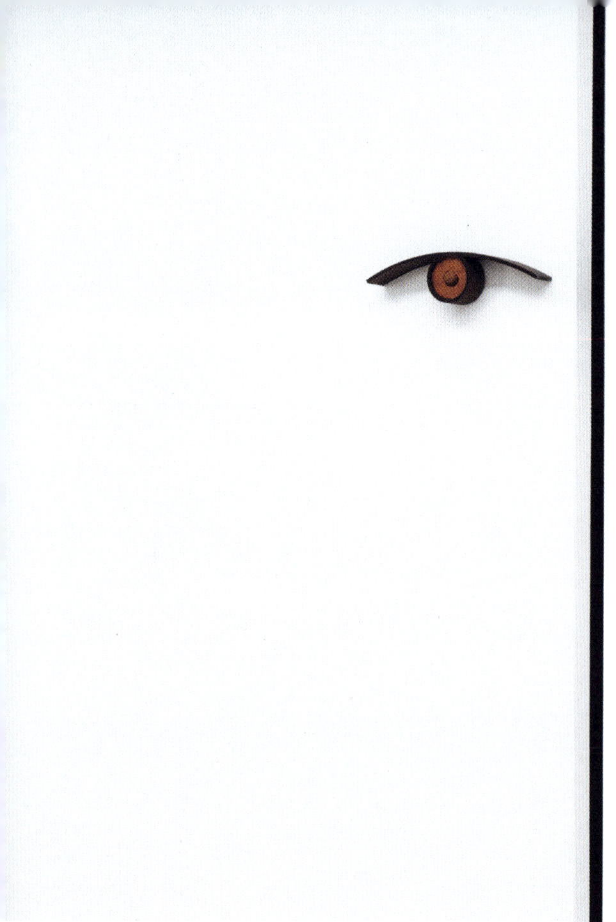

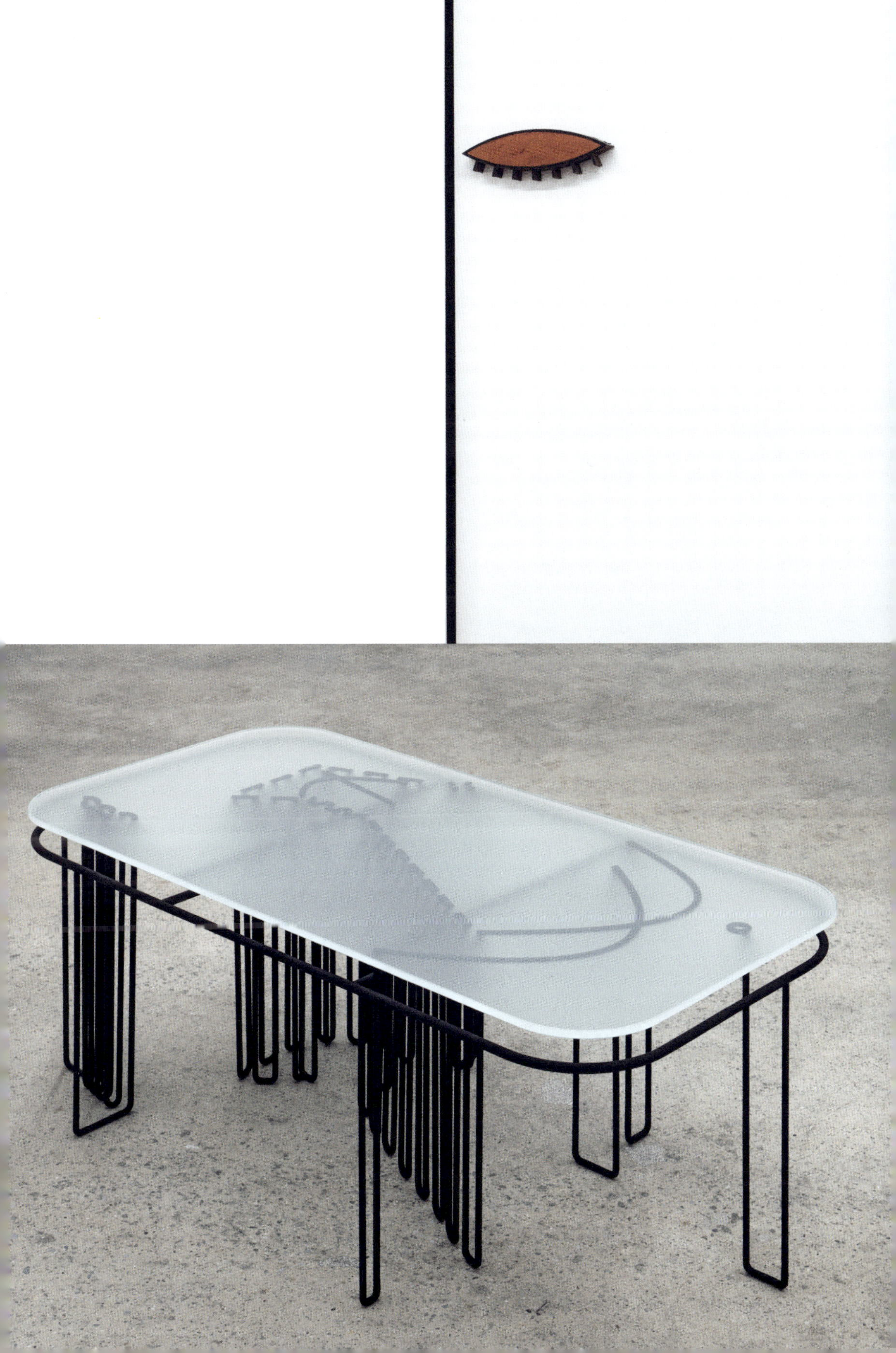

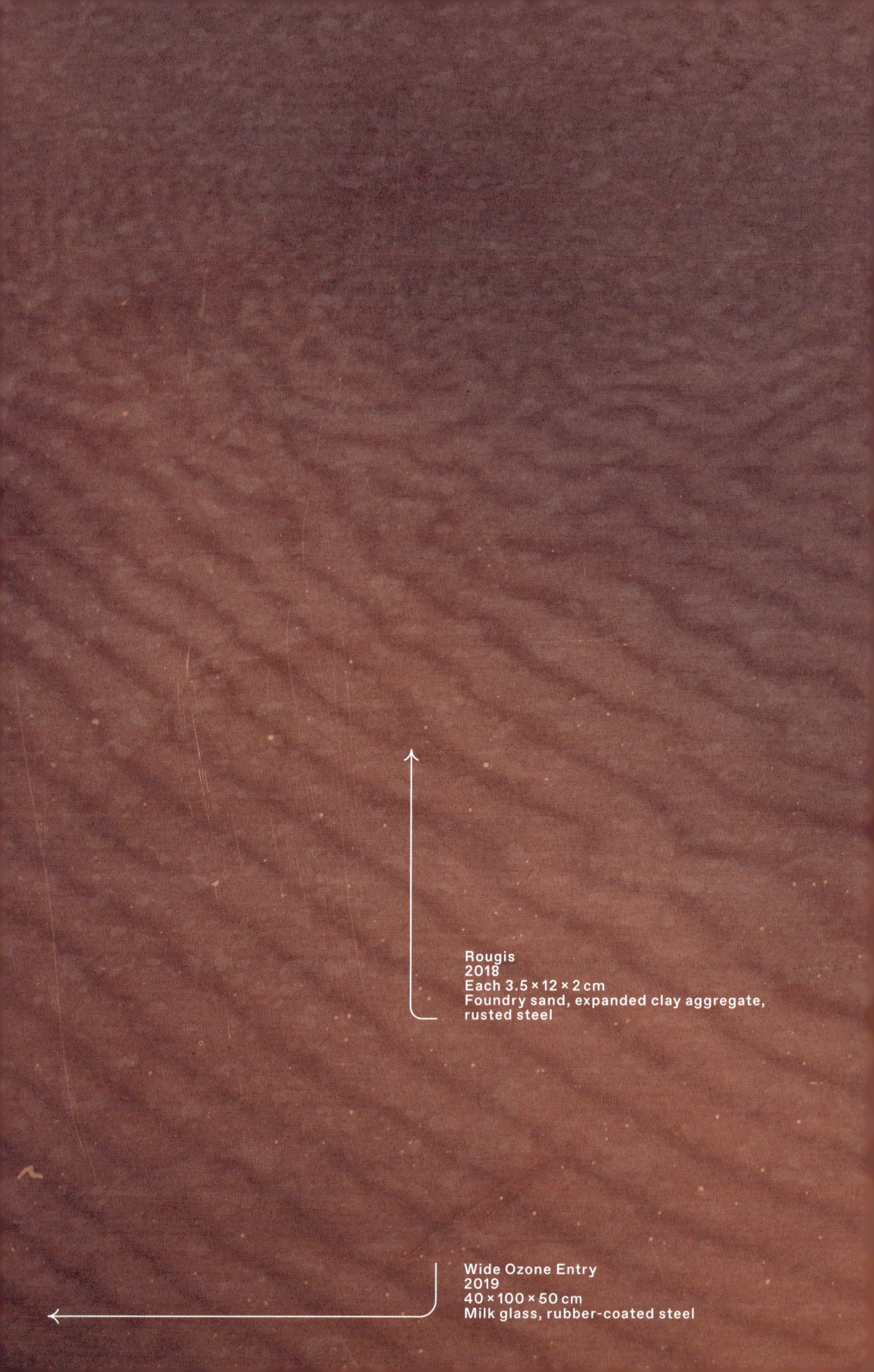

Rougis
2018
Each 3.5 × 12 × 2 cm
Foundry sand, expanded clay aggregate, rusted steel

Wide Ozone Entry
2019
40 × 100 × 50 cm
Milk glass, rubber-coated steel

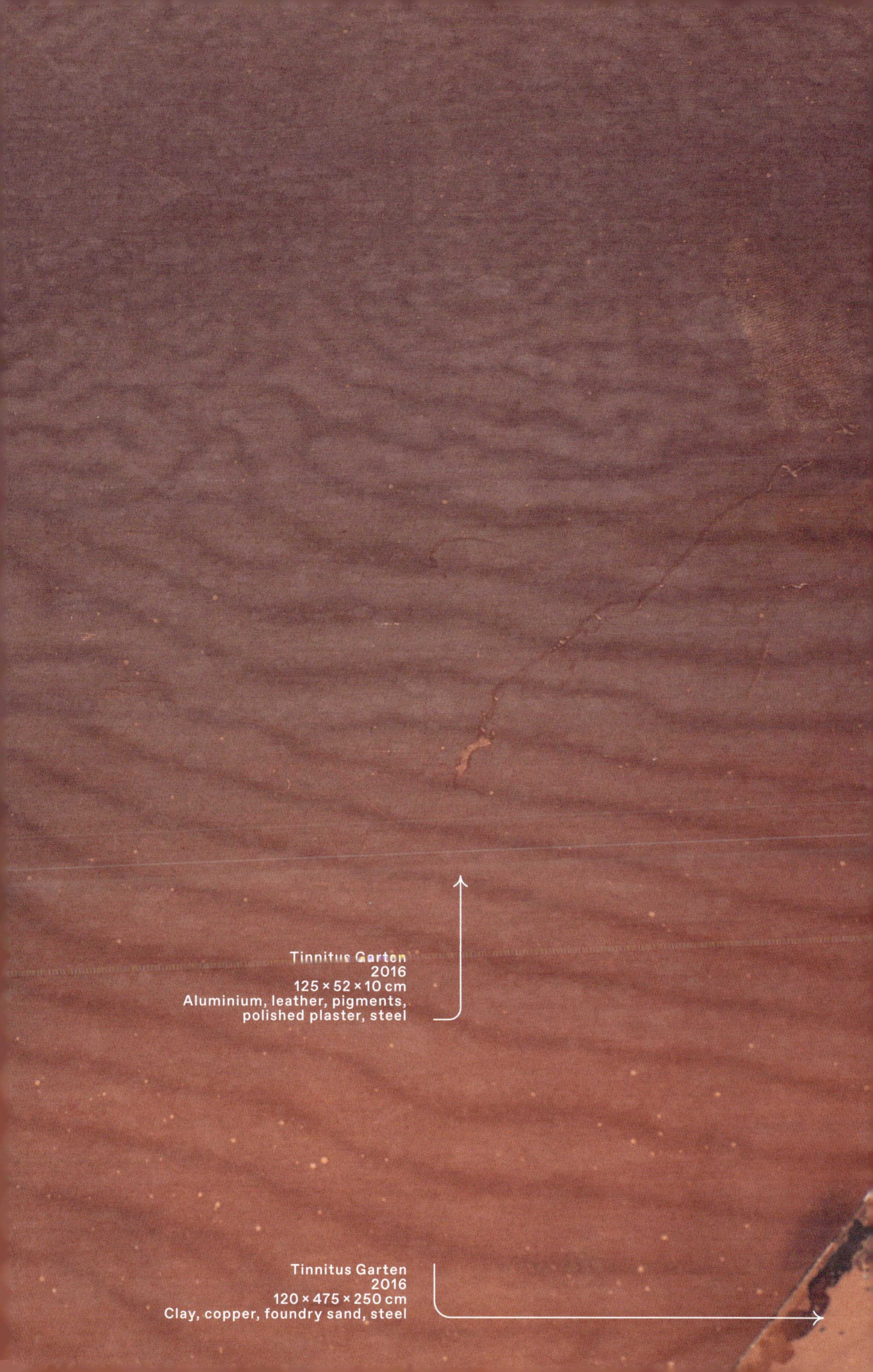

Tinnitus Garten
2016
125 × 52 × 10 cm
Aluminium, leather, pigments,
polished plaster, steel

Tinnitus Garten
2016
120 × 475 × 250 cm
Clay, copper, foundry sand, steel

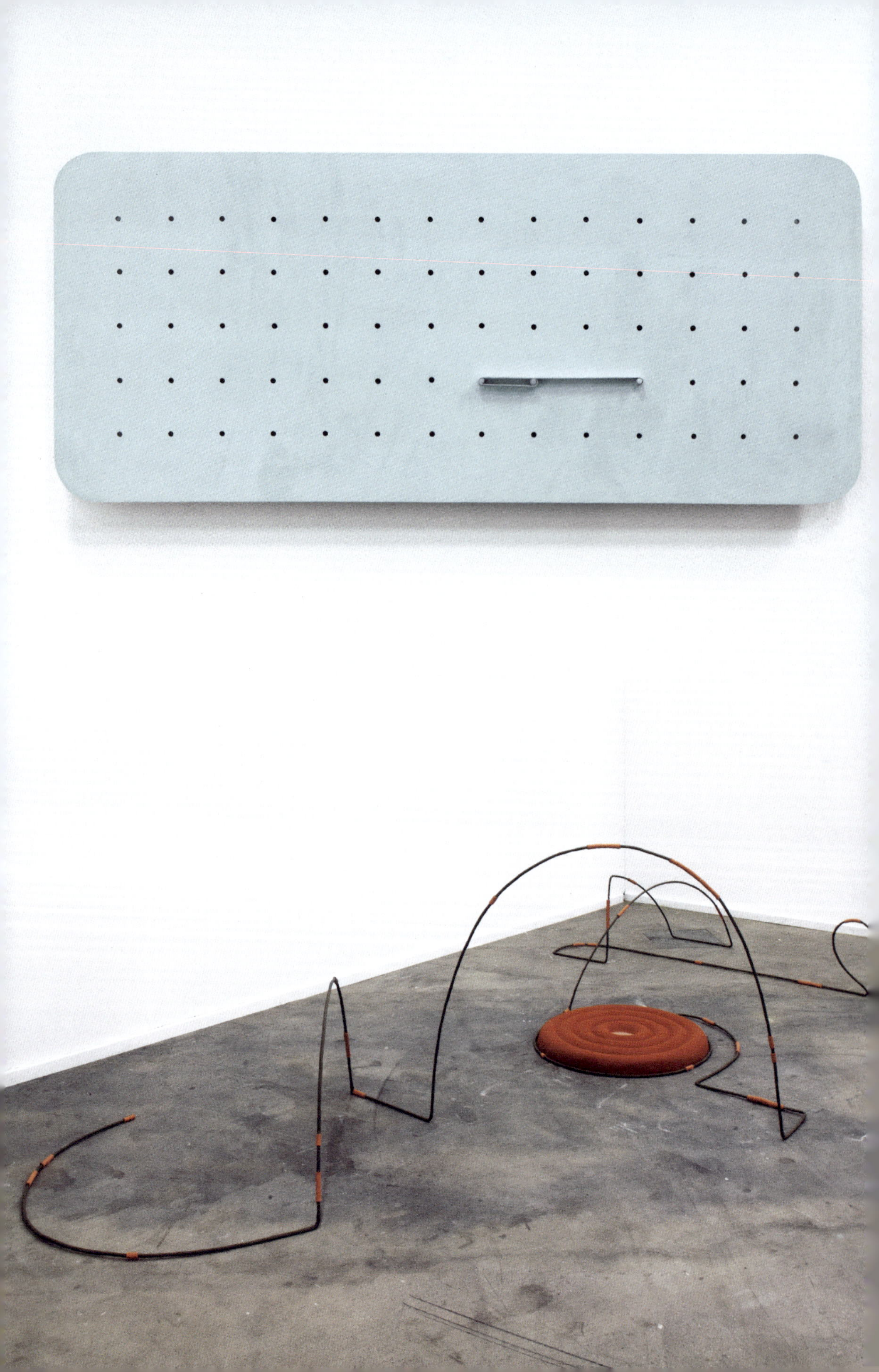

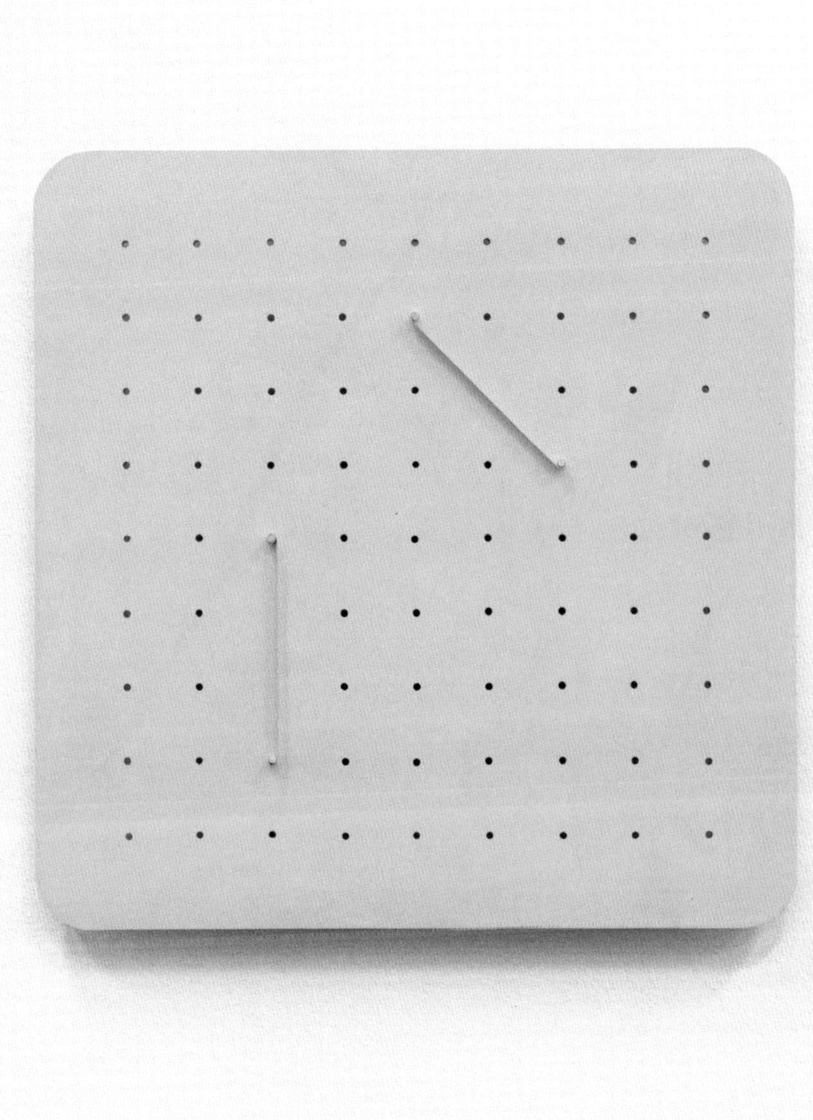

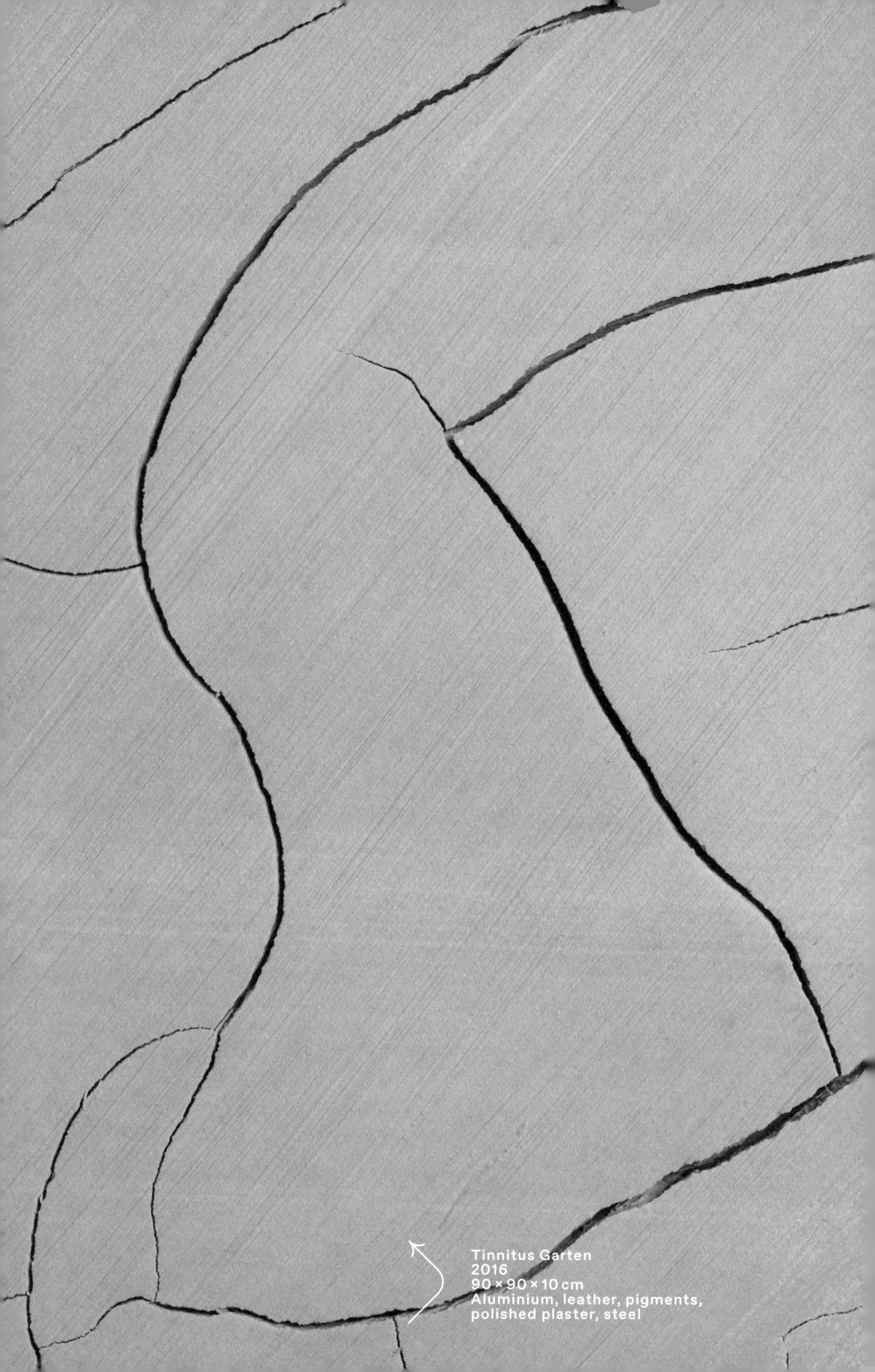

Tinnitus Garten
2016
90 × 90 × 10 cm
Aluminium, leather, pigments,
polished plaster, steel

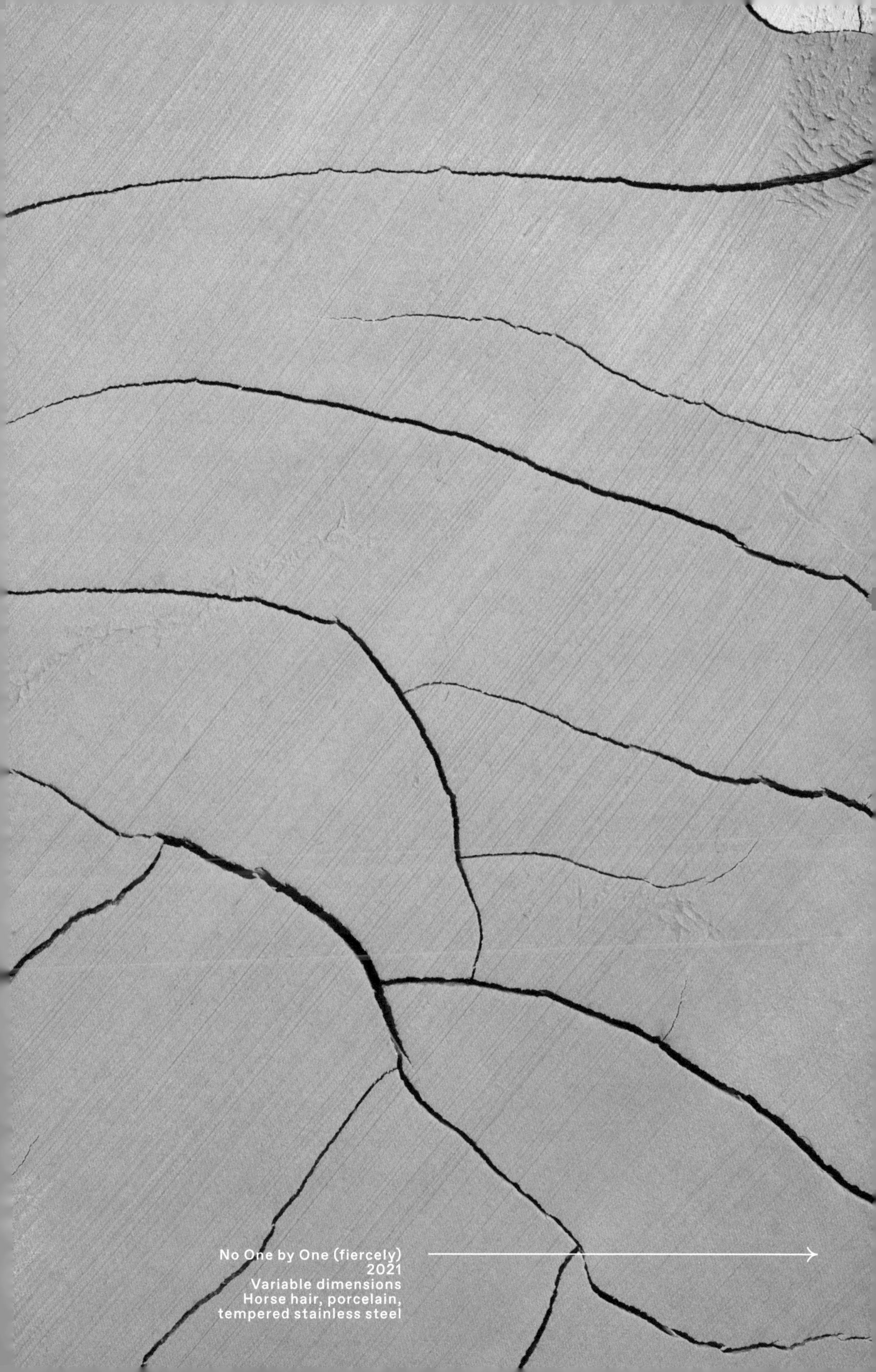

No One by One (fiercely)
2021
Variable dimensions
Horse hair, porcelain,
tempered stainless steel

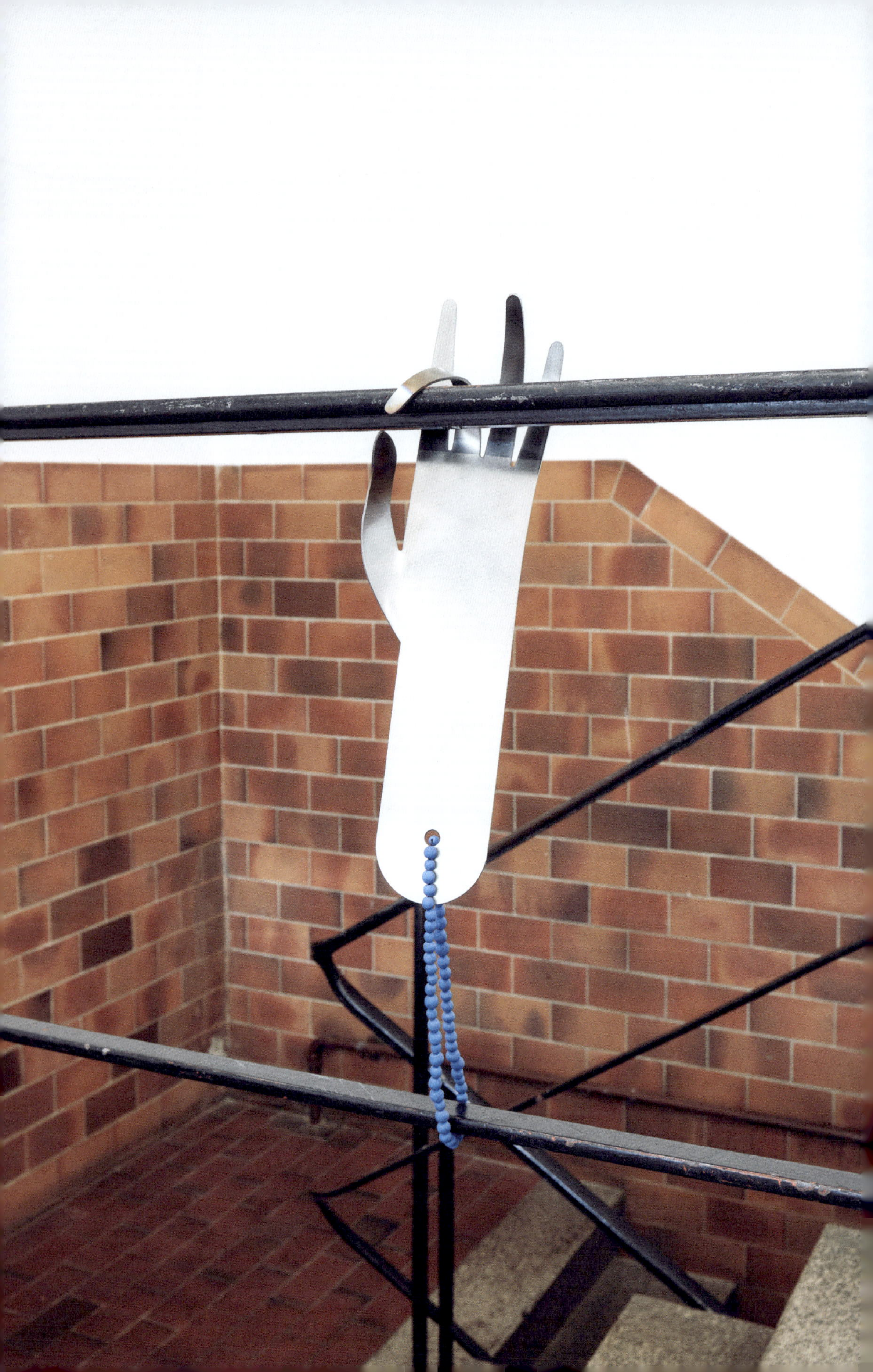

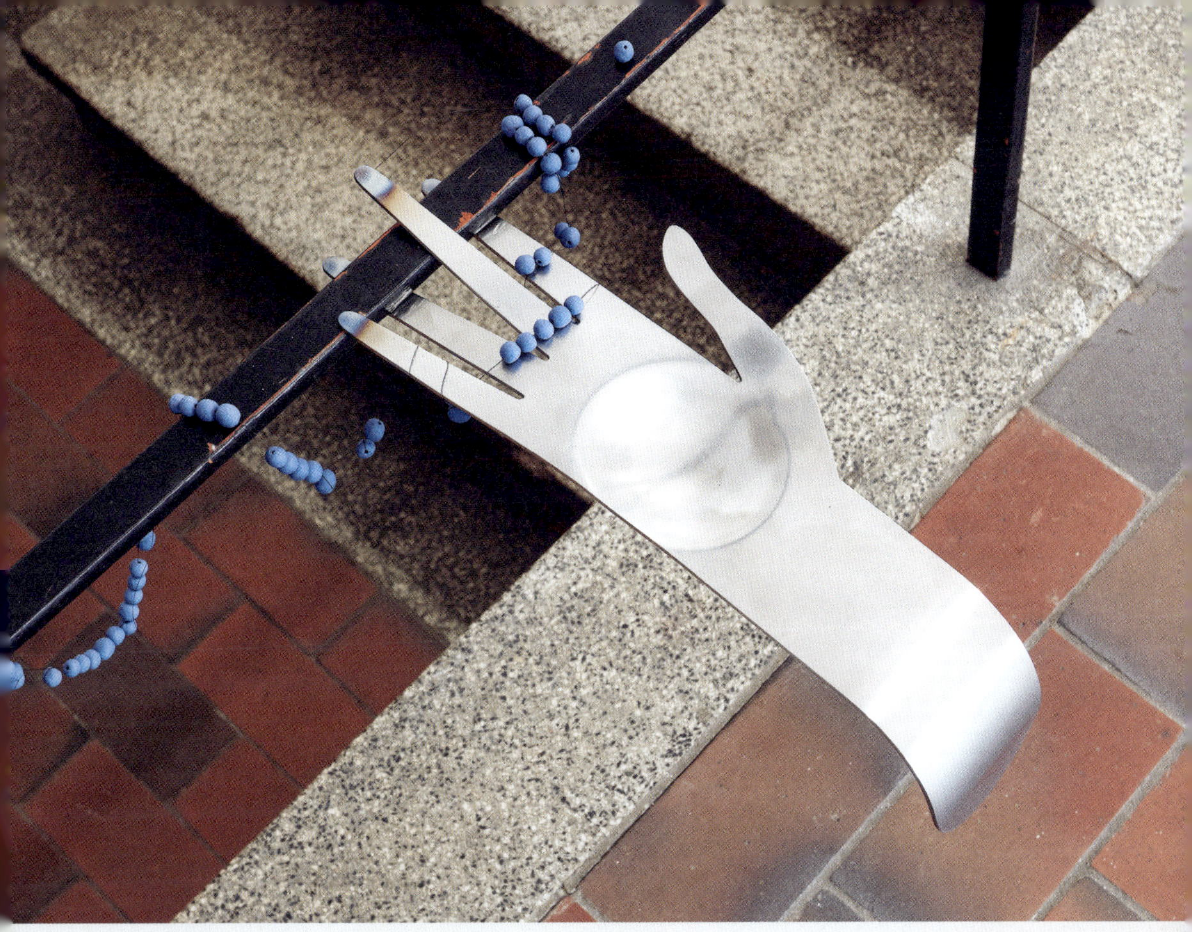

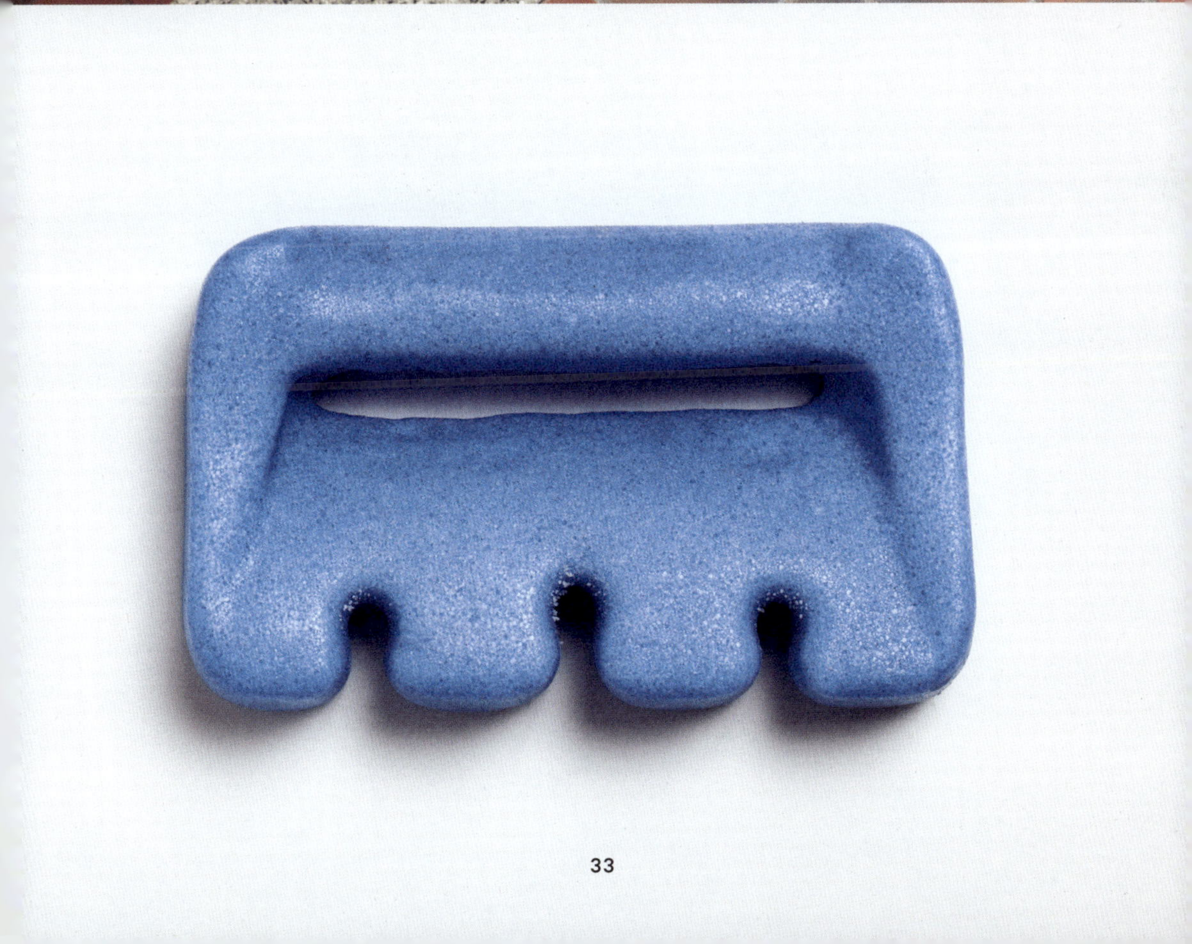

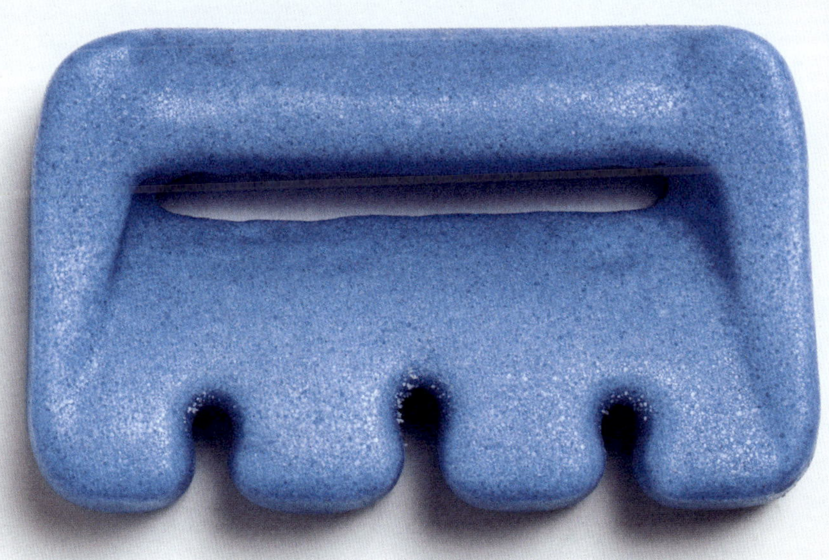

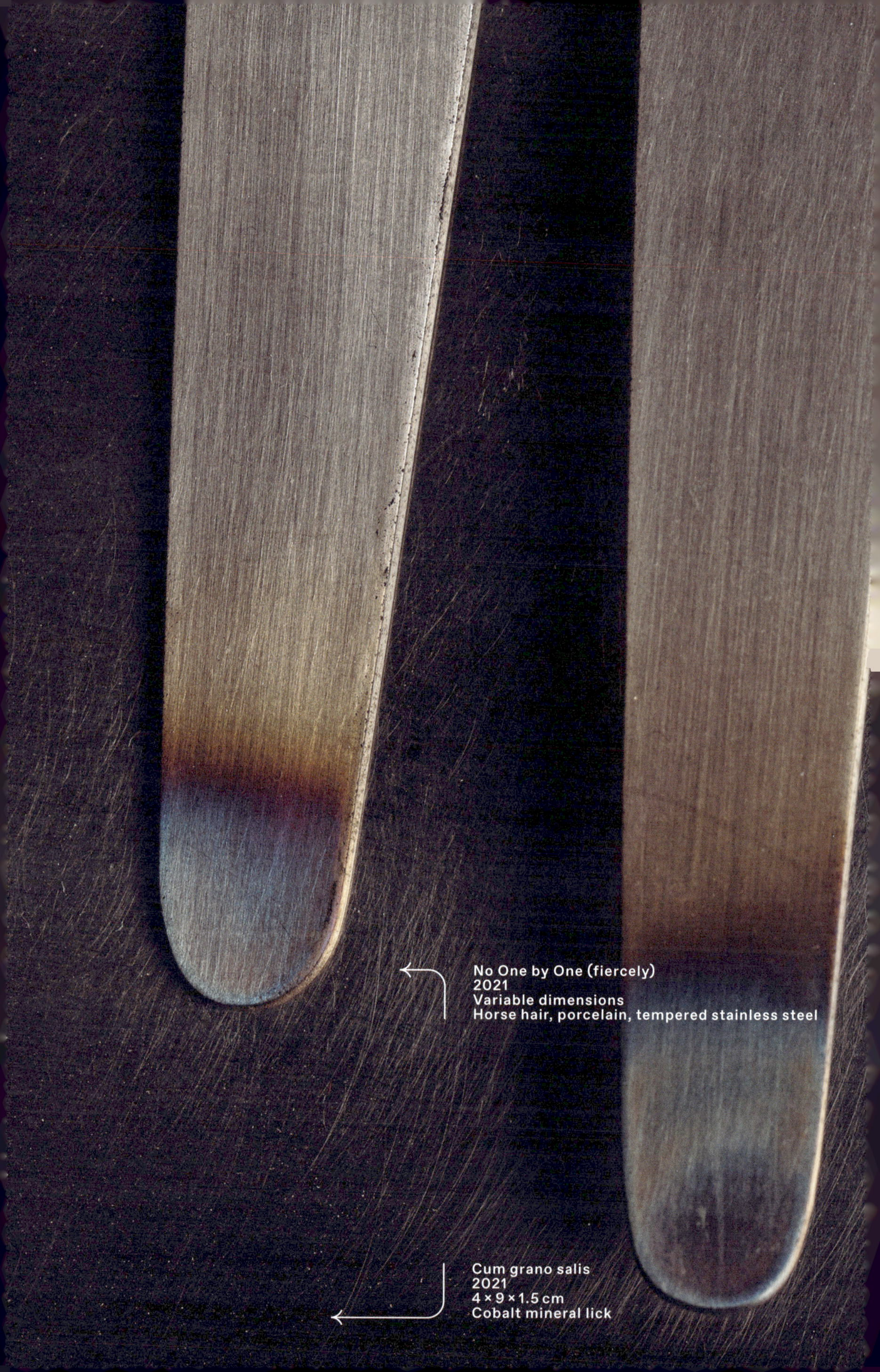

No One by One (fiercely)
2021
Variable dimensions
Horse hair, porcelain, tempered stainless steel

Cum grano salis
2021
4 × 9 × 1.5 cm
Cobalt mineral lick

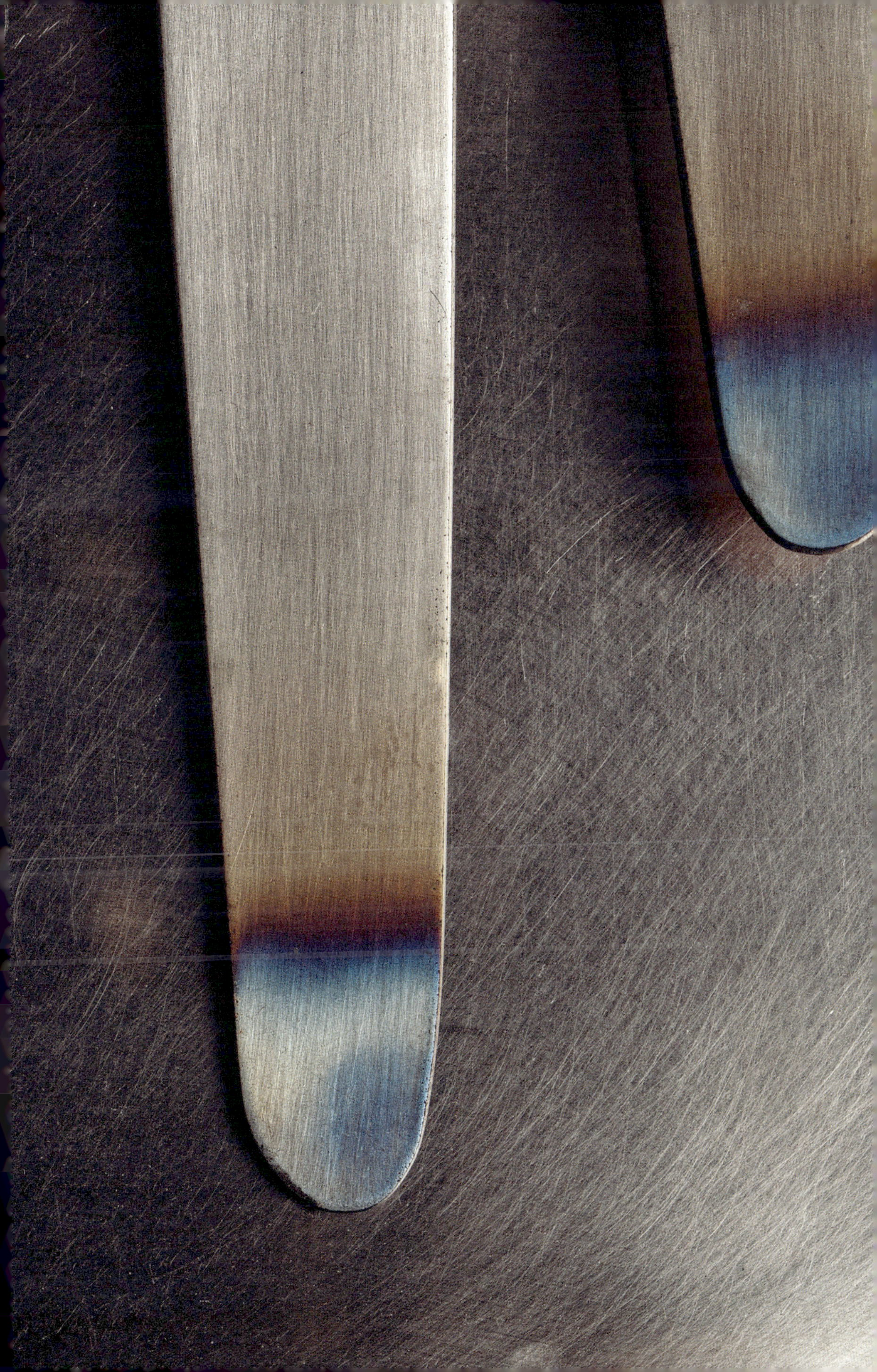

Cric crac croc
mes pieds sont encore
sortis de mes gougounes
en raphia.

Mon talon gauche pilonne
un plan de chardon.

Je peste et pique un fard
aussi sec, cinglée par
une pensée pour mon
enfance sauvage et ses
étés passés nu-pieds
à m'en semeler les plantes
de corne; elle a depuis
longtemps fait peau
de chagrin et me voici
réduite à masser mes orteils
et décanter les ferments
de mon repentir*, paumée
au milieu du sentier.

* avoir négligé mes arbres totems, m'être civilisée à force de lèche-vitrine en ligne et de microdosage de mondanités, être, en somme, devenue une citadine de bon ton

Du temps d'avant
je ne regrette pourtant
ni les limaces
qui s'écrasaient entre
les orteils — le prix à payer
pour fouler la rosée —,
ni le rituel du mois de mai
qui flanquait l'apparition
des maringouins —
décompte journalier
des piqûres, grattage
jusqu'au sang, arrachage
méthodique des croûtes
sans espoir de cicatrisation.

Non plus que les ratons
laveurs, par ailleurs
si trognons, qui zigouillaient
nos chatons portée
après portée, bien aises
d'avoir trouvé le jackpot.

Pas un soupir non plus
pour les routes
poussiéreuses perdues
dans le bois où,
adolescente à vélo,
il ne faisait pas bon croiser
quelqu'un et où,
plus souvent qu'autrement,
montait au loin
le mugissement d'une
cohorte de quads —
et avec lui
mes sueurs froides.

Ce coin précis
de la cambrousse
québécoise (J0K 1L0),
hanté par le fantôme
de la lecture de Cujo,
NE ME MANQUE PAS.

Bref,
j'étais une sylvestre
(et si l'imparfait
de cette formule m'éprouve,
remiser la nostalgie
n'en reste pas moins
le mot d'ordre).

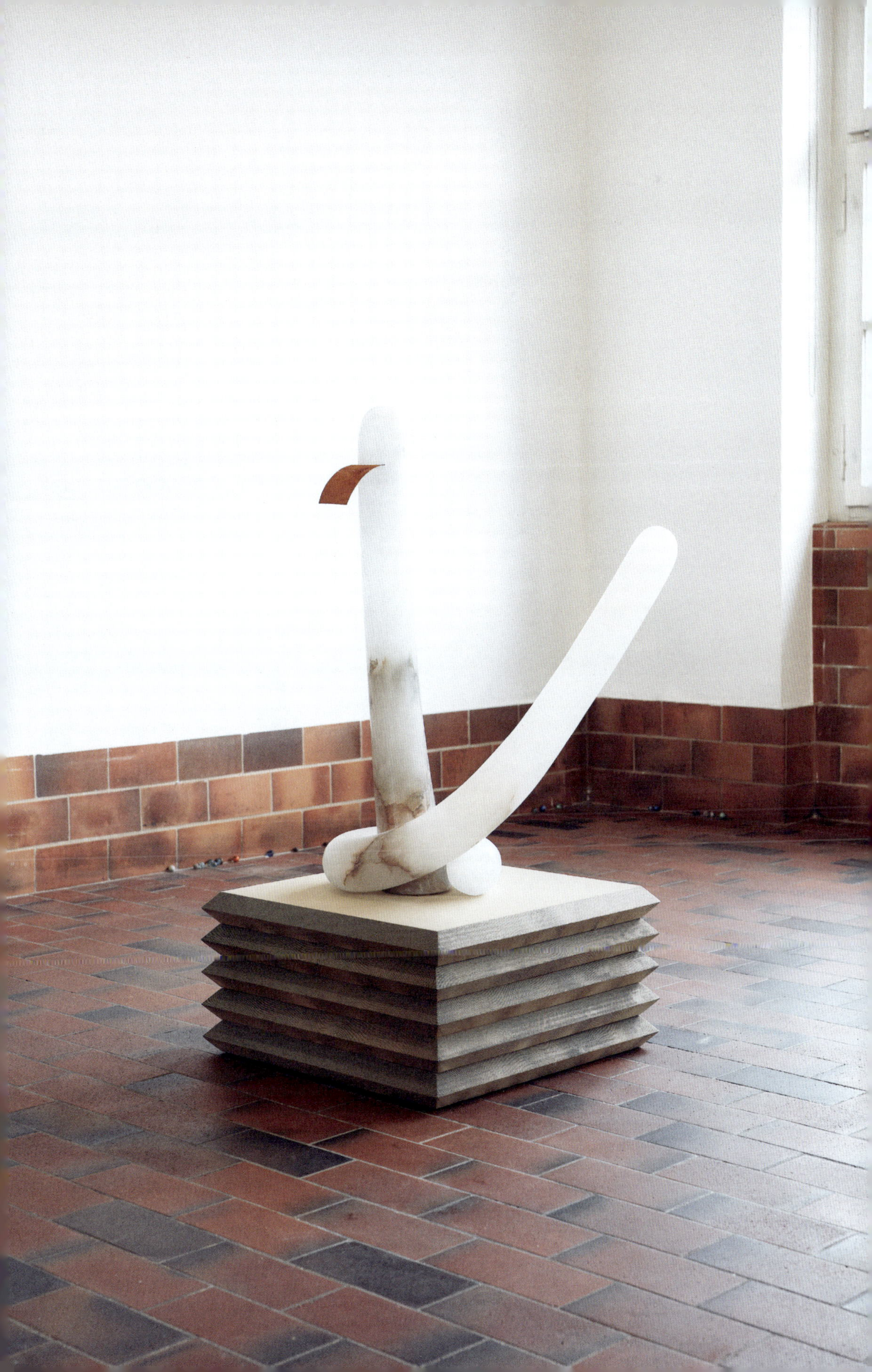

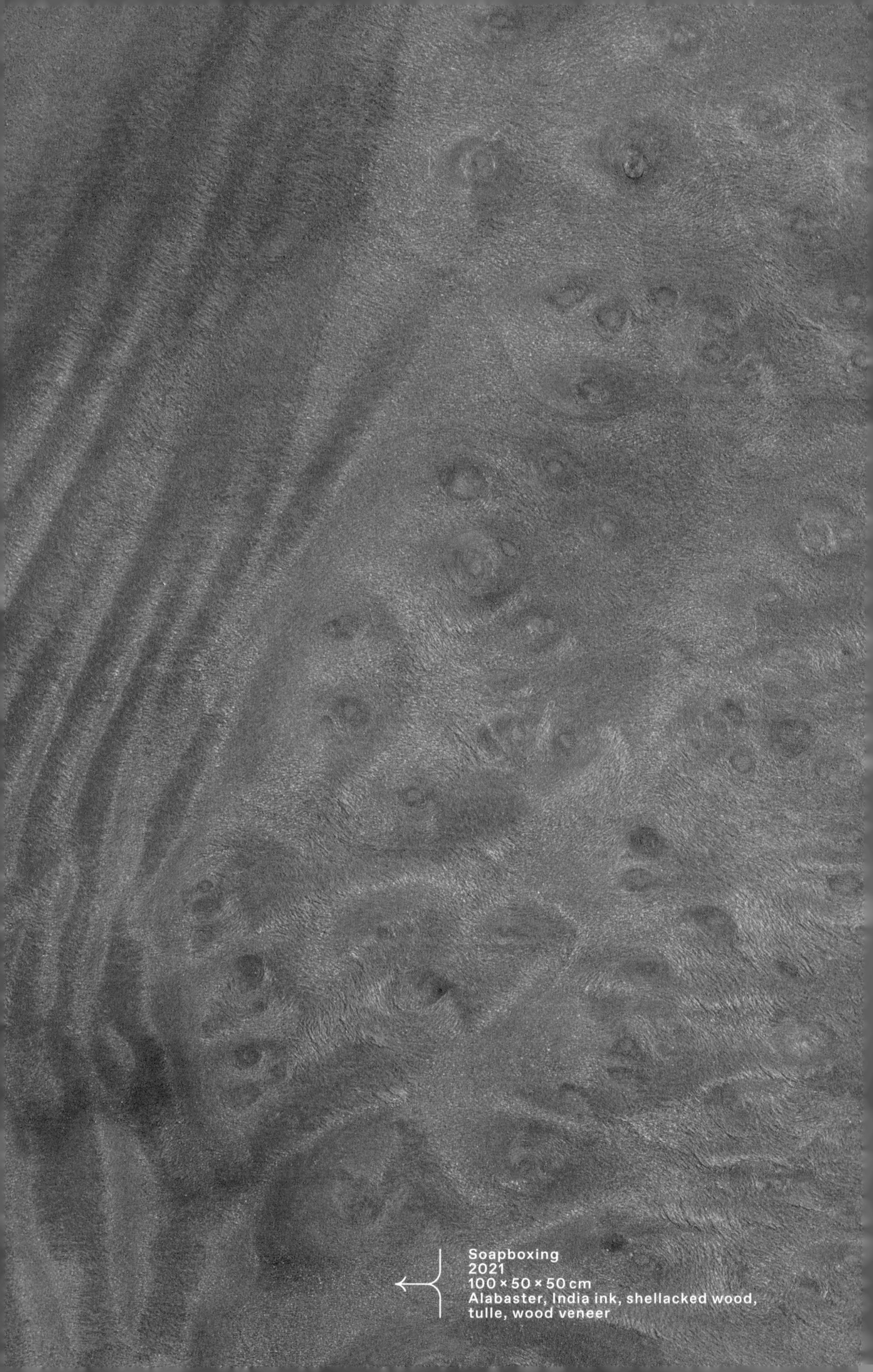

Soapboxing
2021
100 × 50 × 50 cm
Alabaster, India ink, shellacked wood,
tulle, wood veneer

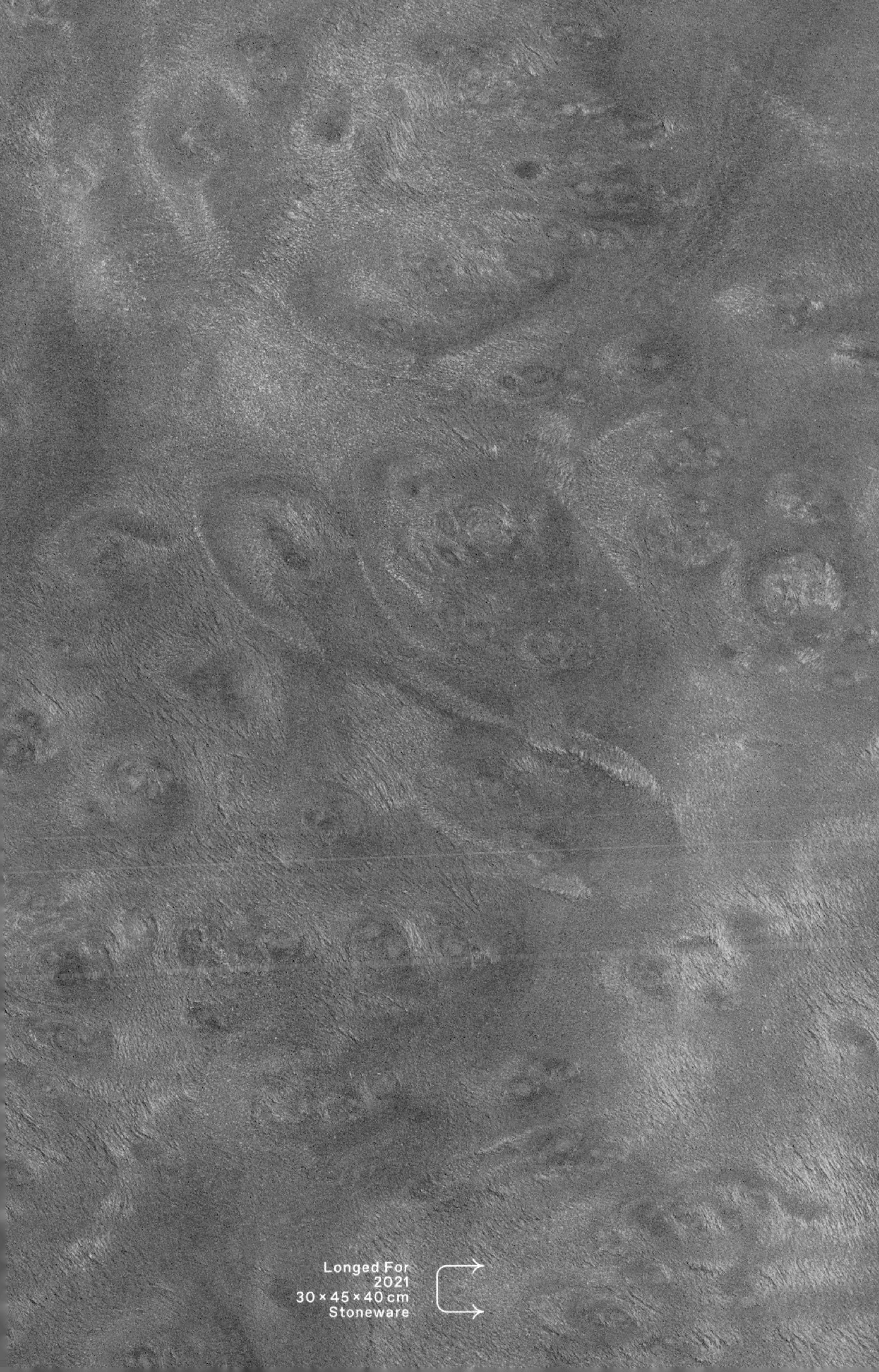

Longed For
2021
30 × 45 × 40 cm
Stoneware

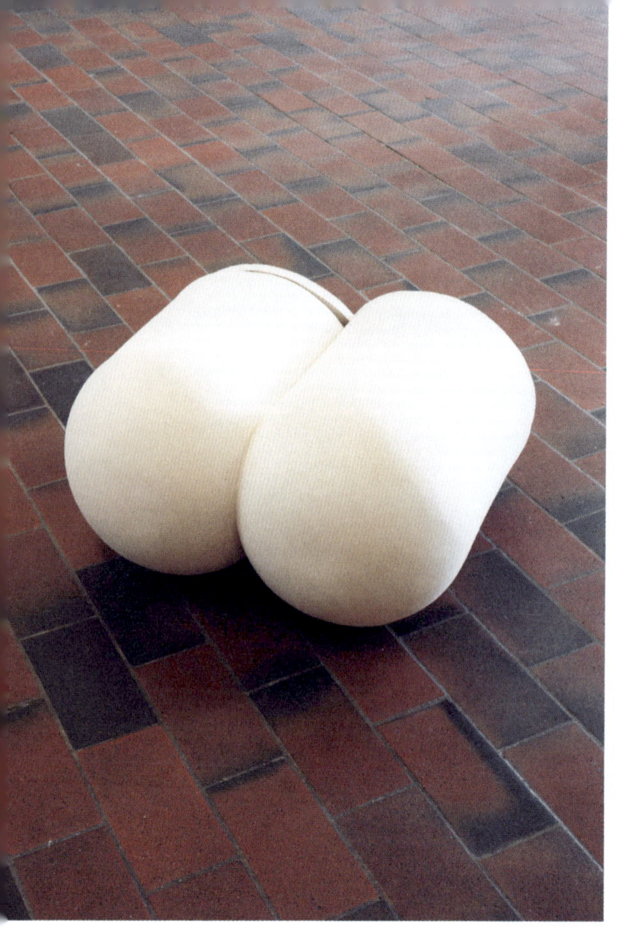

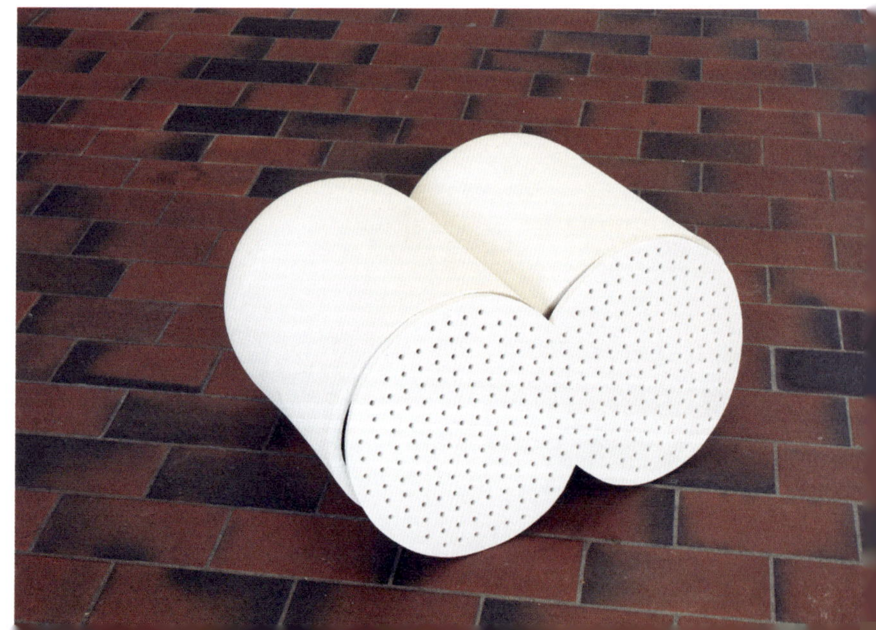

Abricots potelés,
jarre pleine de fiel,
colchiques en giration,
tenture de brocart mité.

Ajoutez à cela
une frénésie
de mini-maracas
en guise de bande-son
pour la chance
qui hoquète,
éreintée
par les bides chroniques
et les après-midis
qui s'étirent
sous le platane
à écluser coupes,
flutes et ballons
à n'en plus finir.

Ouf.

Le décor planté
appelle les trois coups,
que nul
ne vient frapper.

Sa panse
est pleine à craquer,
il est minuit
moins cinq.

Poussif,
peinant à s'accouder,
sa couleur préférée
reste celle
du Chavo double,
déposé avec superbe
sur le zinc.

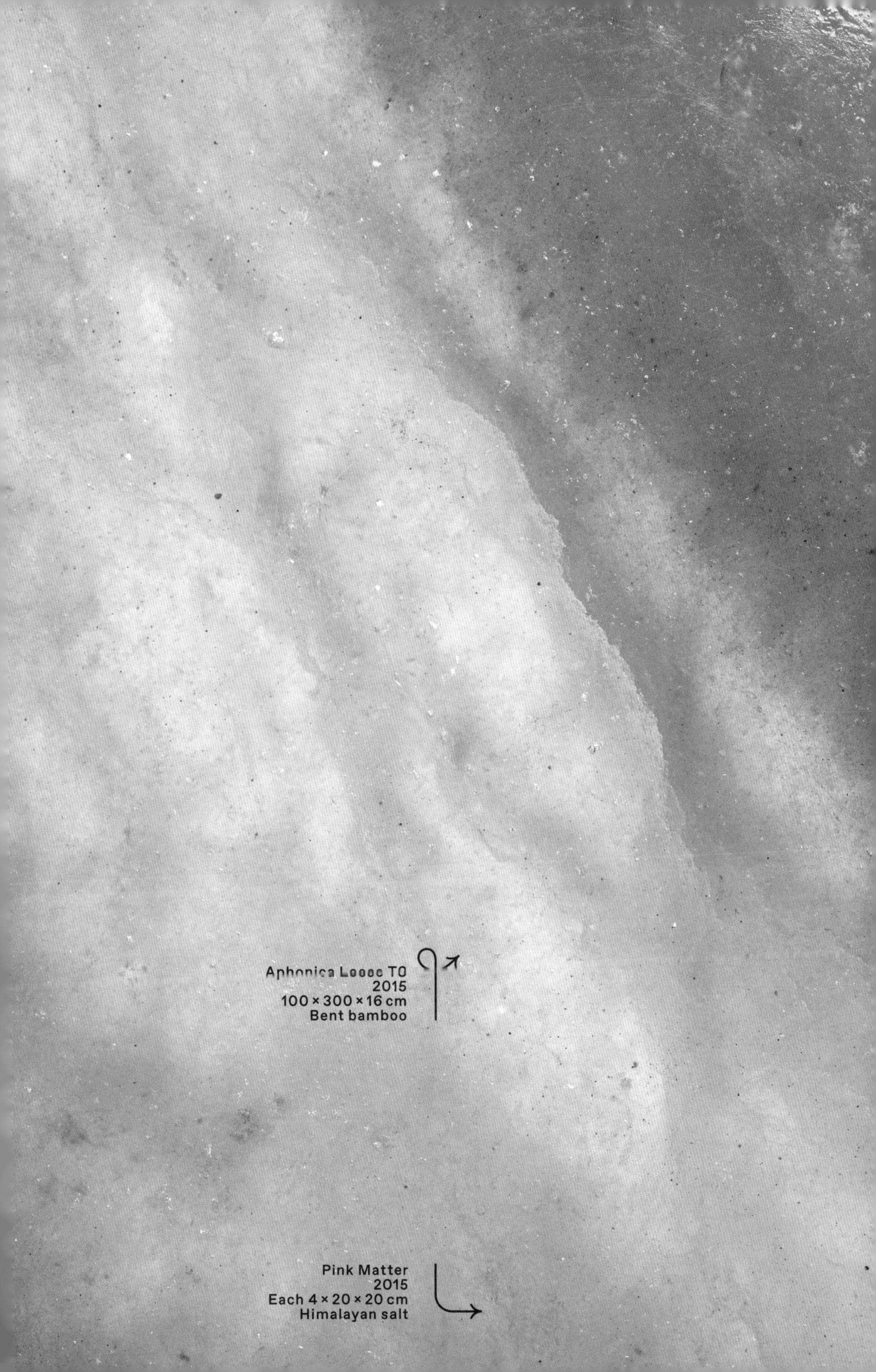

Aphonica Loose T0
2015
100 × 300 × 16 cm
Bent bamboo

Pink Matter
2015
Each 4 × 20 × 20 cm
Himalayan salt

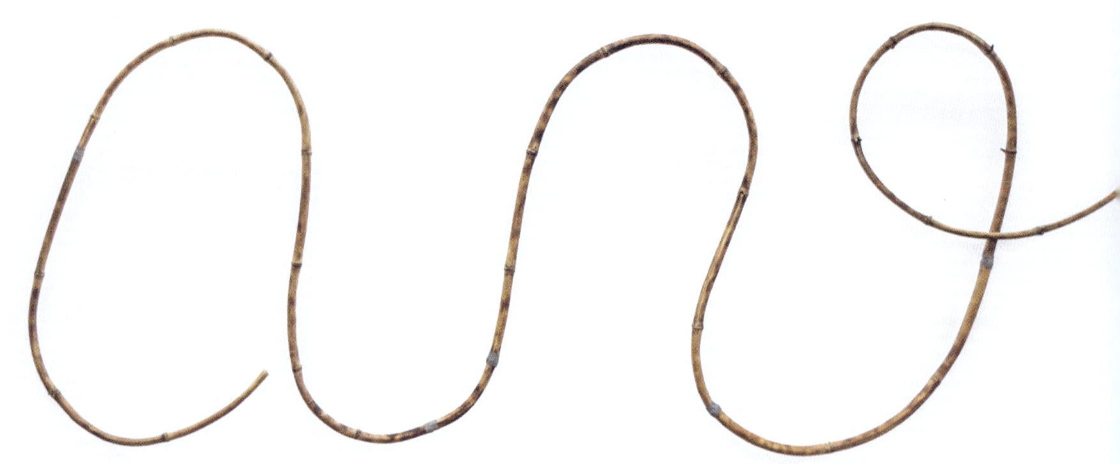

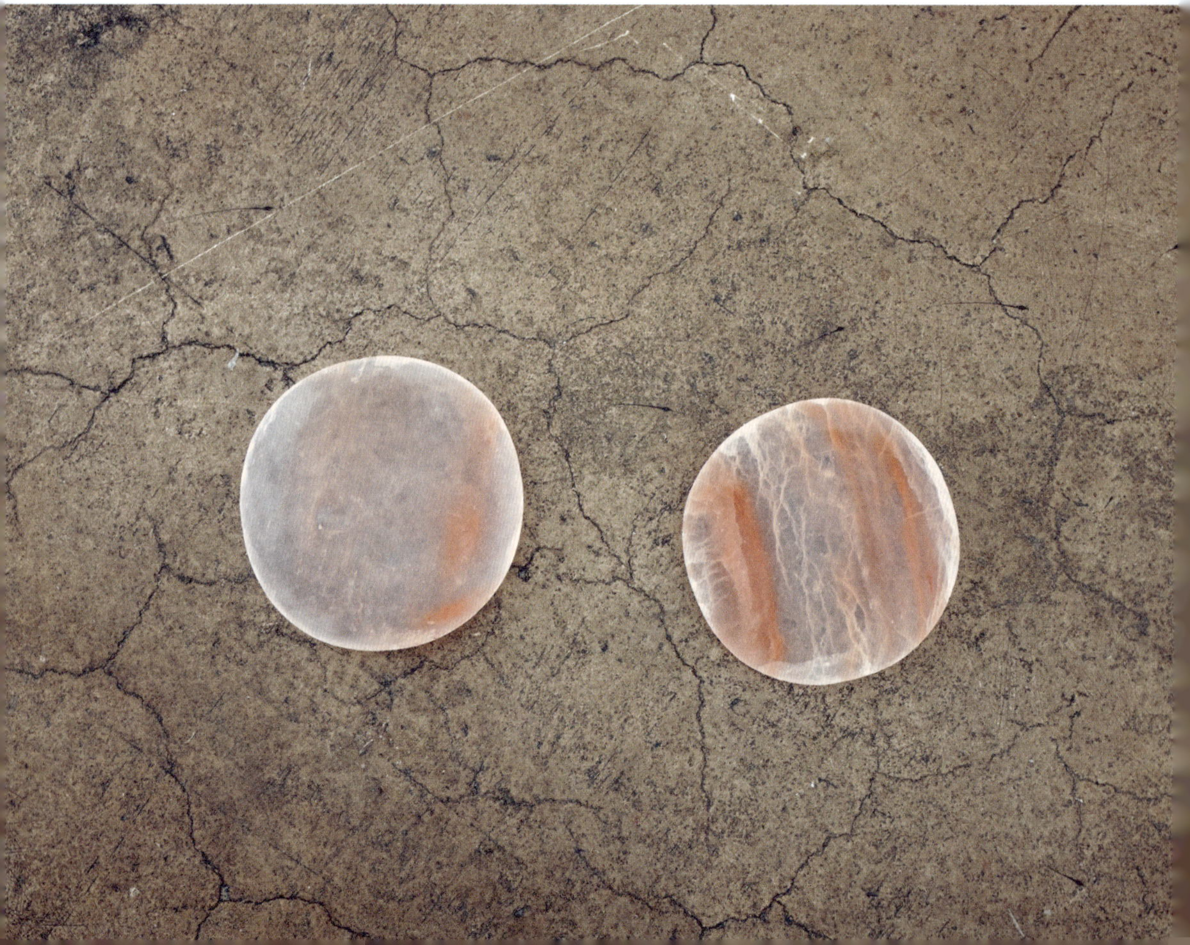

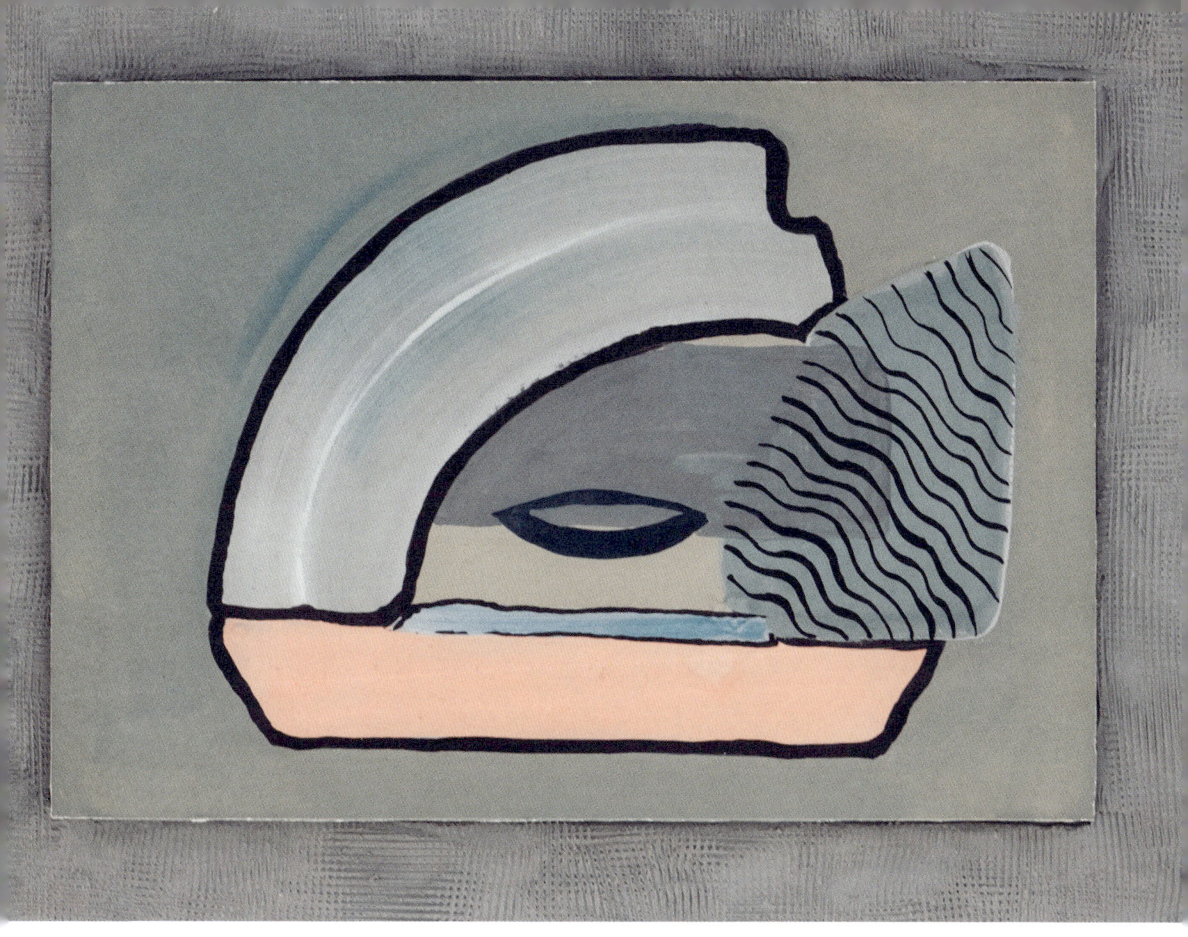

Tohu-bohu
2015
16 × 25 × 1 cm
Gouache embedded in plastiline-covered plates

Digression
2016
60 × 300 × 8 cm
Himalayan salt, industrial plastiline,
pleated silk, steel

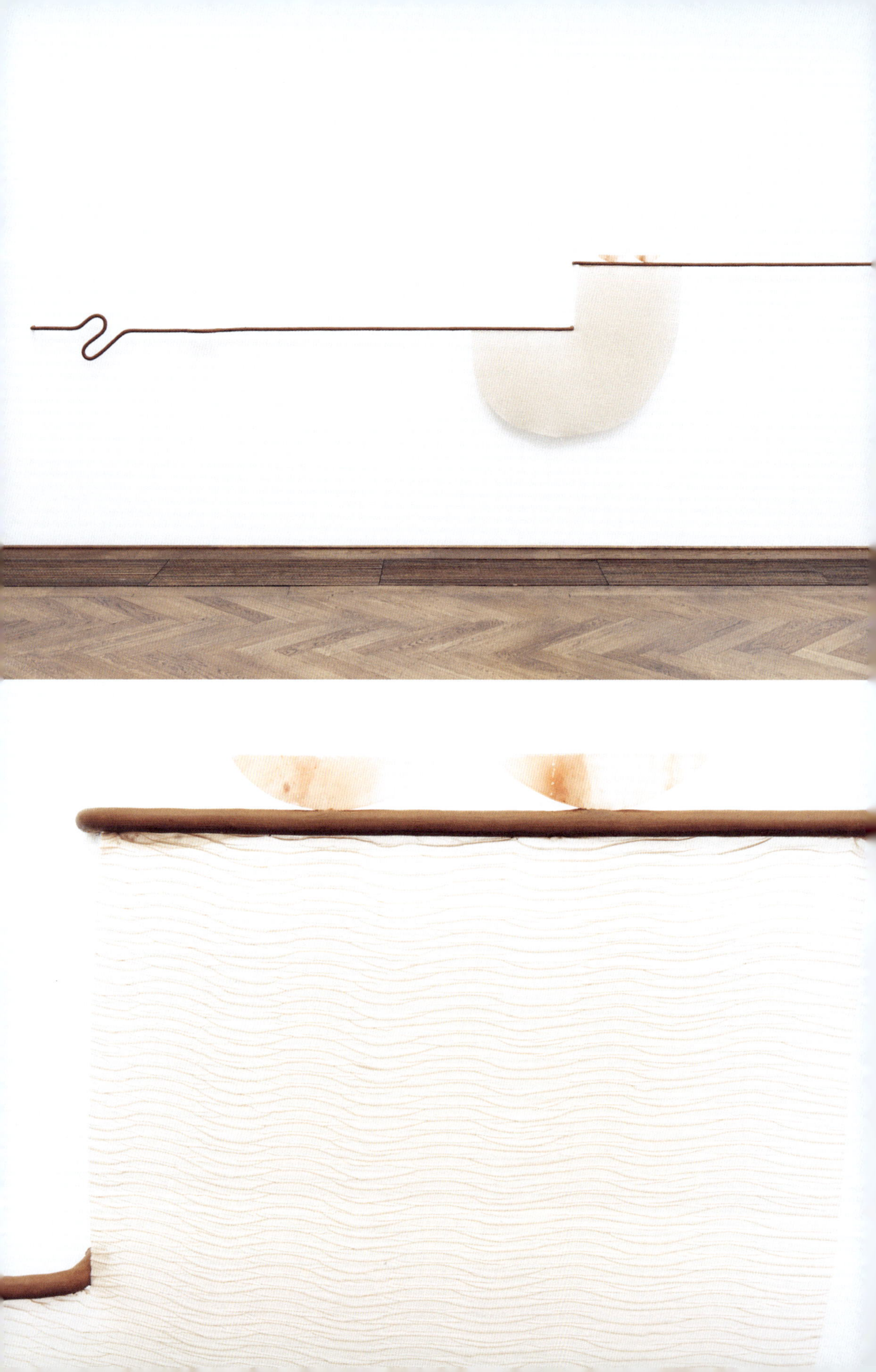

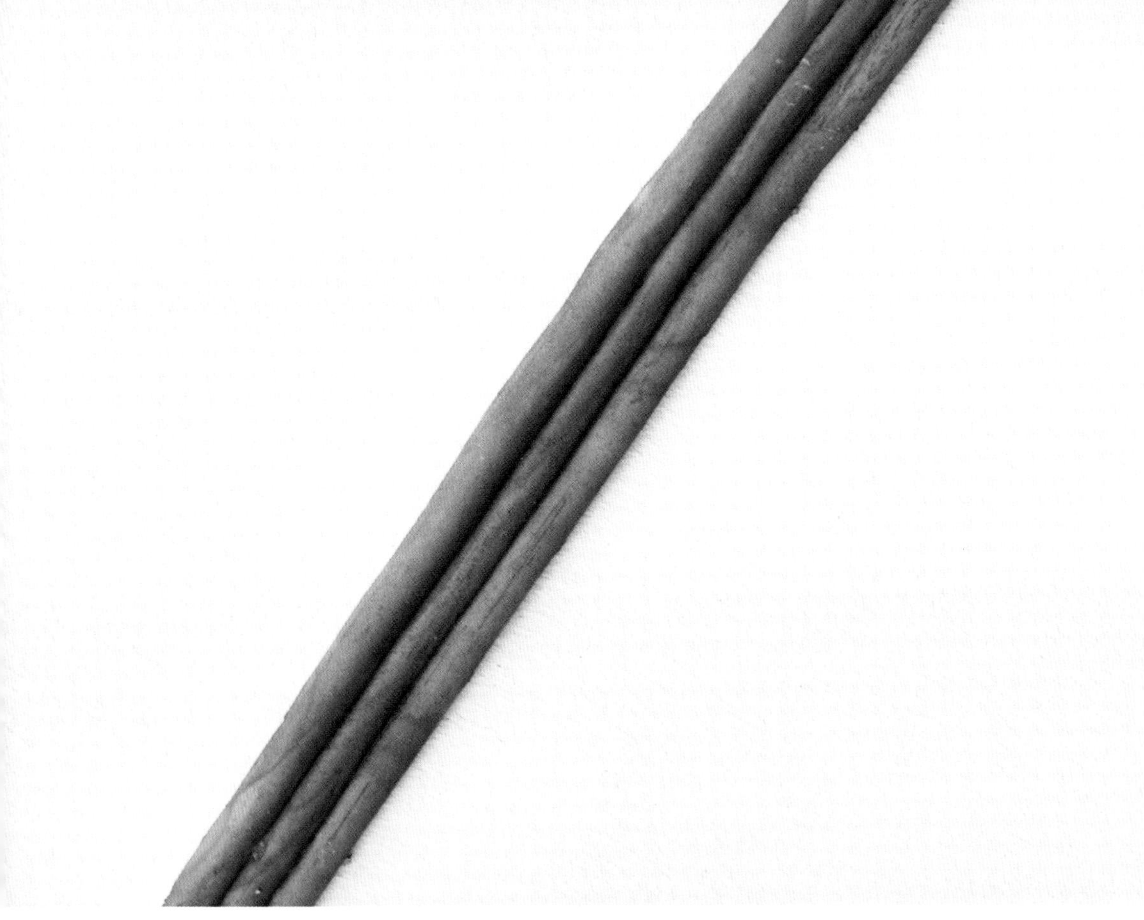

Unterschiedlich grosse Stücke aus zwei verschiedenen Materialien — leuchtendes Einwegspiegelglas und kreideartige Schuppen — sind abwechselnd aufeinandergeschichtet und bilden eine Trennwand zwischen zwei zentralen Säulen.

Das ebenso bescheidene wie prominente Konglomerat vermittelt, je nachdem auf welcher Seite man steht, den Eindruck, festzementiert oder in der Schwebe zu sein.

Doppelgesichtige Assemblage, ein namenloser Janus. Warum nicht?

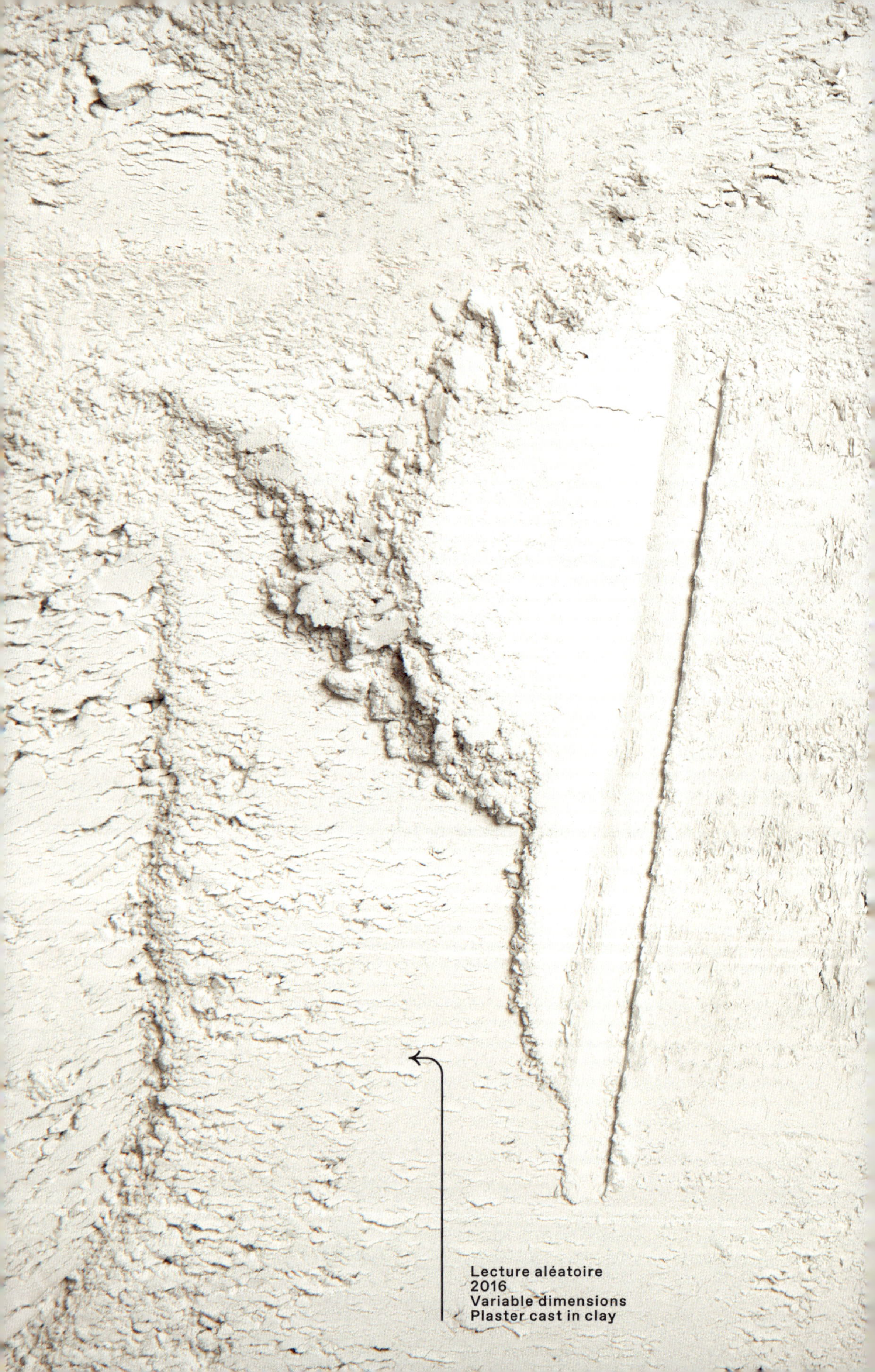

Lecture aléatoire
2016
Variable dimensions
Plaster cast in clay

Lecture aléatoire
2016
Variable dimensions
Plaster cast in clay

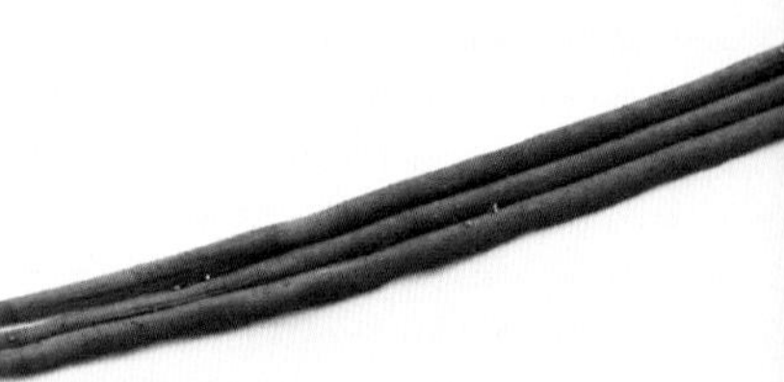

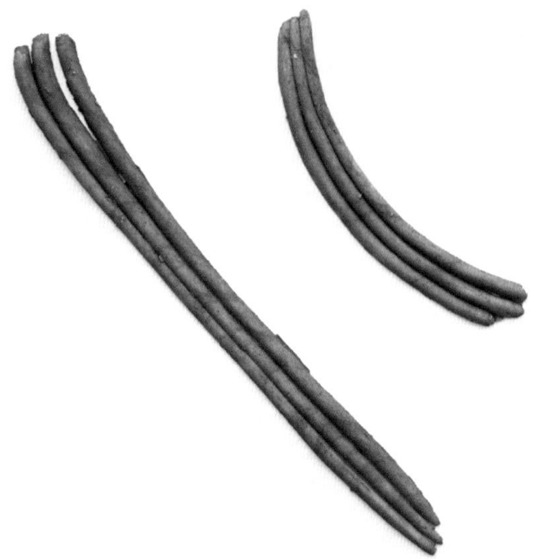

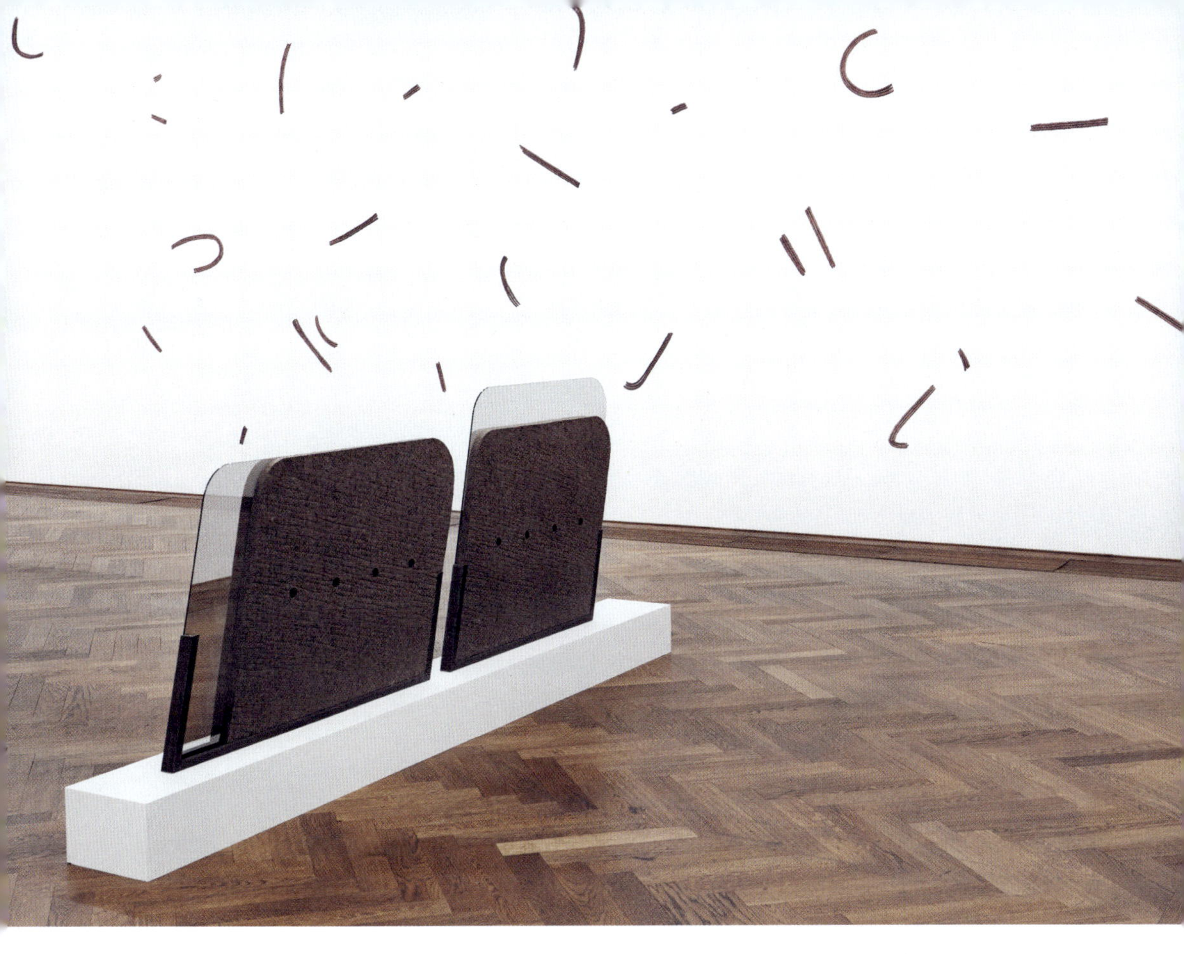

écoute, la croûte se fend

les sucs ont taché ses doigts

tire-toi

songe à l'arc, que nul ne tend

la boucle est bouclée,

Breathe In / Breathe Out
2016
80 × 135 × 4 / 95 × 130 × 4 cm
Felt, steel, two-way mirror

I Owe You a Yo-yo
2019
140 × 35 × 30 cm
Bent bamboo, plaster cast in clay

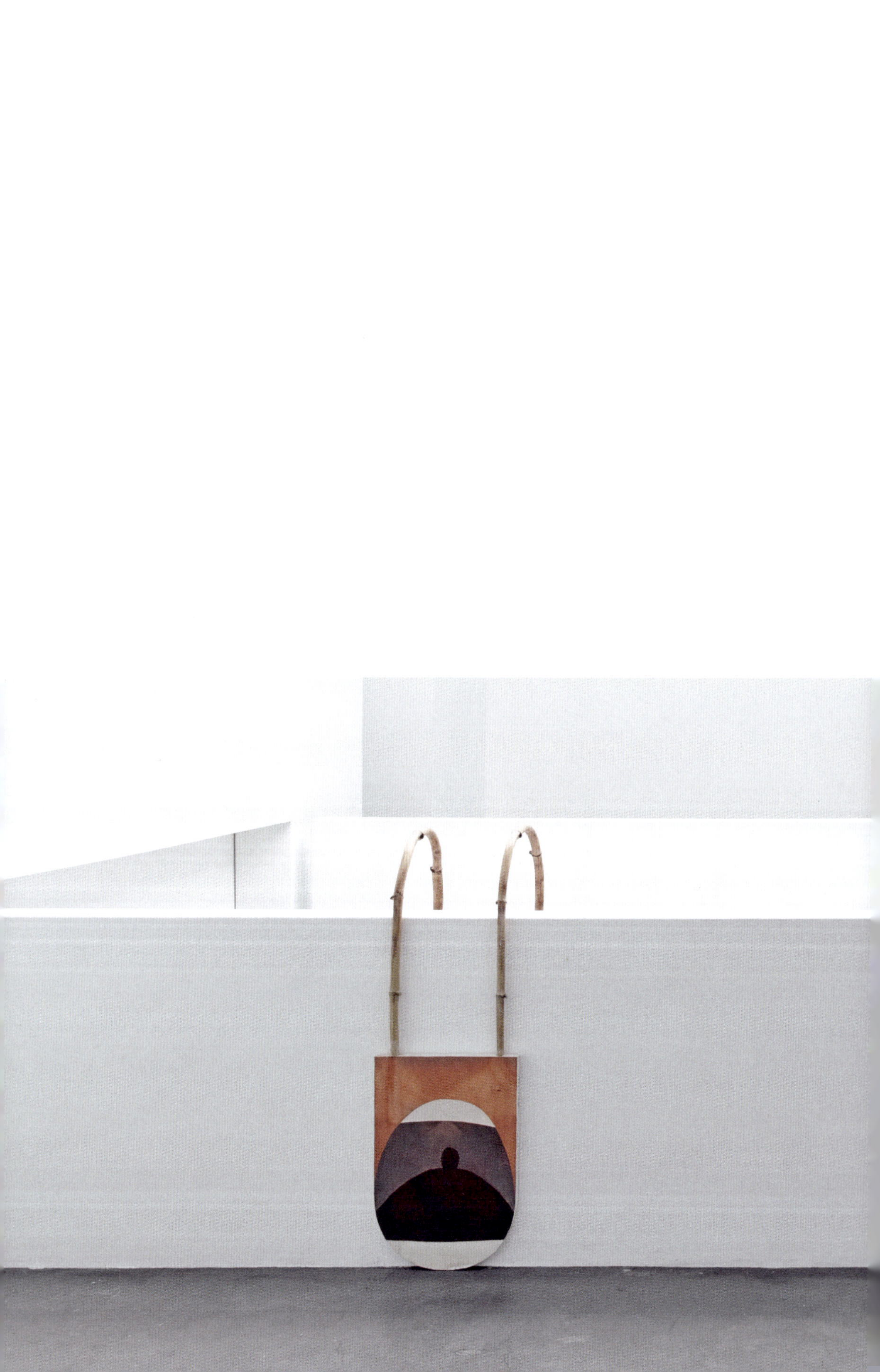

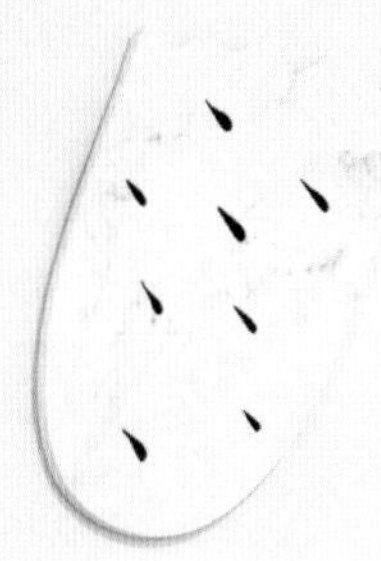

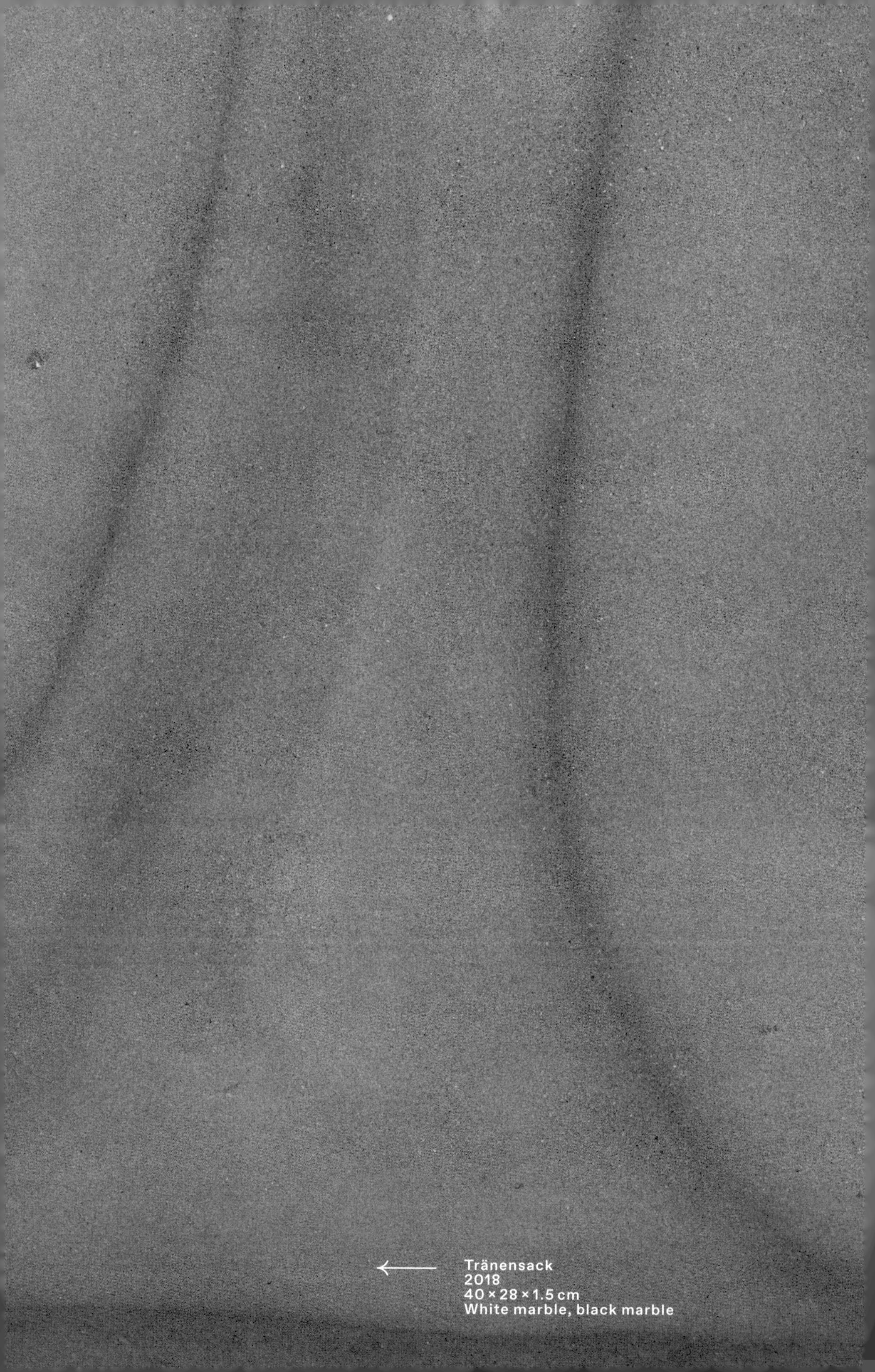

←

Tränensack
2018
40 × 28 × 1.5 cm
White marble, black marble

Clay Tablet
2017
62 × 130 × 4 cm
Plaster cast in clay

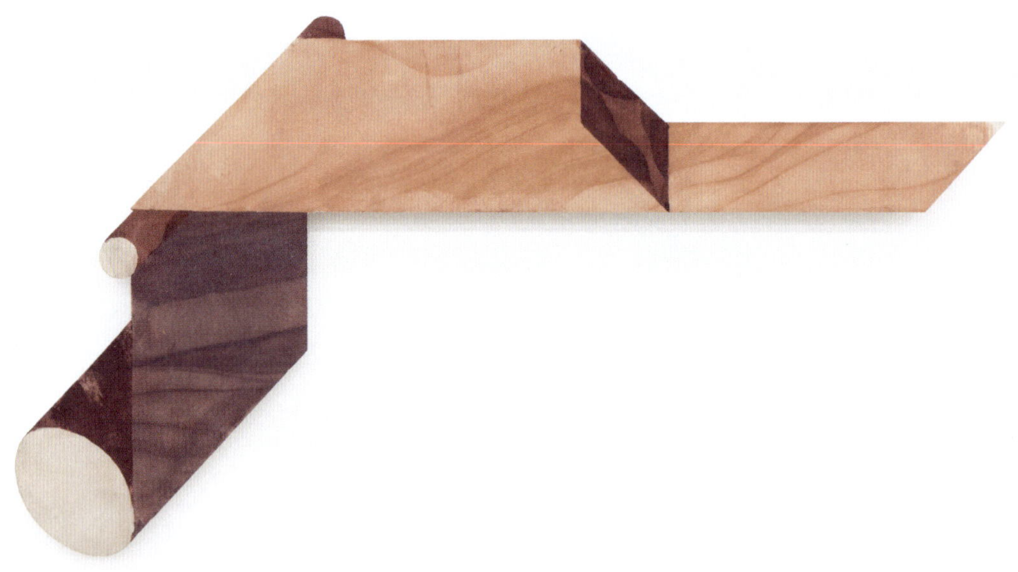

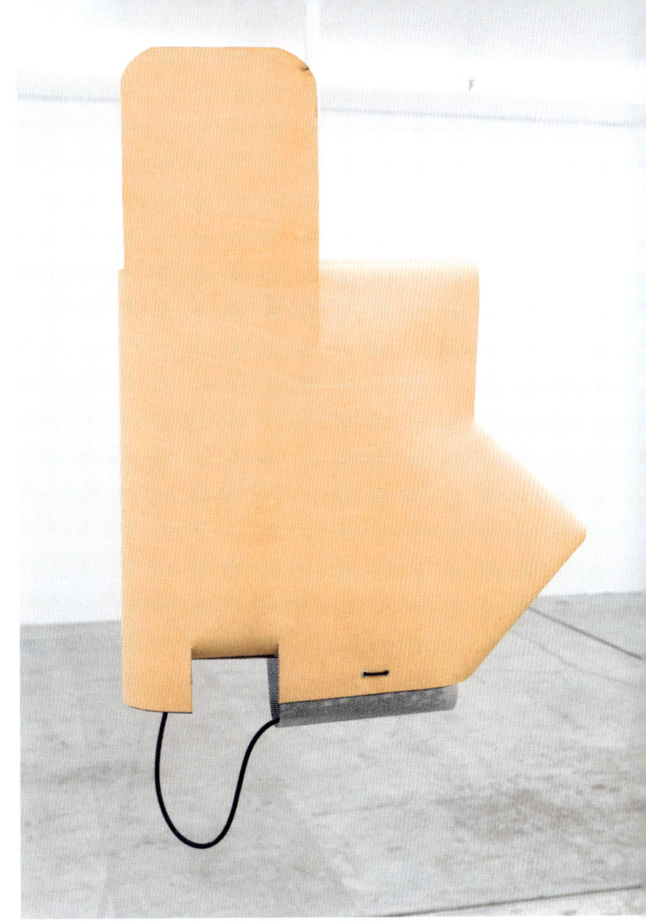

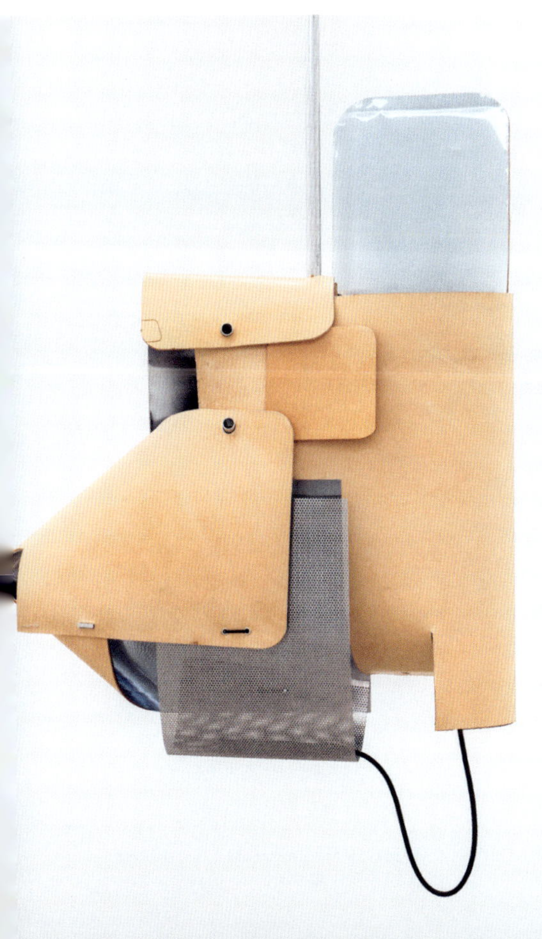

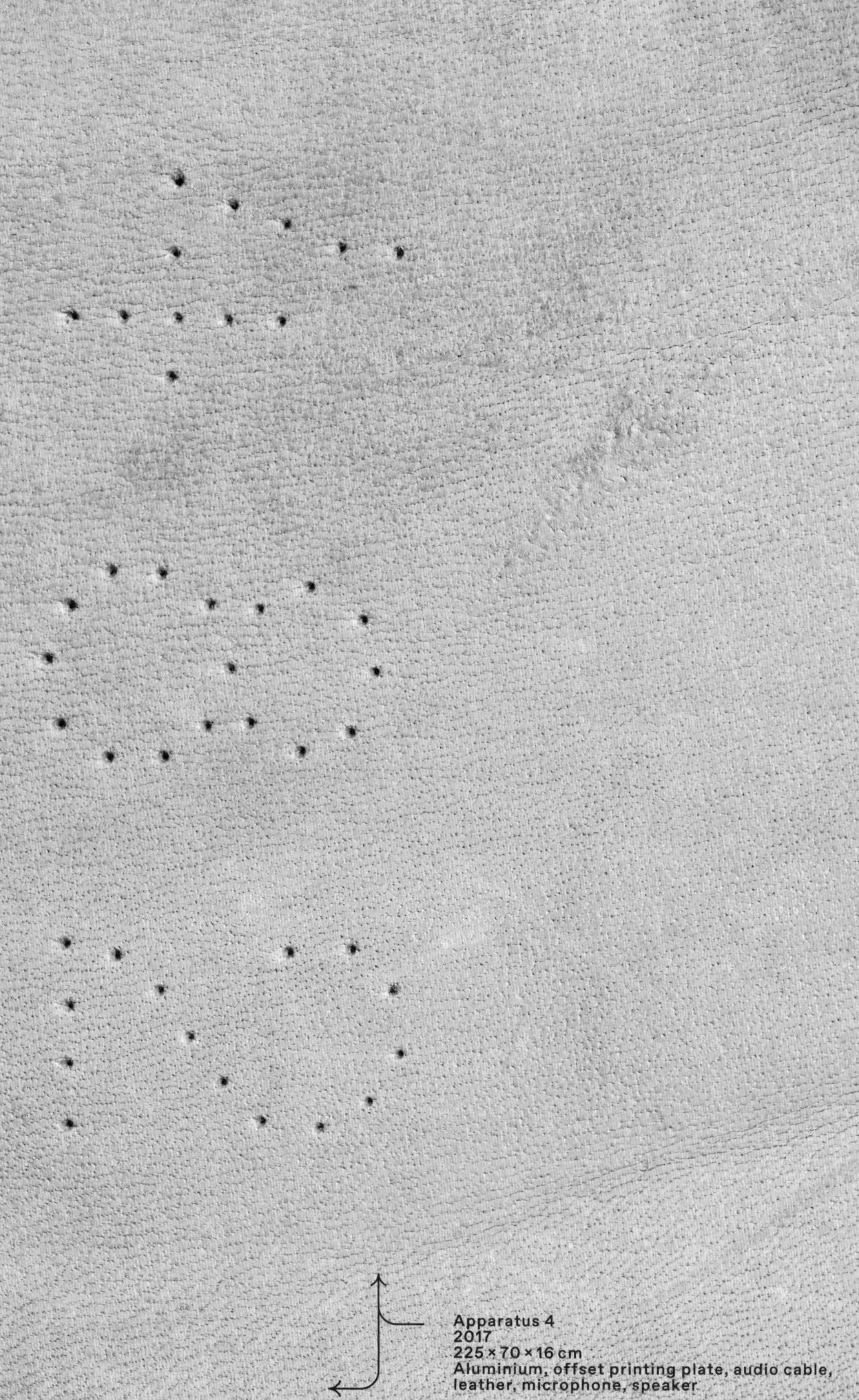

Apparatus 4
2017
225 × 70 × 16 cm
Aluminium, offset printing plate, audio cable, leather, microphone, speaker

Apparatus 3 →
2017
225 × 80 × 20 cm
Aluminium, audio cable, leather,
microphone, polished plaster, speaker

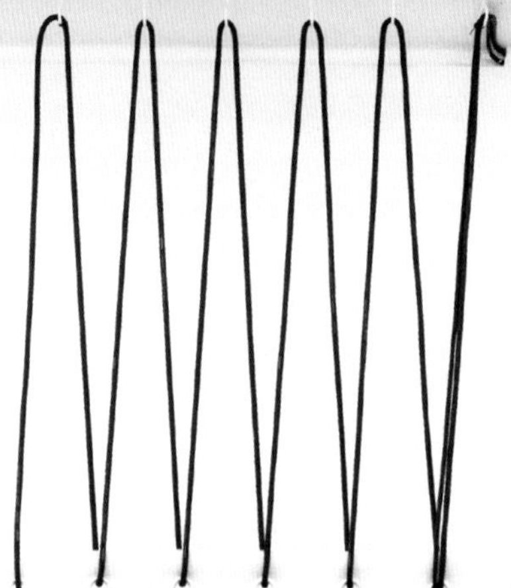

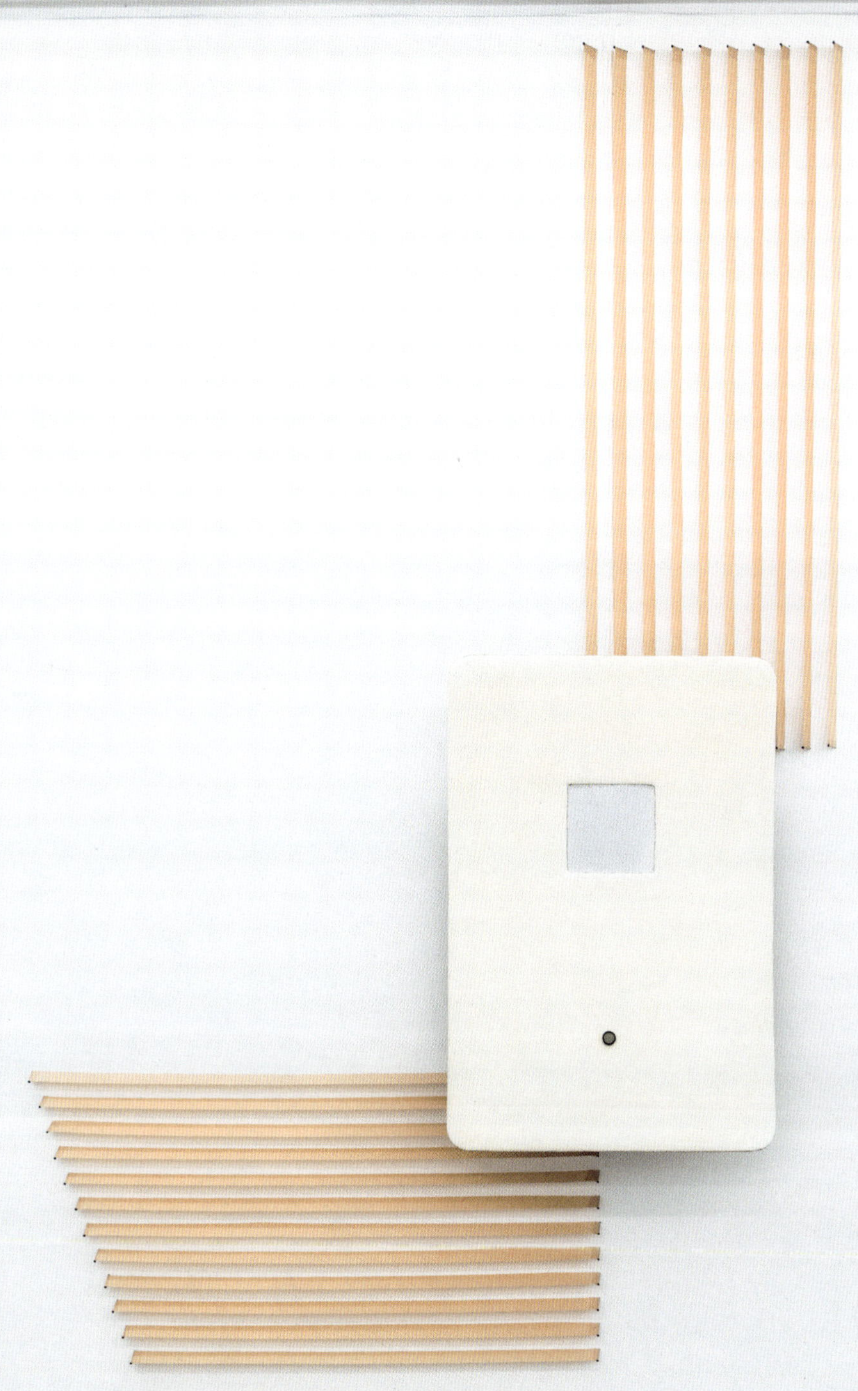

←

Apparatus 2
2017
225 × 160 × 35 cm
Audio cable, cork, fabric, microphone,
crepe masking tape, speaker, wood, wood paste

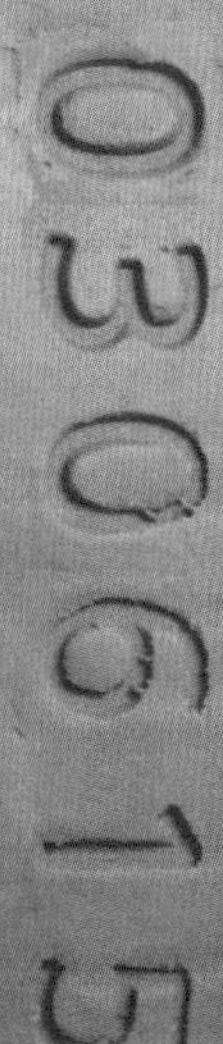

Apparatus 1
2017
42 cm high
Audio cable, brass, microphone,
industrial plastiline, speaker

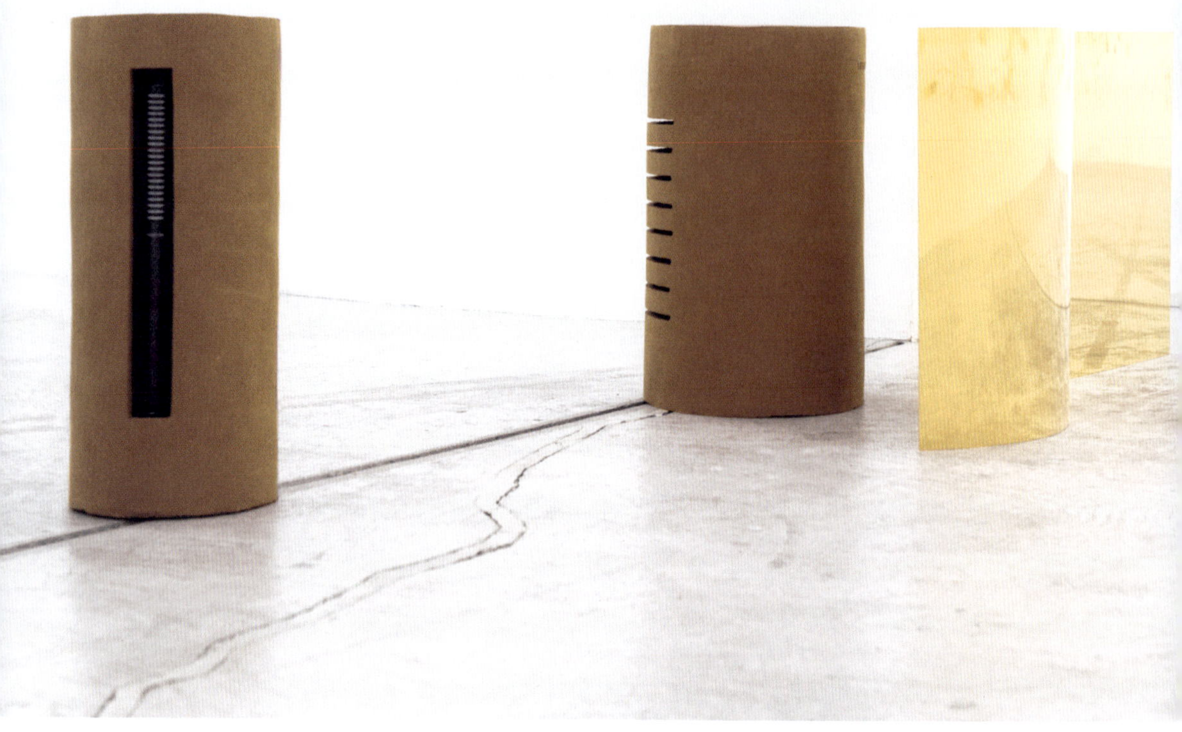

The long thin blades of grass flitting between our fingers non-stop, so beautiful. And supple. We have to take advantage of it as long as they're still juicy because the minute they start drying up, they get brittle and crumble—puff! all in unison. In their altered state, they fill up and saturate all the air imprisoned under the tin roof, making it even stuffier. So you just take a deep breath, roll up your sleeves and tackle the next job. Once the dear, low-key dust has settled, you fill it into the burlap bags lined up in a stepped row on the rammed earth, then you stack them on the poorly carpentered slats of the feeding troughs, lined up along the freshly whitewashed walls as far as the eye can see. The bags will be stored there indefinitely since using drones to distribute them has been prohibited, rightfully so and much to everyone's relief. Everybody without exception criticised this pompous crop that smacked of political strategy. No dusting, no white lying on the fields this year.

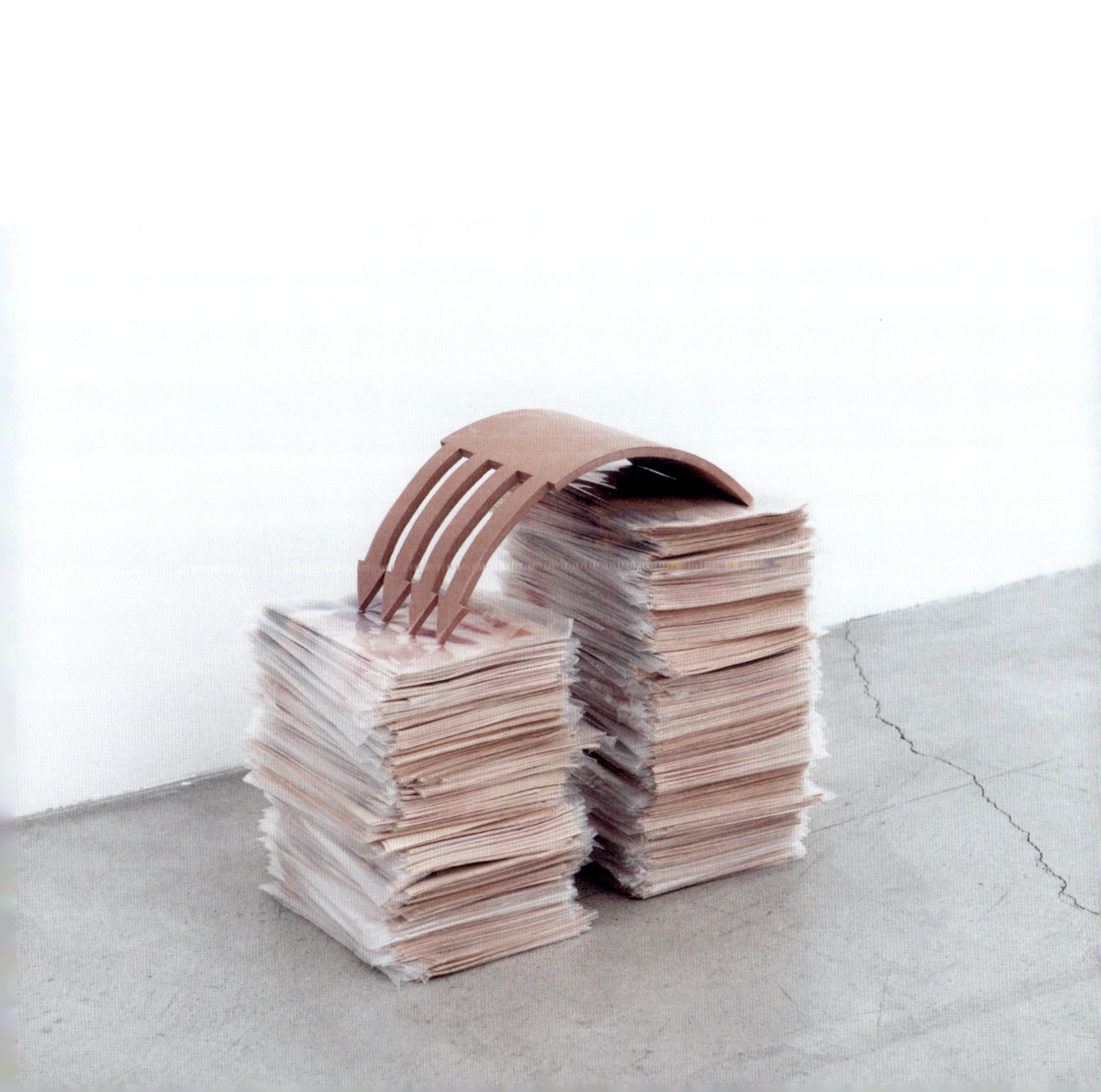

Untitled
(with Marie-Michelle Deschamps)
2017
55 × 50 × 30 cm
Artist edition printed on newsprint,
polythene seal, stoneware

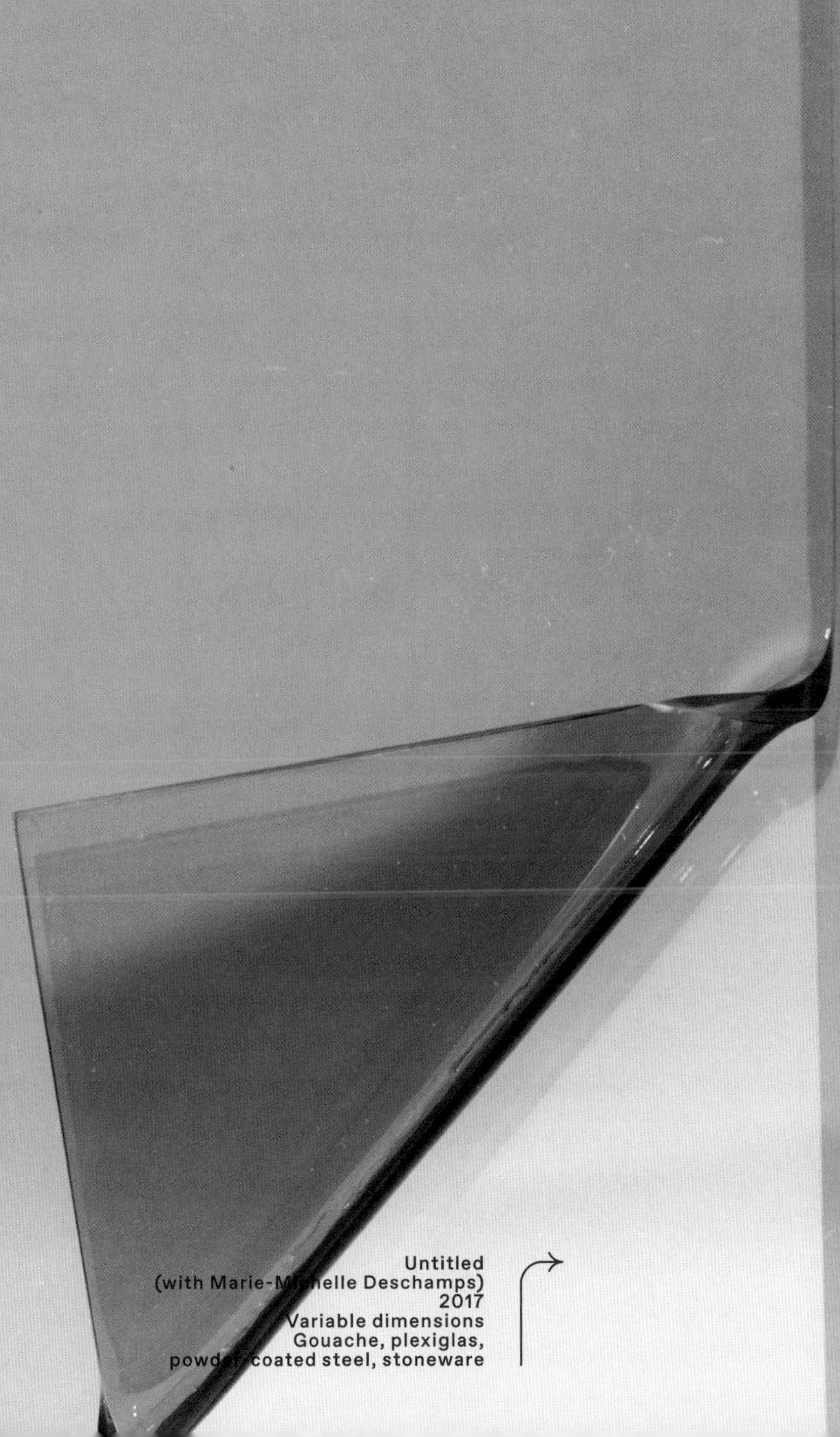

Untitled
(with Marie-Michelle Deschamps)
2017
Variable dimensions
Gouache, plexiglas,
powder-coated steel, stoneware

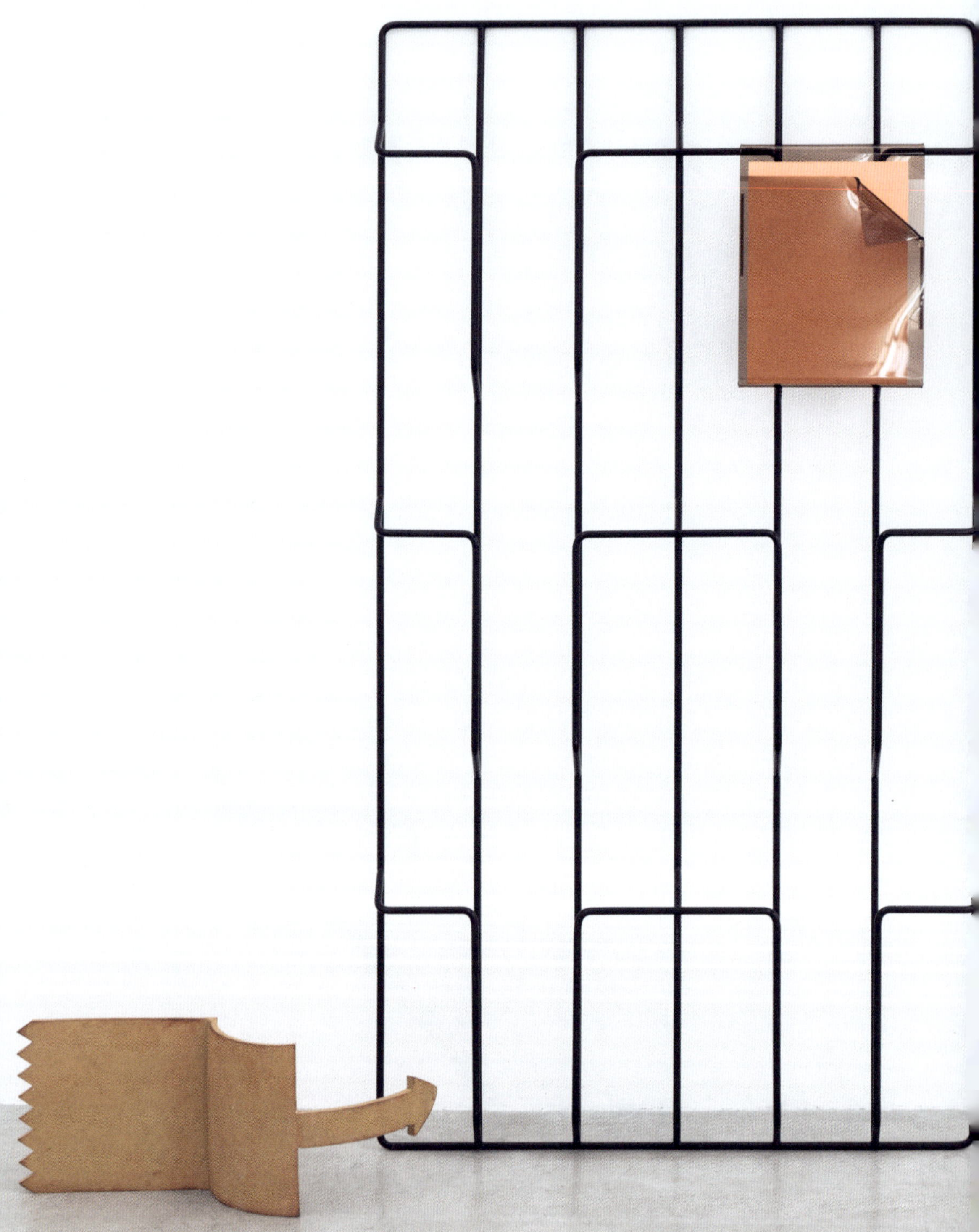

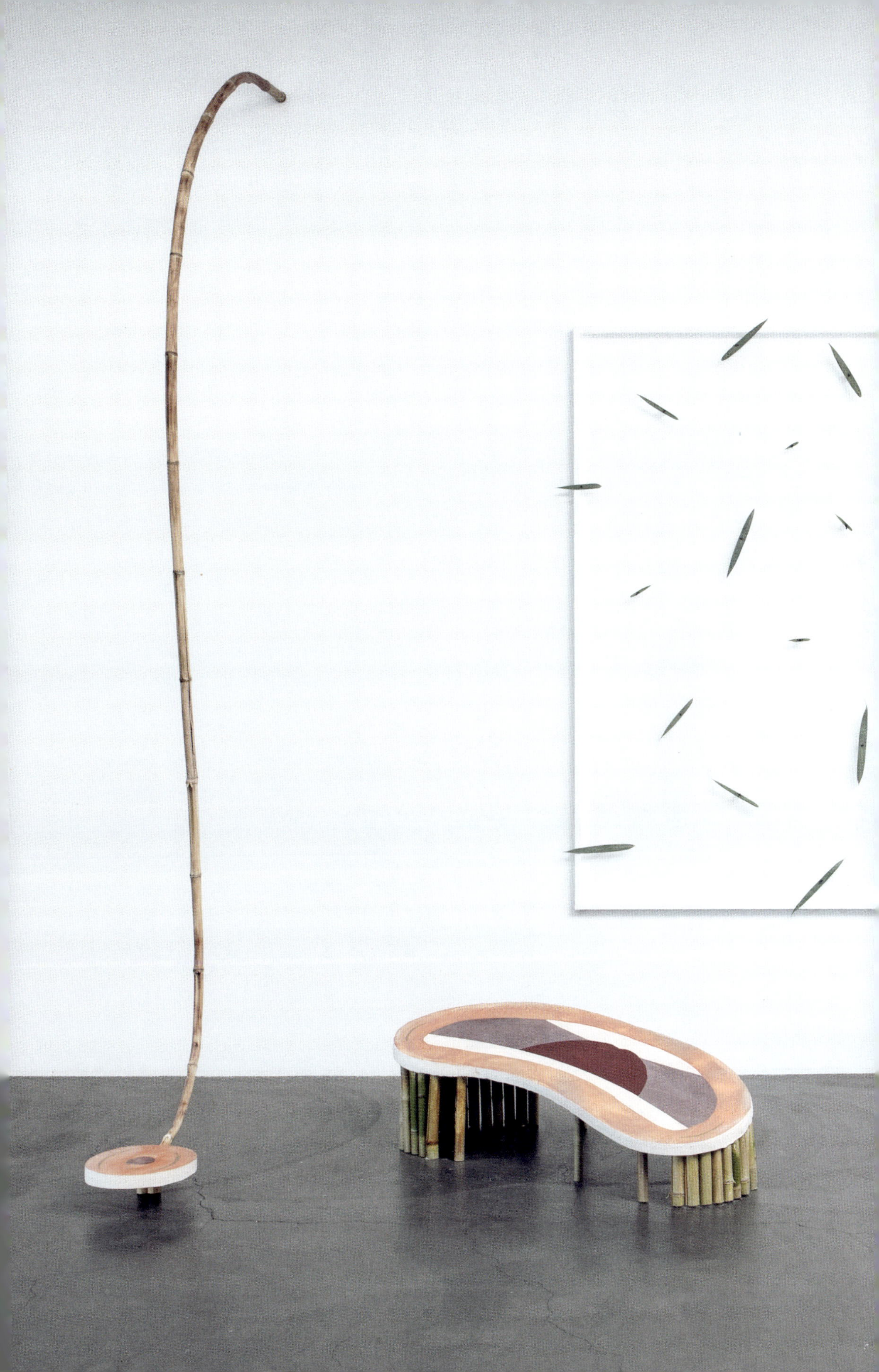

I Owe You a Yo-yo
2019
Variable dimensions
Bamboo leaves, bent bamboo,
insulating plastic film, magnets,
plaster cast in clay, steel powder

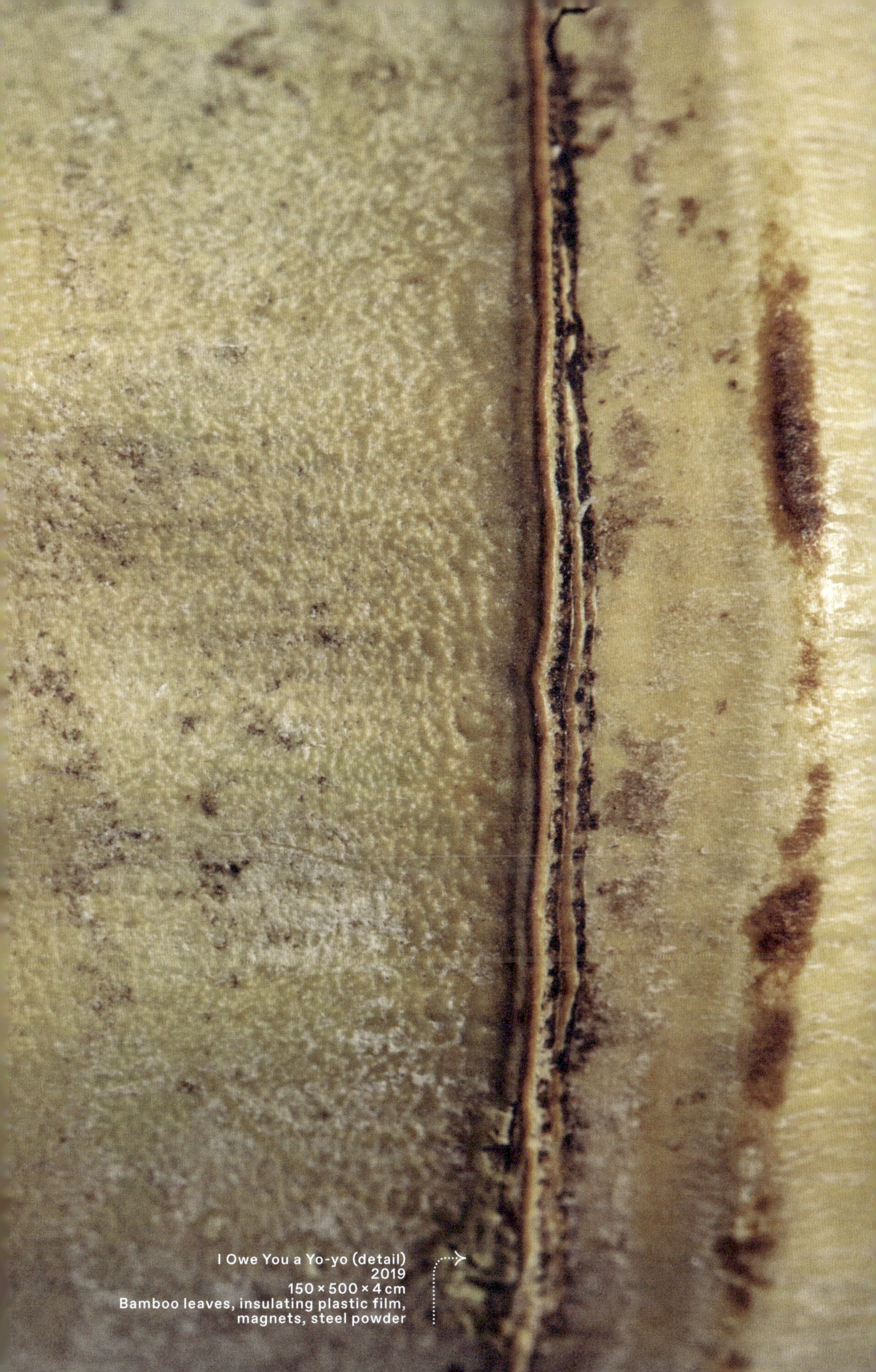

I Owe You a Yo-yo (detail)
2019
150 × 500 × 4 cm
Bamboo leaves, insulating plastic film, magnets, steel powder

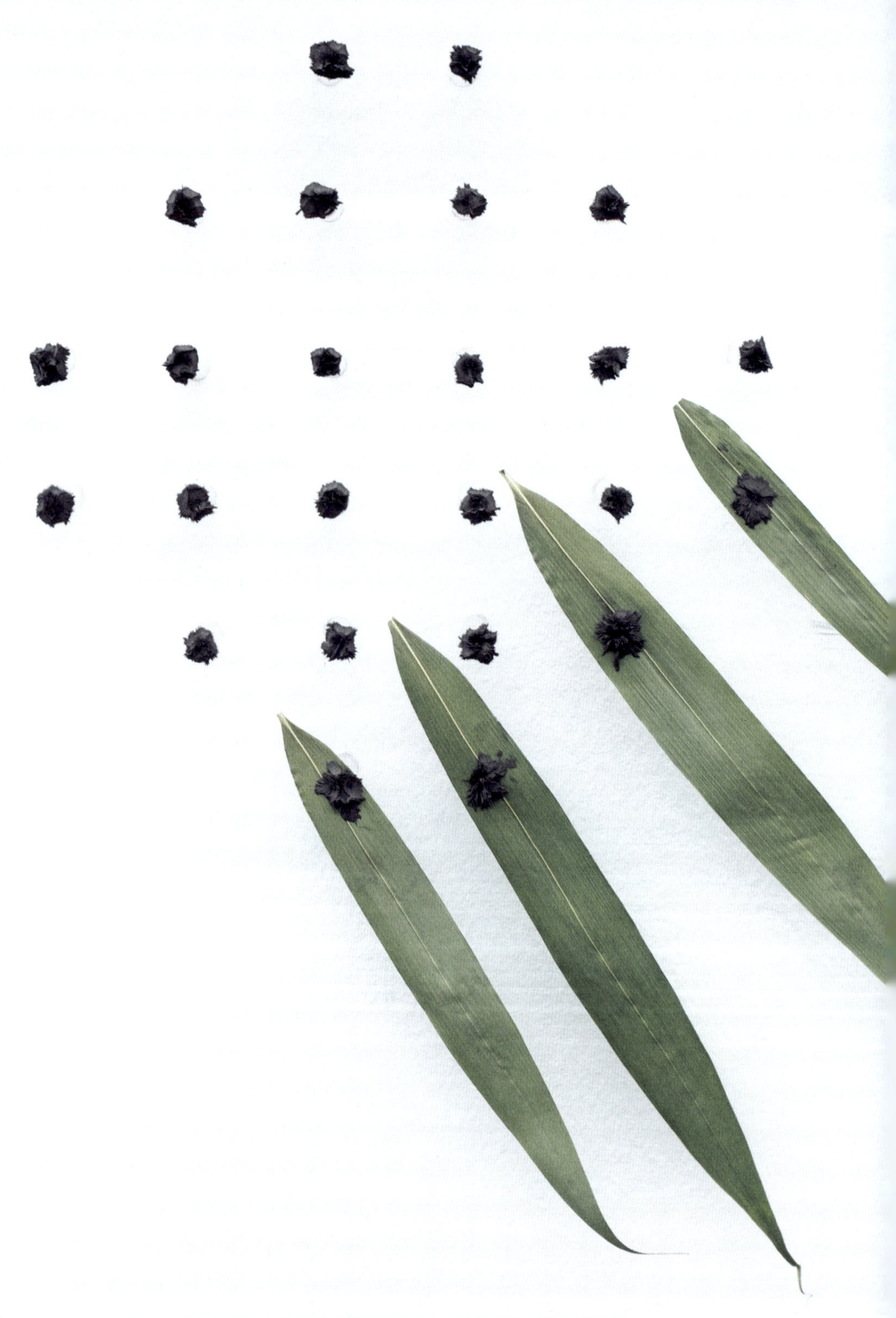

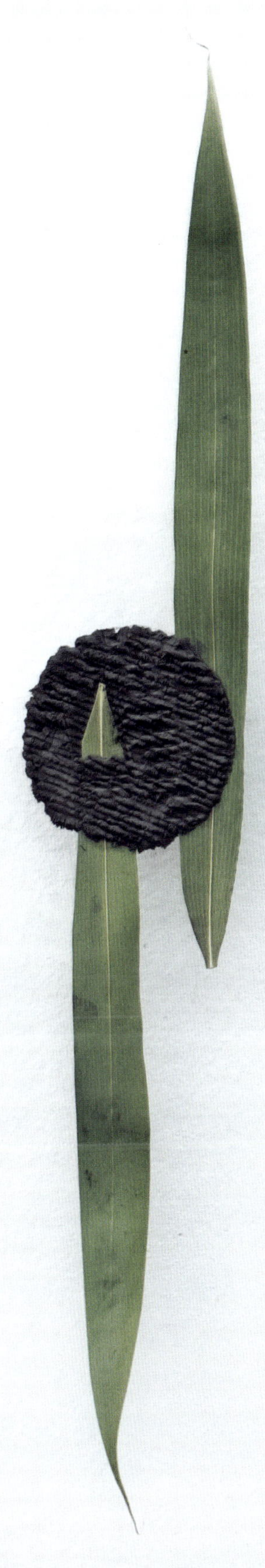

I Owe You a Yo-yo (detail)
2019
150 × 500 × 4 cm
Bamboo leaves, insulating plastic film,
magnets, steel powder

I Owe You a Yo-yo
2019
150 × 500 × 4 cm
Bamboo leaves, insulating plastic film, magnets, MDF, steel powder

I Owe you a Yo-yo
2019
45 × 120 × 130 cm
Bent Bamboo, plaster cast in clay

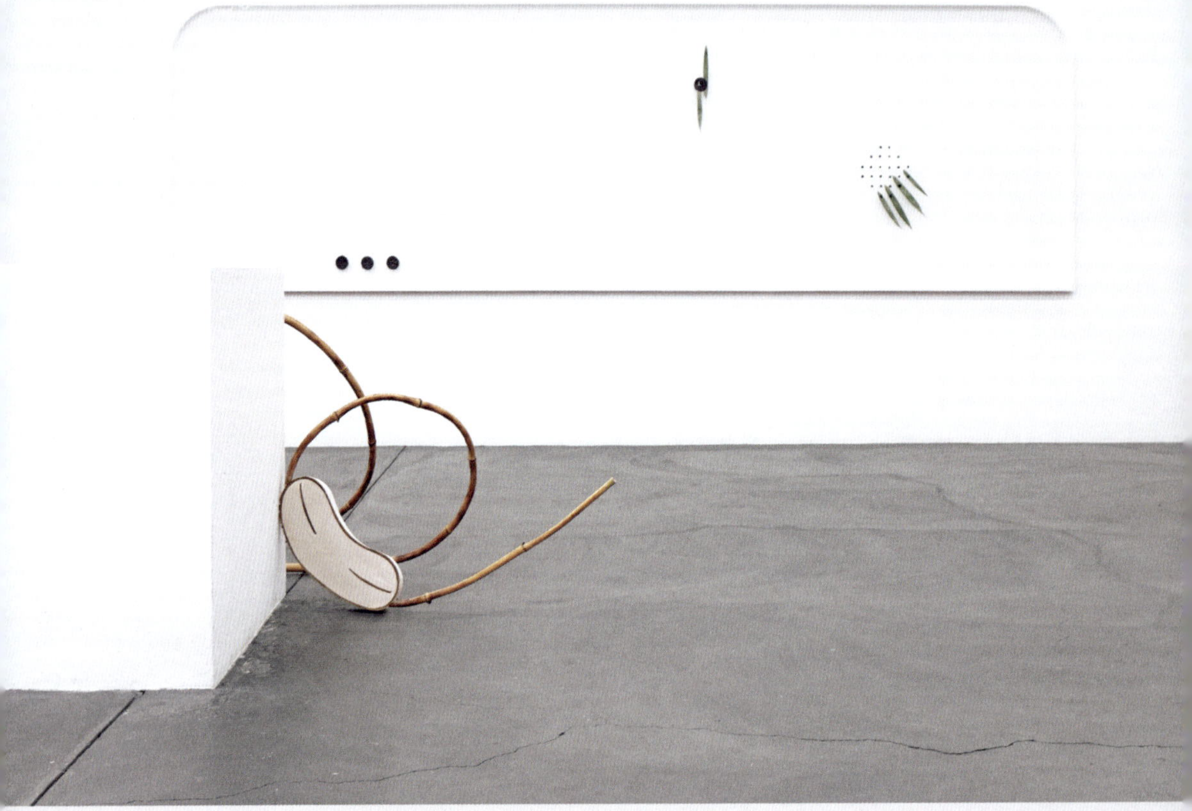

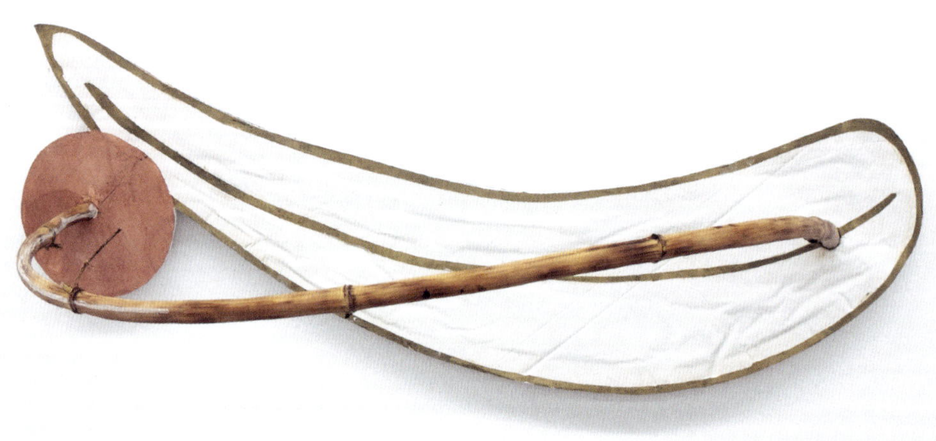

Toute ma peau ici, debout, maintenant[1]

Jeremy Narby

Ma première rencontre avec le tabac remonte à 1985, alors que je vivais en Amazonie péruvienne dans une communauté ashaninka dont les membres pensent que les plantes, et celle du tabac en premier lieu, peuvent transmettre des connaissances à celleux qui les consomment. Lorsque les Ashaninkas sont confronté·e·s à un problème ou une maladie, iels consultent le·la *seripari*, ce qui signifie « tabac-chamane » dans leur langue.

Pour ma part, je n'avais aucune affinité particulière avec les cigarettes ou les cigares, et je ne pensais pas non plus que l'on puisse apprendre quoi que ce soit en les fumant. Jeune anthropologue fraîchement sorti des bibliothèques universitaires, je souhaitais simplement comprendre les points de vue des peuples indigènes amazoniens.

Après un an dans la communauté, un vieux chamane m'a permis d'essayer sa pâte de tabac. Il m'a tendu sa gourde, et j'y ai trempé un bâtonnet pour l'enduire de la substance noirâtre qu'elle contenait. Je l'ai alors mis entre mes lèvres, puis je me suis assis en retrait. Un peu plus tard, j'ai passé la langue sous mes dents de devant ; elles m'ont paru particulièrement longues et pointues. Des moustaches de félin semblaient pousser sur les côtés de mon visage, me permettant de mieux percevoir l'environnement alentour. J'avais un goût de sang dans la bouche, et je l'ai trouvé agréable, alors que je suis végétarien. Je me sentais devenir félin. Je ne pensais pas que ce genre de choses était possible, mais l'impression était bien réelle, palpable, et se manifestait par une sensation de chaleur, de puissance et de sagesse. J'ai observé des poules en train de glousser à proximité et, comme un jaguar bienveillant, j'ai décidé de *ne pas* leur sauter dessus. Je me souviens m'être dit : « On sait que la pâte de tabac est forte quand l'anthropologue se met à attaquer les poules ! ».

L'acuité de cette impression féline et prédatrice me reste aujourd'hui encore ; je peux la convoquer à volonté et je m'en sers comme source de force et de courage. Mais il aura fallu du temps avant que je me sente capable de raconter cette expérience. J'ai longtemps évité le sujet avec les Occidentaux car il semblait les mettre mal à l'aise. J'ai dû moi-même faire un long cheminement, déjà pour suspendre mon incrédulité, et plus encore pour en parler ouvertement. J'ai franchi ce cap dans un désir de réciprocité envers le peuple ashaninka : en diffusant la validité de leurs connaissances botaniques ; en reconnaissant qu'elles proviennent de l'ingestion de substances psychoactives dérivant de plantes enseignantes ; et en témoignant de leur rapport au monde plus-qu'humain, j'espère donner en retour à ces gens qui m'ont tant appris et apporté — et c'est là le travail de toute une vie.

1 Propos extraits des écrits de Jeremy Narby et d'un entretien réalisé avec l'artiste le 10 mars 2023. L'ajout de l'écriture inclusive est une initiative de Maude Léonard-Contant en accord avec l'auteur.

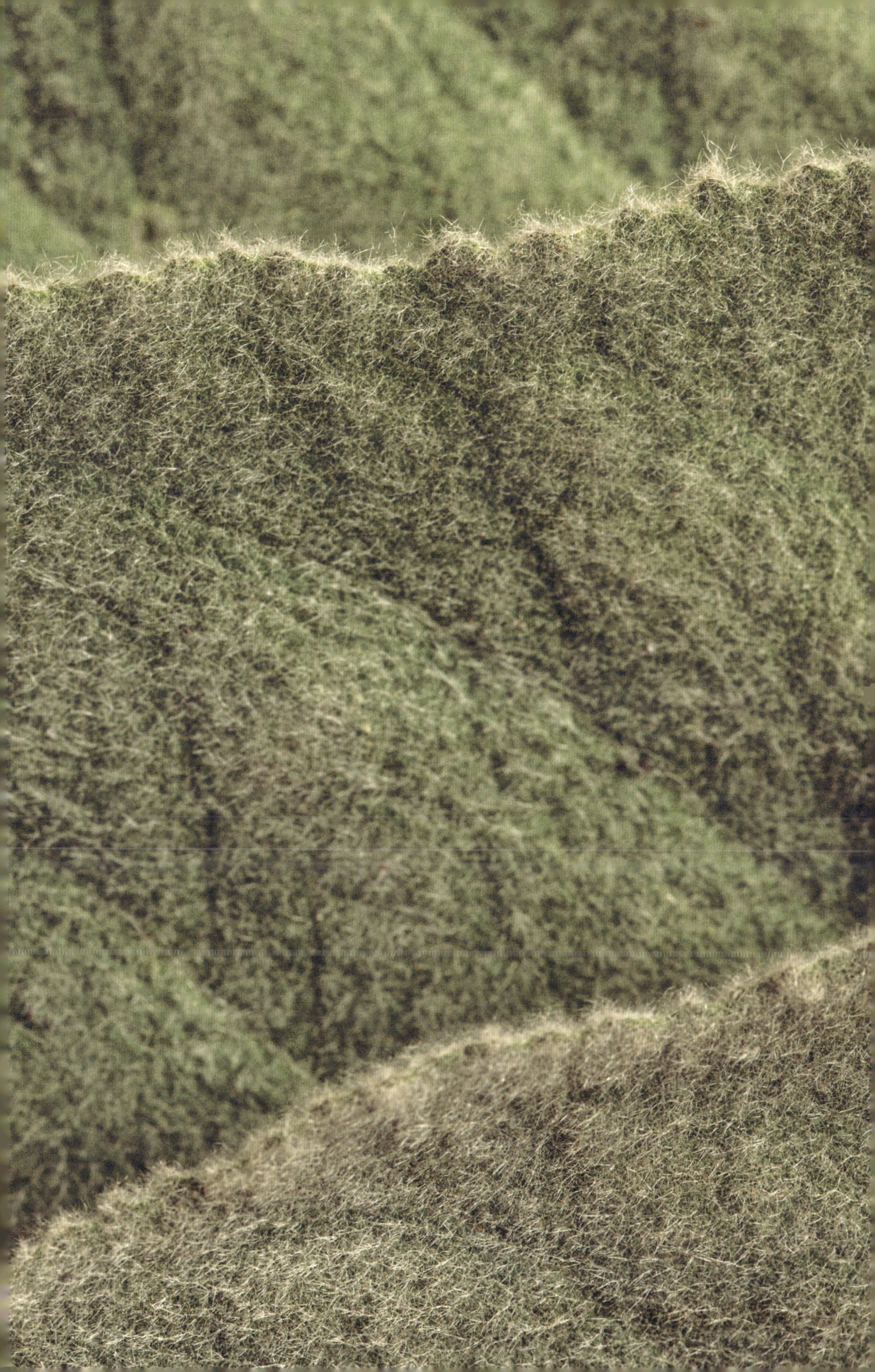

Je suis allé vivre chez les Ashaninkas pour réaliser une étude anthropologique sur la façon dont iels utilisent leurs ressources naturelles, et pour tenter de comprendre leur relation avec la forêt tropicale. Il se trouve que les Ashaninkas n'ont pas de mot pour décrire ces ressources ni même la notion de nature. Selon la définition qu'en donne le dictionnaire anglais Oxford, « nature » désigne tout ce qui se trouve en dehors de la sphère humaine, mais il s'agit avant tout d'un concept suprématiste anthropique qui n'existe pas au-delà des cultures occidentales.

Pour la première fois, je rencontrais des êtres humains qui parlaient des plantes et des animaux comme de personnes intelligentes, mues par une volonté propre et des intentions, capables de communiquer non seulement entre elles mais avec nous. Selon les Ashaninkas, des entités invisibles animent les plantes, les animaux et tous les êtres vivants ; elles forment la base de la parenté qui nous relie avec le monde plus-qu'humain. Ainsi, chaque espèce a une entité qui lui est associée, en charge de chacun de ses individus ; les Ashaninkas parlent alors du « propriétaire », de la « mère » ou du « père » de cette plante ou de cet animal. Ce point de vue implique de traiter ces individus non-humains comme des parent·e·s ou des allié·e·s. Les plantes bienfaisantes comme le manioc, le maïs ou le palmier pêche sont appelées frères ou sœurs parce qu'elles sont bonnes et généreuses. En revanche, les espèces chassées sont traitées avec plus de distance, tel·le·s des parent·e·s par alliance. Quant aux plantes comme l'ayahuasca et le tabac, elles sont des alliées puissantes, et donc potentiellement dangereuses. Dans tous les cas, le recours aux plantes et aux animaux implique nécessairement de reconnaître la relation que l'on entretient avec elleux.

Pour me familiariser avec la vie des Ashaninkas, je les ai accompagné·e·s dans leurs activités, en forêt notamment. Je me suis alors rendu compte qu'iels possédaient un savoir botanique encyclopédique. Des anthropologues et agronomes belges qui travaillaient dans la vallée avoisinante ont délimité un peu au hasard dix mètres sur deux dans la forêt, puis leur ont demandé de désigner les espèces qu'iels connaissaient sur cette surface. À leur grande surprise, les Ashaninkas ont su nommer 95% des plantes et ont pu donner les propriétés de la moitié d'entre elles ; cicatrisantes, anti-diarrhéiques, soulageant le mal de dos, antidote pour le venin de tel ou tel serpent. Chaque fois que l'occasion s'en présentait, j'ai moi-même essayé ces remèdes, vérifiant empiriquement leur efficacité. Quand je finis par demander d'où leur venaient ces connaissances, les Ashaninkas répondirent simplement « des plantes elles-mêmes » ; après avoir bu une mixture hallucinogène, les chamanes communiquent avec les essences animées, ou esprits des plantes, au sein même de leurs visions, pour obtenir ces informations. Inversement, les transes provoquées par les plantes donnent aux autres espèces l'occasion d'exprimer leurs plaintes et leurs exigences, que les humains peuvent ensuite prendre en considération.

Selon elleux, la nature est intelligente et utilise un langage visuel, non seulement au travers d'hallucinations et de rêves, mais aussi par des signes concrets, perceptibles au quotidien. Par exemple, la plante qui possède à la base de ses feuilles deux crochets blancs similaires à ceux du serpent « fer-de-lance » guérit de la morsure de ce dernier, comme si une même intelligence animait le buisson et le reptile.

Les Ashaninkas recherchent généralement des plantes amères, âcres ou toxiques, sans faire de distinction radicale entre un «remède» et un «poison». Certaines langues amazoniennes utilisent d'ailleurs un seul et même mot pour ces deux concepts. Le tabac, par exemple, est à la fois une plante toxique et médicinale. À l'instar d'autres plantes enseignantes psychoactives comme l'ayahuasca, le palmier chambira ou le toé, le tabac a deux âmes, l'une pour la médecine, l'autre pour la malice. Pour les Amazonien·ne·s, travailler avec ces plantes implique de développer avec elles une relation basée sur le respect. Iels considèrent par exemple que l'ayahuasca est un être à part entière et qu'il faut tenir compte de la personnalité de sa mère lors des échanges avec elle. À la fois mâle et femelle, elle peut prendre différentes formes; femme, homme, colibri, boa noir, boa jaune, jaguar—même si, du point de vue amazonien, l'ayahuasca n'a pas de personnage fixe. Pour certain·e·s chamanes, c'est avant tout une plante diplomate qui aime aider à résoudre des conflits.

Parler de la réalité amazonienne dans une langue indo-européenne n'est pas sans difficultés. En essayant de l'appréhender, j'ai beaucoup appris sur les limites de ma langue maternelle et de la pensée occidentale, qui tend à dichotomiser le corps et l'esprit. Les Ashaninkas ne font pas cette distinction. Pour «corps», iels disent «toute ma peau ici, debout, maintenant», ce qui illustre bien la fluidité inhérente à leur rapport au monde, laquelle fait clairement défaut aux langues indo-européennes. L'ayahuasca a augmenté mon attention aux mots, à la façon de les prononcer, au son de la voix; ce que l'on dit participe à la création du monde. Je pense que nous (les Occidentaux) ne réussiront pas à descendre du piédestal sur lequel nous nous sommes mis·e·s si nous continuons à parler de «nature». Les mots comptent.

Quand je témoigne du lien que les Ashaninkas entretiennent avec les êtres plus-qu'humains, ainsi que des savoirs qui en résultent, et plus spécifiquement de leur relation à la «mère» ou au «propriétaire» d'une plante, je préfère parler de «personnalité». Par exemple, si vous allez à la rencontre du tabac (en l'absorbant d'une façon ou d'une autre) comme d'un être à la personnalité difficile, vous entrez en relation avec lui plutôt que vous ne le consommez. Dans la compréhension de Rafael Chanchari[2], la mère du tabac est un grand homme brun, puissant et ambigu—une vision capable de provoquer plus de vigilance qu'aucune campagne de prévention.

Les scientifiques ont souvent de la peine avec le concept animiste de plante enseignante. Concernant ces questions, la position de chacun·e dépend de sa propre compréhension de la réalité. Pour ma part, en m'ouvrant à la validité du savoir indigène et à sa capacité de compléter la science, je me sens mieux armé face au monde—parce que je dispose de plus de concepts, d'angles et de scénarios possibles pour le comprendre. Je compare l'utilisation simultanée de ces deux systèmes de savoir au bilinguisme. Penser le monde en anglais, en français ou en allemand n'est pas la même chose, même pour une personne qui manie parfaitement les trois langues. Bien entendu, la traduction est toujours possible. Mais les traducteur·ice·s professionnel·le·s le savent bien: traduire revient souvent à trahir et certains concepts sont intraduisibles. Cela n'implique aucune hiérarchie entre les langues, juste que bien les parler et pouvoir faire des allers-retours demande une pratique constante, laquelle prédispose forcément à l'ouverture et à la rencontre avec l'autre.

2 Enseignant, guérisseur, jardinier et penseur amazonien domicilié à Iquitos au Pérou et co-auteur avec Jeremy Narby de *Deux Plantes Enseignantes: Le Tabac et l'Ayahuasca* (Mama Editions, Paris, 2021).

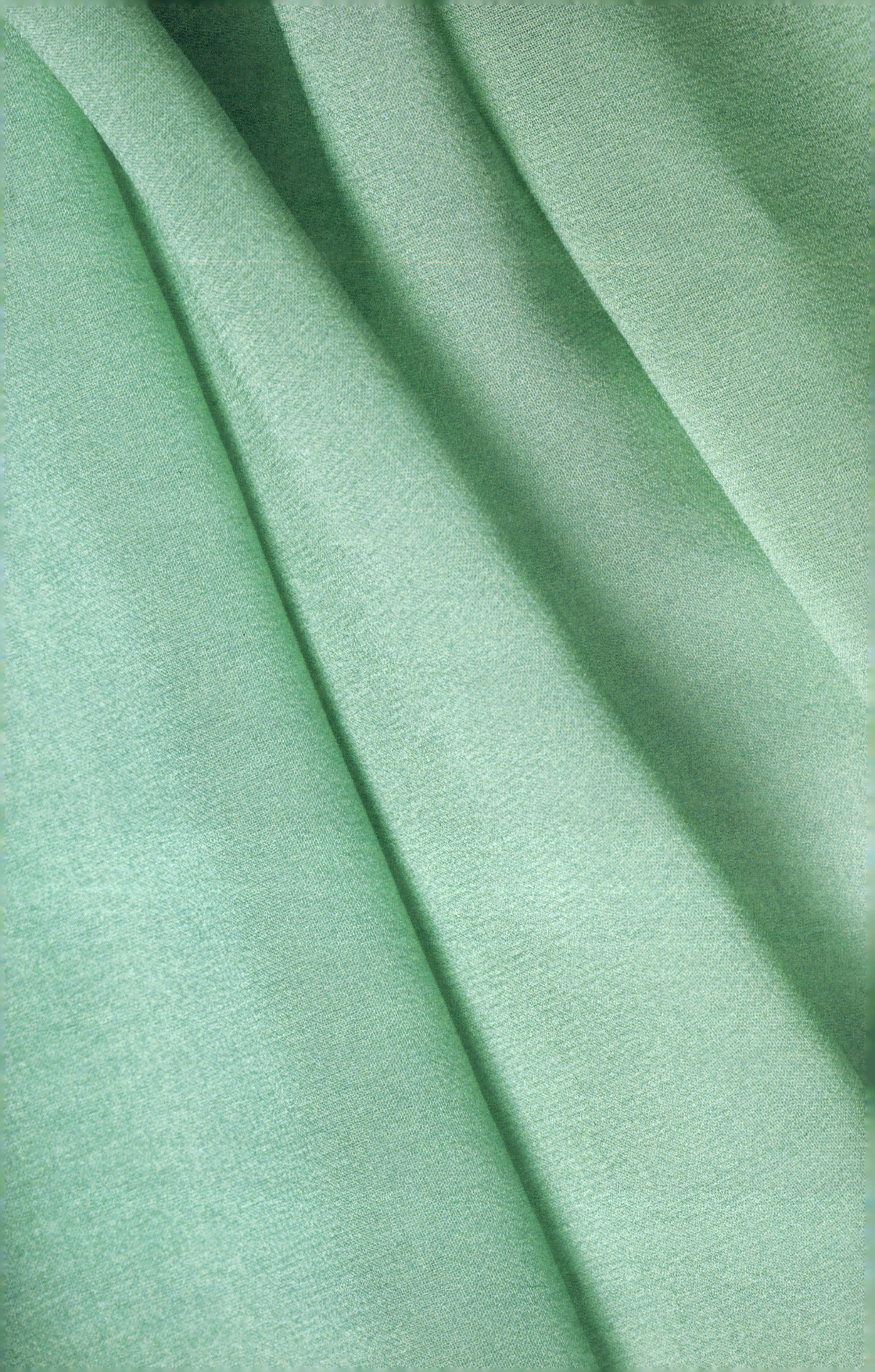

Pulmoni
2015
23 × 26 × 3.5 cm
Glazed stoneware

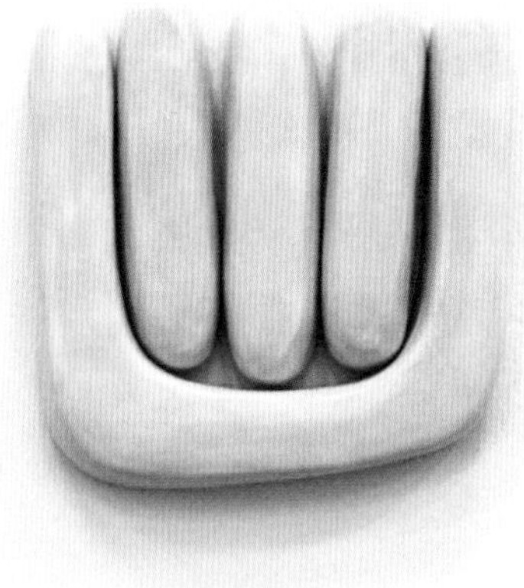

Wieder zu Hause mit vom Harz der Balsam-Tanne verklebten Haaren. Der Vater hat uns erzählt, dass dies der Kaugummi der «Indianer» war (damals sagte man das noch). Die Mutter seufzt beim Stöbern nach der Azetonflasche. Schluck deine Vorwürfe hinunter, Hélène, und mach lieber das scheussliche Shampoo bereit, das unsere Mähnen retten wird. Früher oder später hätten wir ohnehin entdeckt, welche Lust das Ausdrücken der prallen Bläschen auf der sonst so glatten Rinde bereitet.

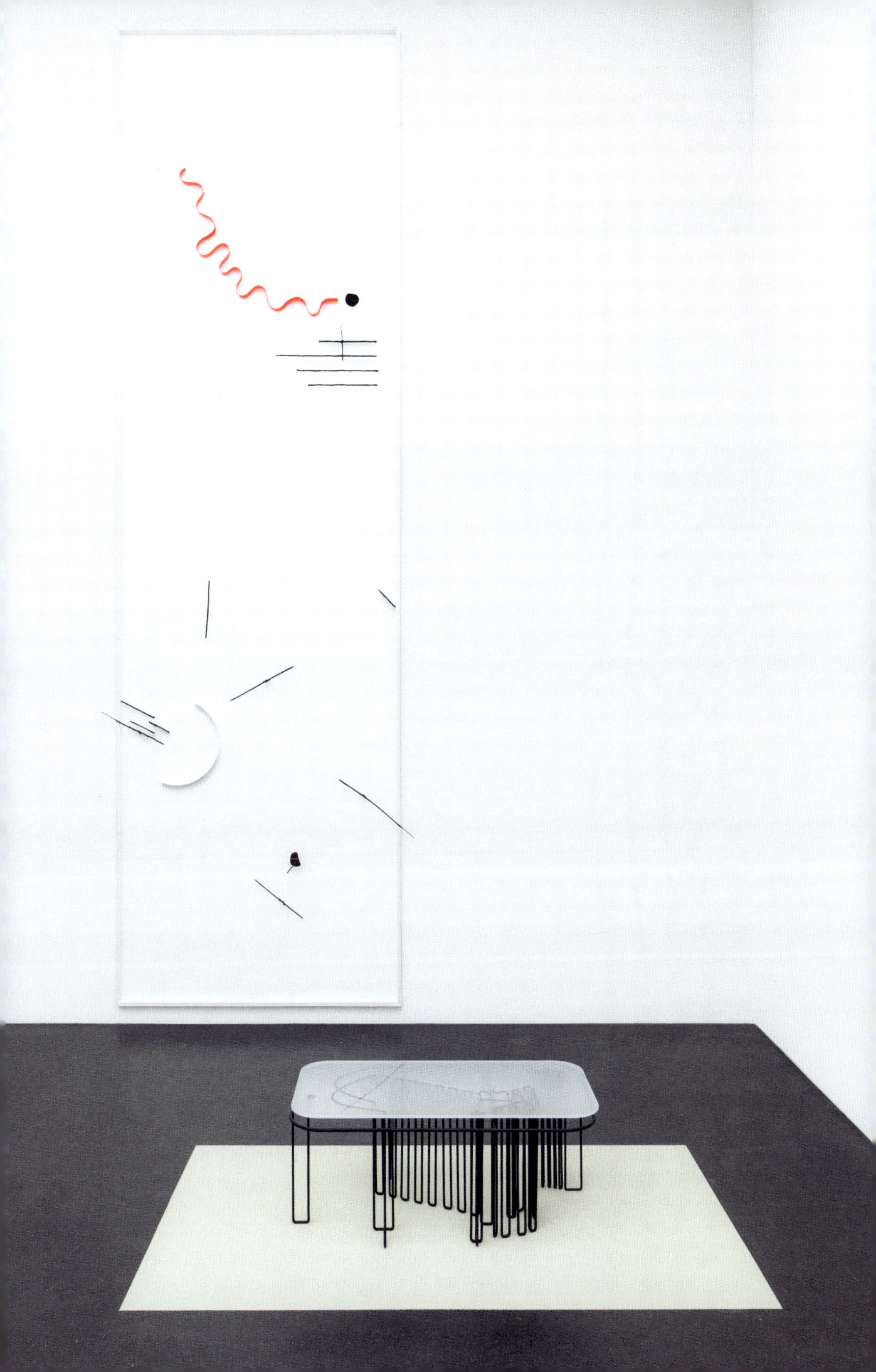

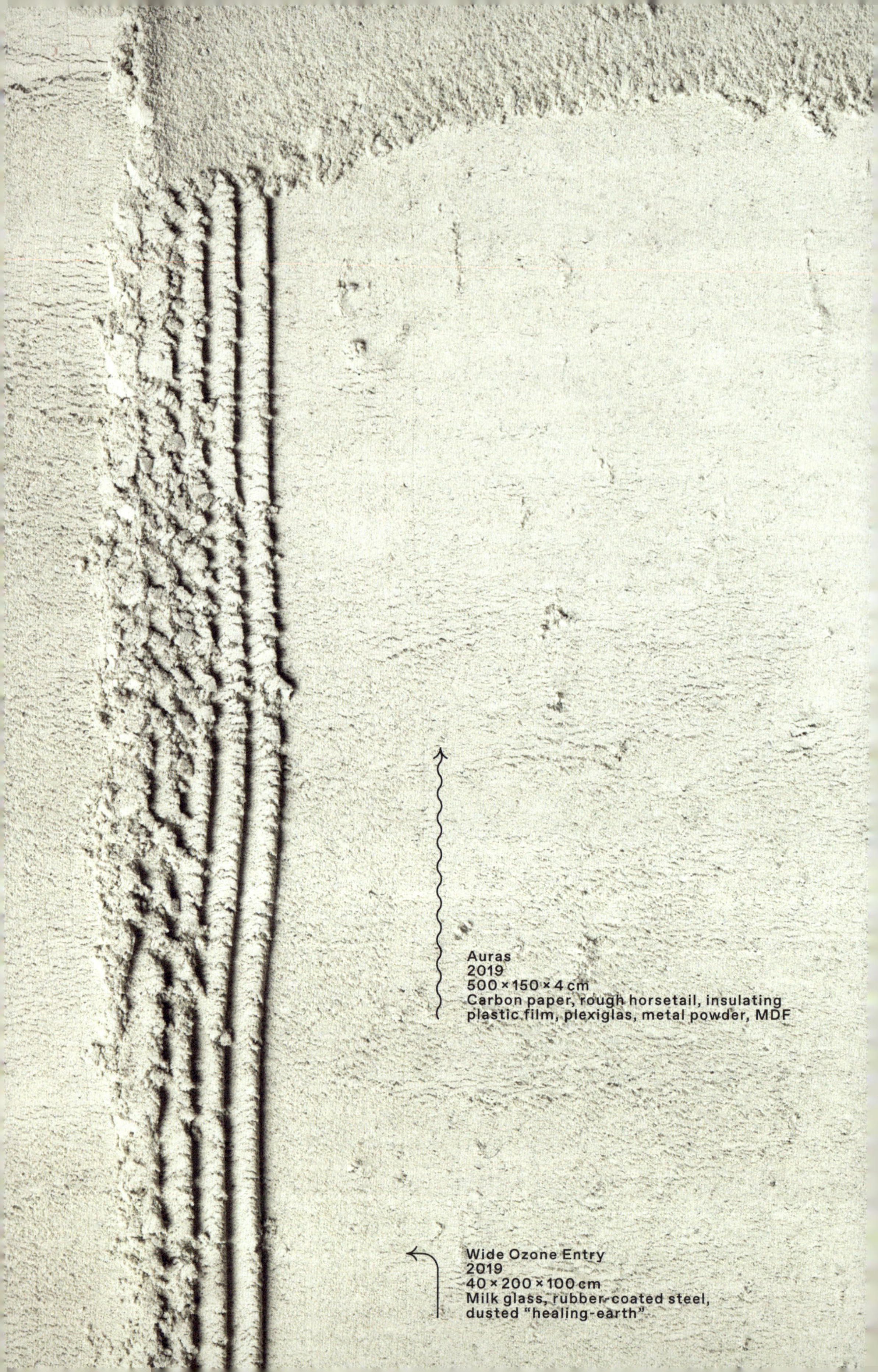

Auras
2019
500 × 150 × 4 cm
Carbon paper, rough horsetail, insulating plastic film, plexiglas, metal powder, MDF

Wide Ozone Entry
2019
40 × 200 × 100 cm
Milk glass, rubber-coated steel, dusted "healing-earth"

À tout vent
2017
230 × 80 × 5 cm
Foundry sand, powder-coated steel

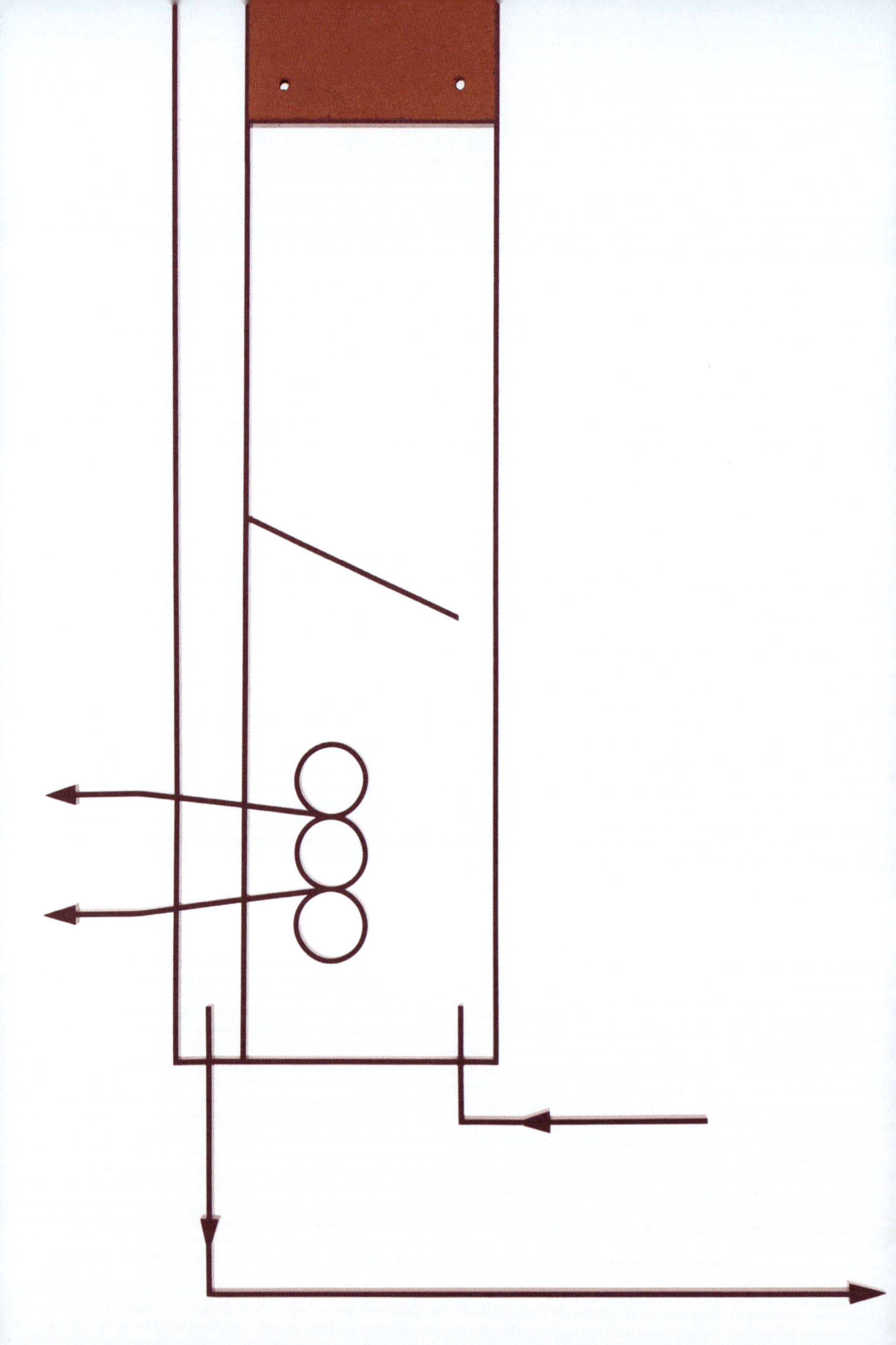

In der Mitte einer frisch gejäteten Lichtung warten, im Kreis aufgestellt, neun weisse Plastikgartenstühle auf die letzten Bewahrer eines althergebrachten Wissens.

Der Siedepunkt des Wassers macht sich leise bemerkbar. In Schwadronen organisiert und ohne Wimpernzucken, dröhnt die Grossfamilie der Fliegen im Schwebeflug. Der Farn stellt seine Fotosynthese ein und im Untergrund schluckt die mikroskopische Gemeinde einmal synchron.

Wo.

sind.

sie.

Hat man je eine derartige Verspätung erlebt?

Um die Erwartung zu überlisten, tritt man weg und sucht nach Läusen. Als die Spannung auf dem Höhepunkt ist, ertönt der Gong und lässt die enttäuschten Erwartungen in einem nie da gewesenen Durcheinander explodieren. Um das Unerklärliche zu erklären, beeilt man sich, dem deplatzierten Röhren eines einsamen Tieres die Schuld zu geben, man fragt sich, ob nicht eher das Fehlen der nach Bergamotte duftenden Blätter, die auf die Schnelle durch einen Aufguss bitterer Gräser ersetzt wurden, für das Ausbleiben verantwortlich sei, man geisselt rundum alles, man schilt um die Wette.

Man kann sich die Haare raufen und mit den Kiefern klappern, so viel man will, es kommt niemand.

Man ballt die Fäuste, man würfelt erneut.

Echt hart, versetzt zu werden.

Savoir-faire
2018
41 × 34 × 1 cm
Foundry sand, granite, marble

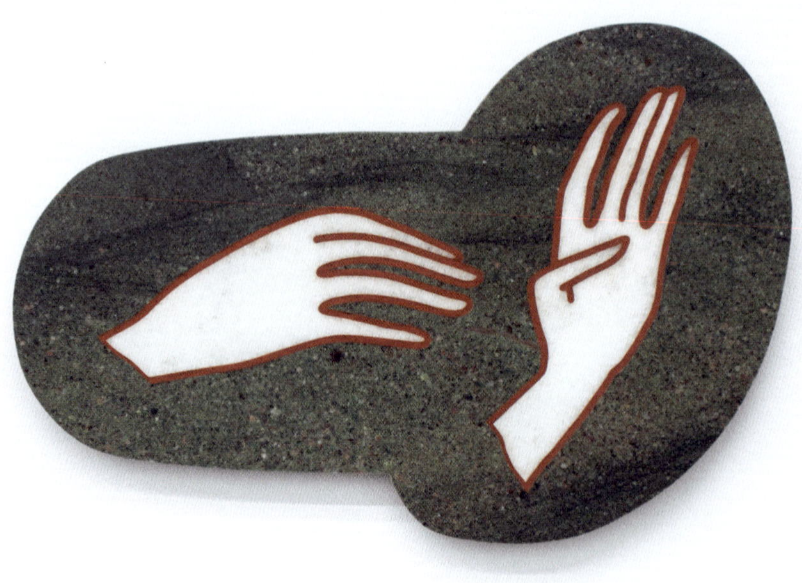

Laissons la paresse venir
puisque l’épuisette
est trouée

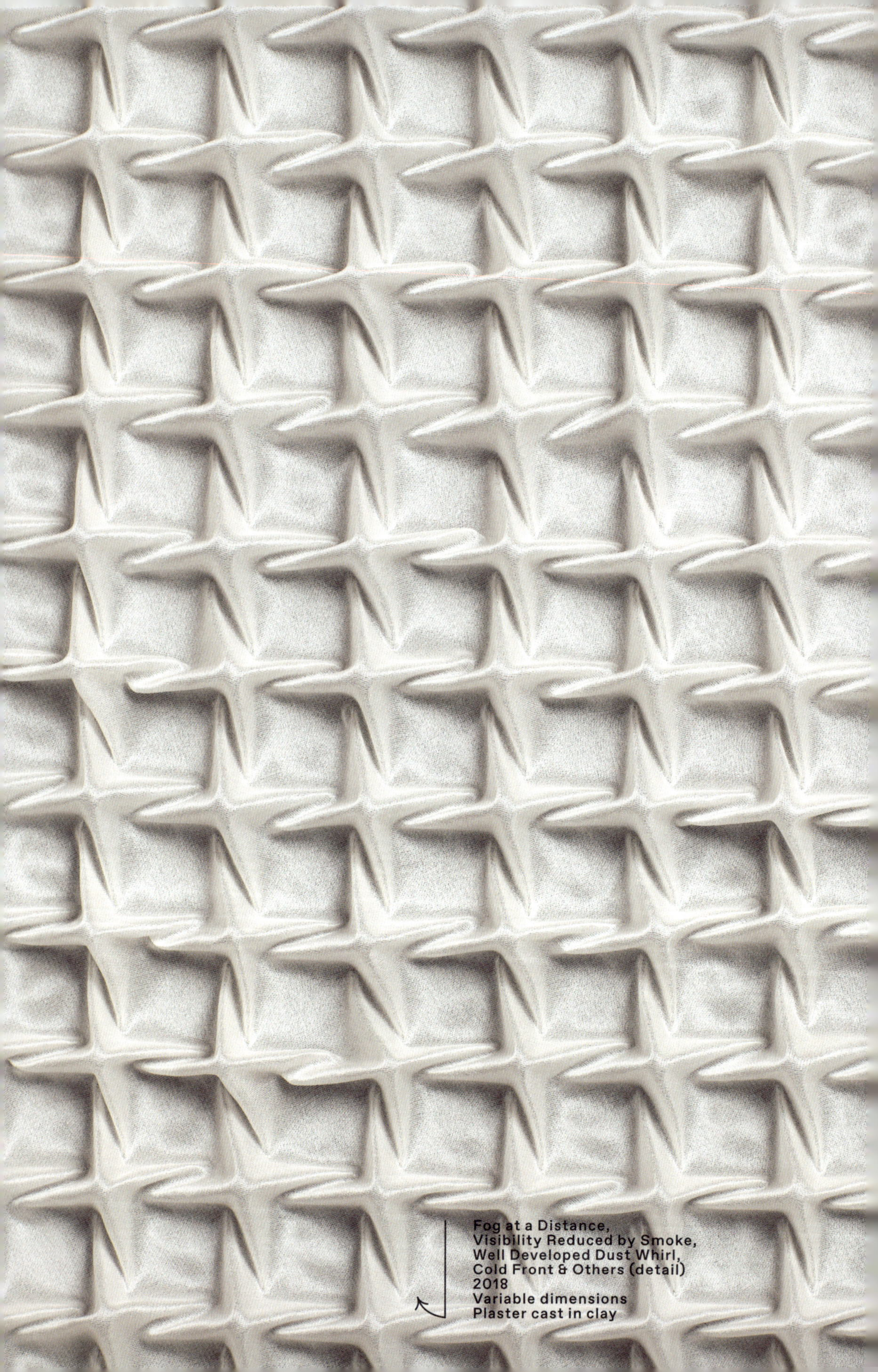

Fog at a Distance,
Visibility Reduced by Smoke,
Well Developed Dust Whirl,
Cold Front & Others (detail)
2018
Variable dimensions
Plaster cast in clay

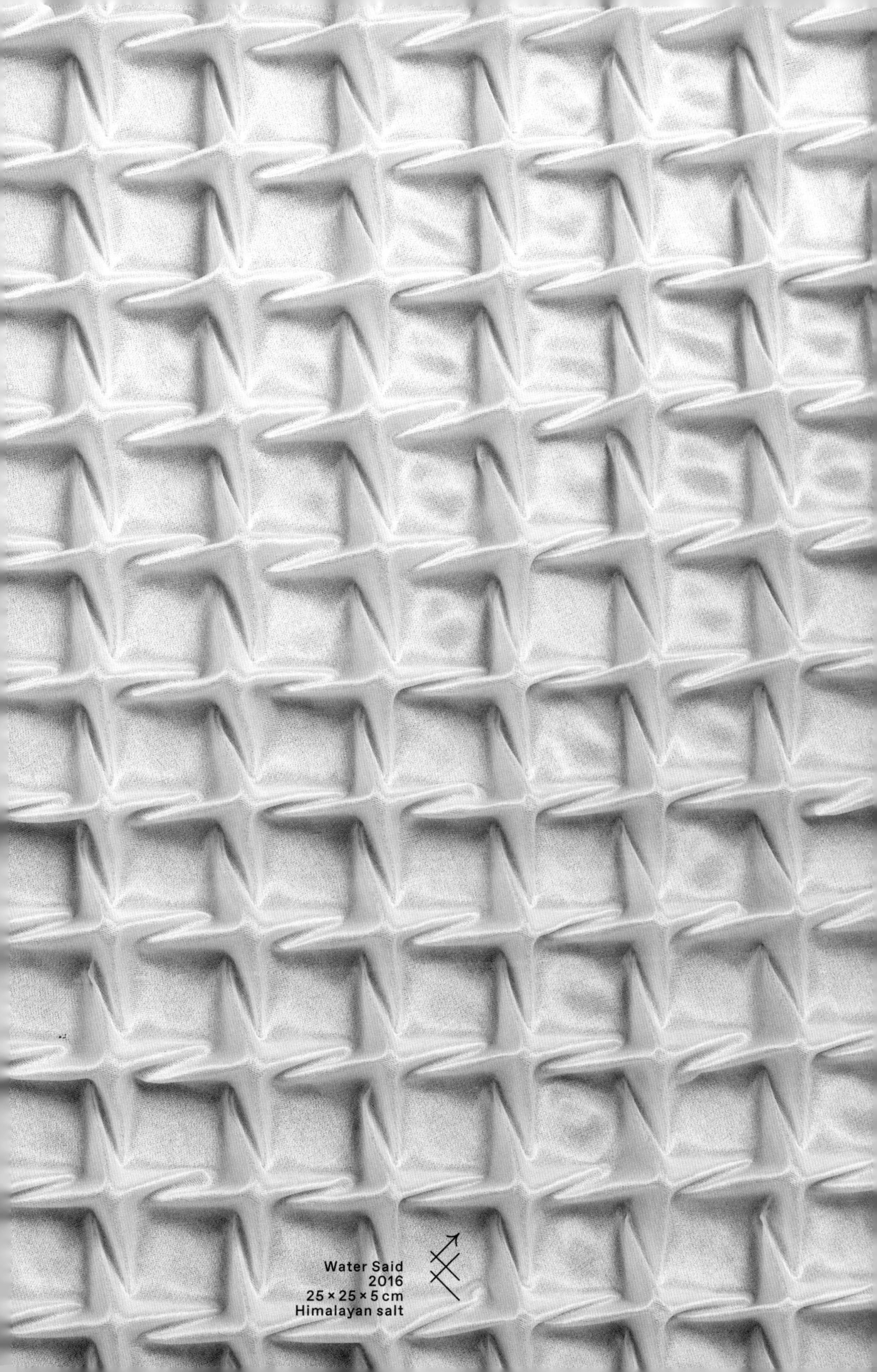

Water Said
2016
25 × 25 × 5 cm
Himalayan salt

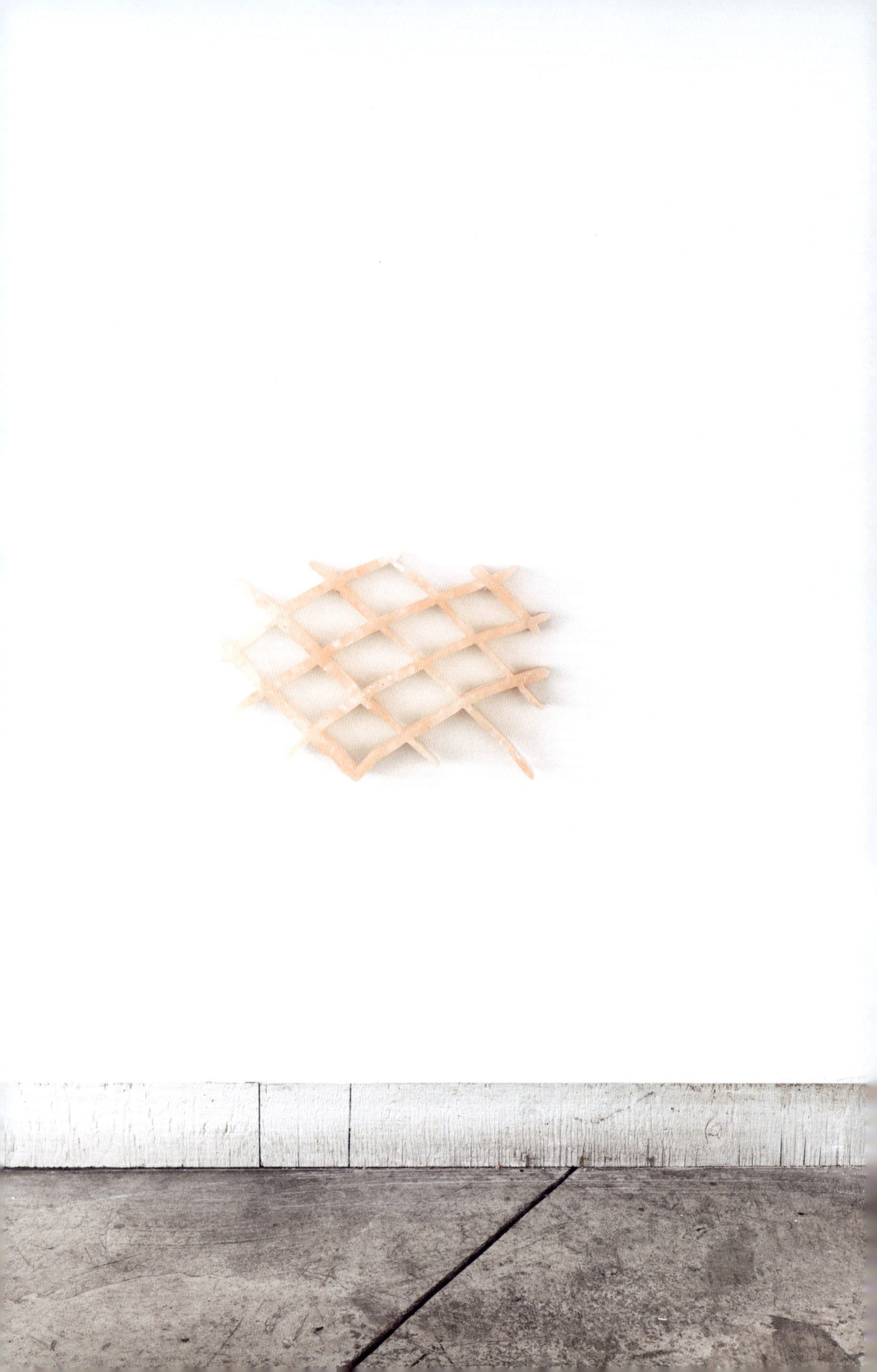

Il a troqué
son lorgnon
cerclé d’écaille
contre une
longue-vue
plus propice
à l’activité
qui l’occupe
depuis
le point
du jour.

Il dénombre
les grappes
de toucans
agrippés
au promontoire
d’en face
en grignotant
des pois chiches
en croûte
de wasabi

Ne vous fiez pas
à son air absent:
il a la dent dure,
mais pas au point
de la congédier
avant qu’elle n’ait fini
son réquisitoire.

Elle se tient en retrait
à vendre sa salade
d’un ton monocorde.

Lui:

soucieux des oiseaux,
somme toute
magnanime et
positivement
antipathique.

Elle:

n’a jamais compté,
dès lors,
comptabilise.

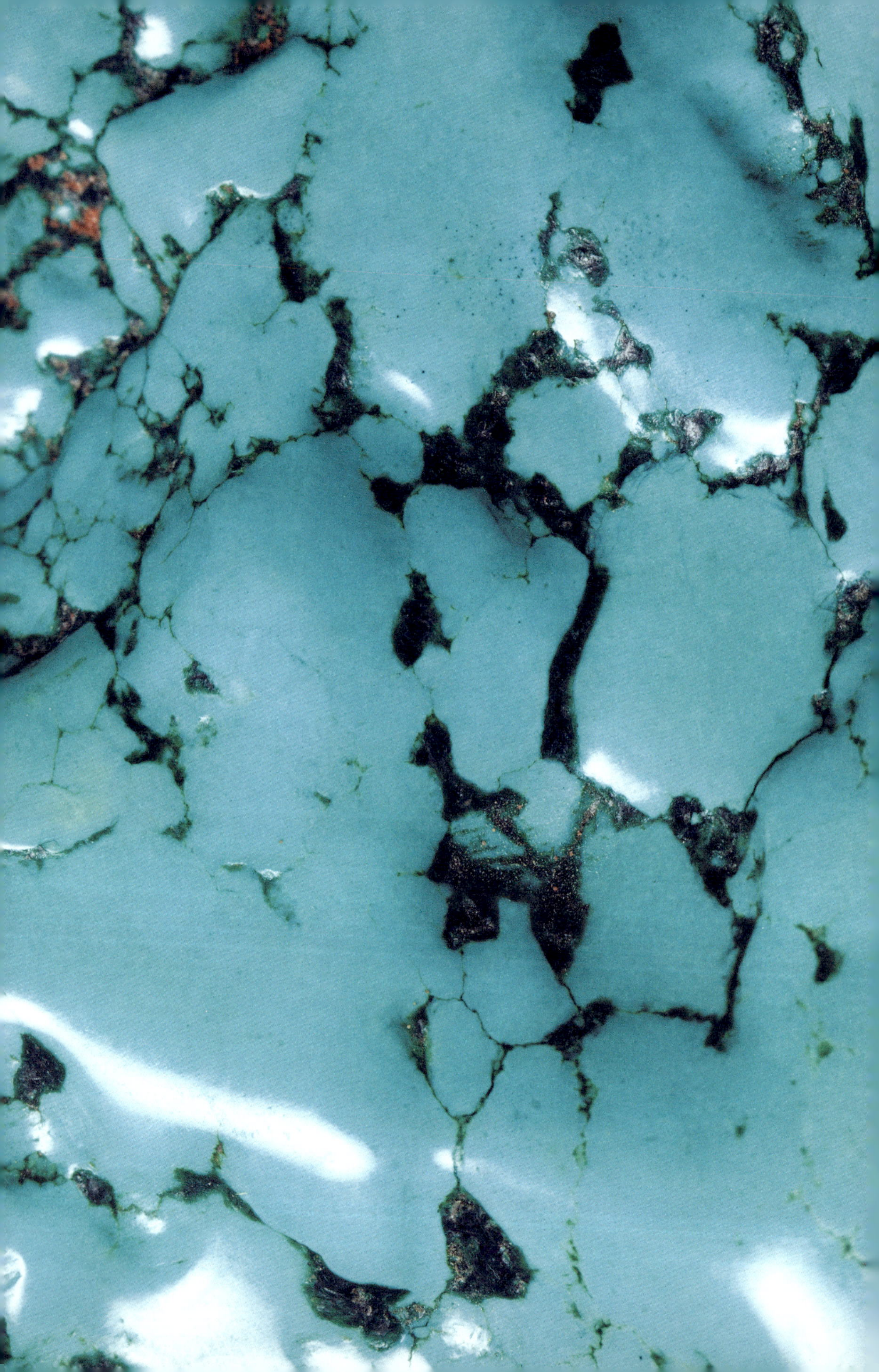

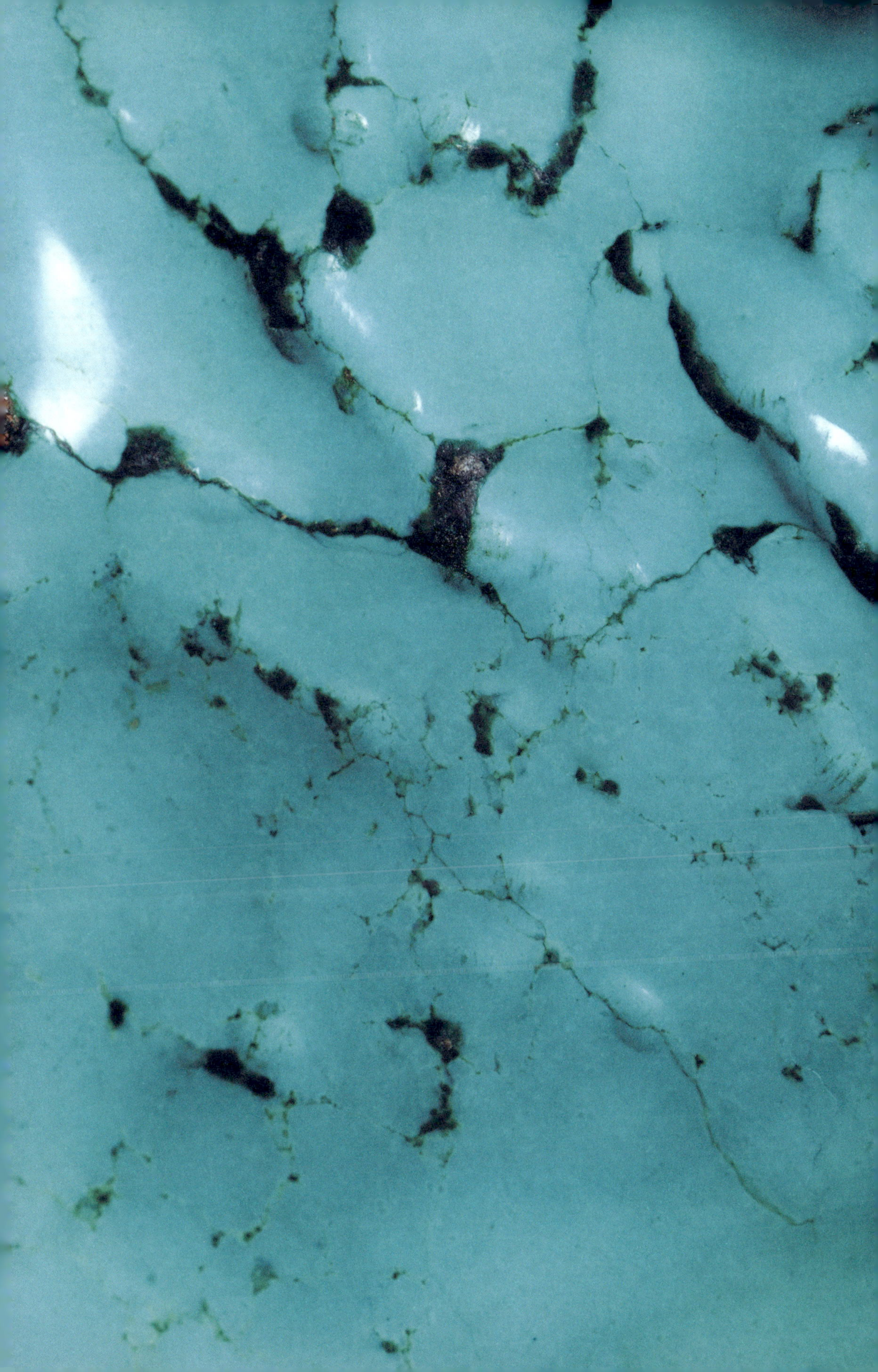

Hankering for peat,
the eel has slithered too far,
too far under the fine sand
compacted by the recent rains.

Blessed showers!

It was high time for it to rain;
the embankment of the frog pond
had even started smelling fetid
by the time the first drops ricocheted off the demijohns/
stomping millstones/
soothing riverside anxiety/
flattening the couch grass/
revitalizing the gutters/
anointing the tender shoots of the new asparagus/

The saturated air is exhilarating after the rain.
Finally breathing fancy free, the cells pleasantly
expanded by the surrounding humidity, and succumbing
to the illusion that this will last forever.

(—and our eel!?)
(—let the dowser decide.)

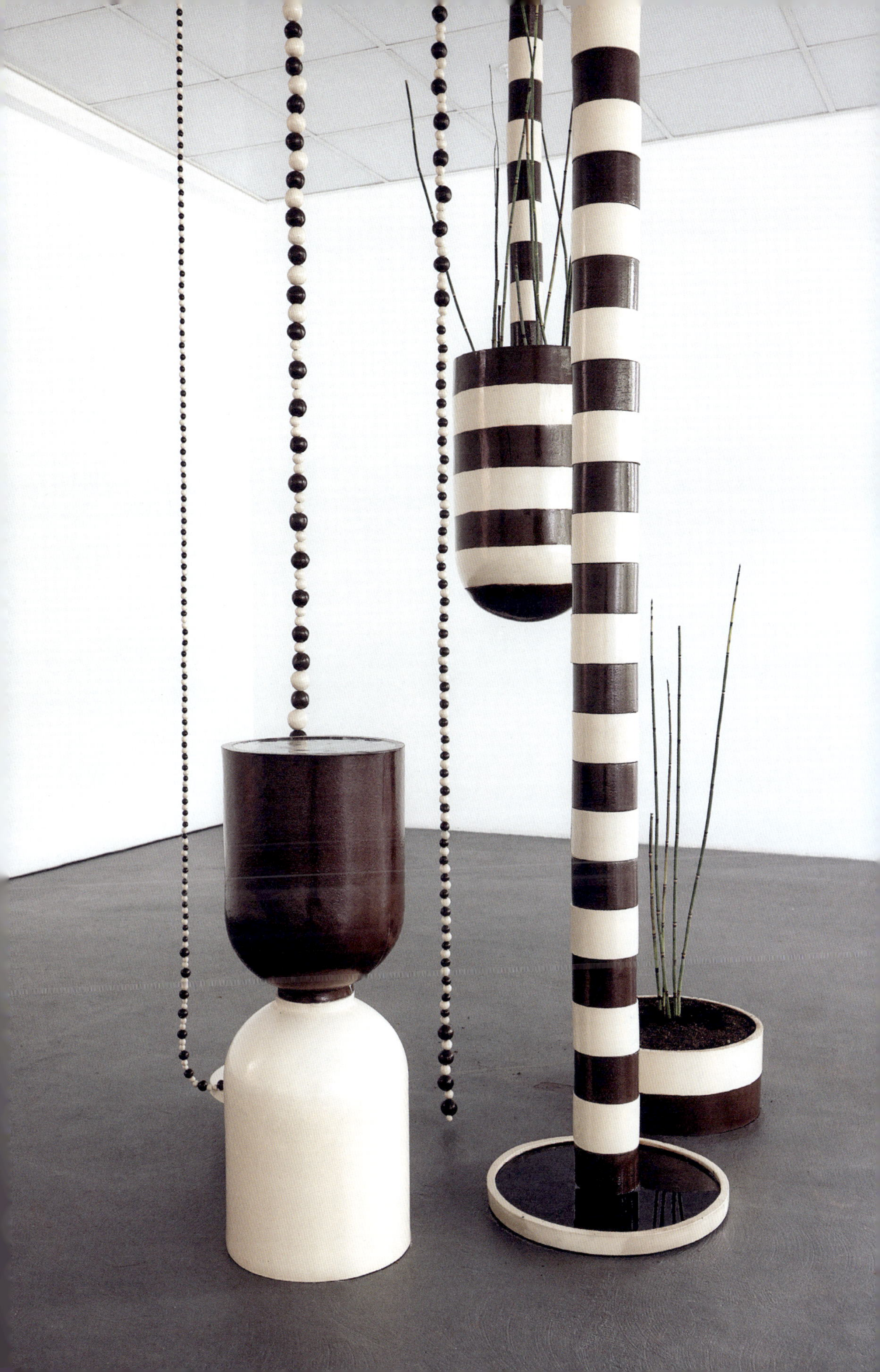

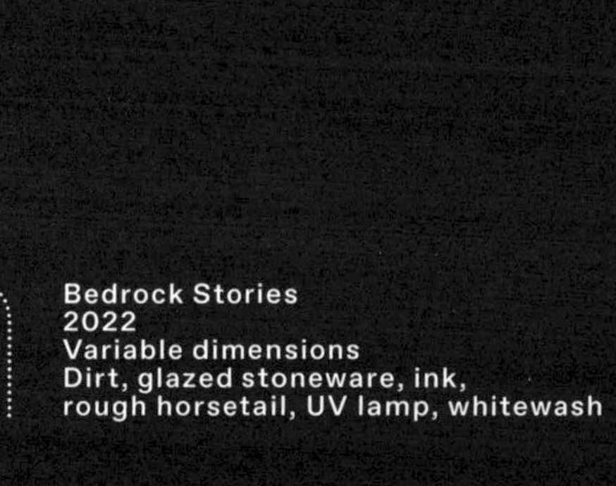

Bedrock Stories
2022
Variable dimensions
Dirt, glazed stoneware, ink,
rough horsetail, UV lamp, whitewash

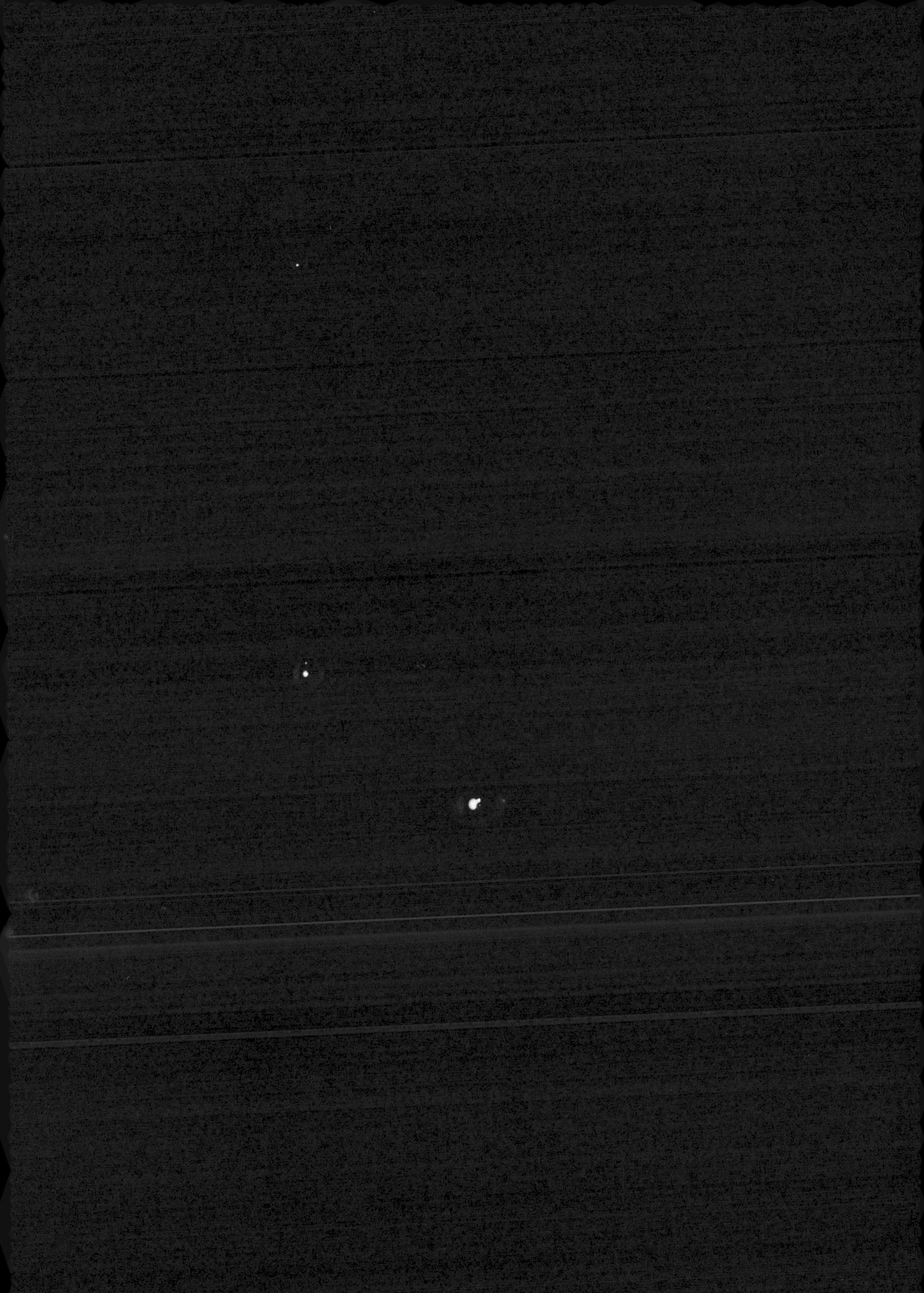

Bedrock Stories
2022
Variable dimensions
Dirt, glazed stoneware, ink, rough horsetail,
sound (recordings in French,
English, German), UV lamp, whitewash

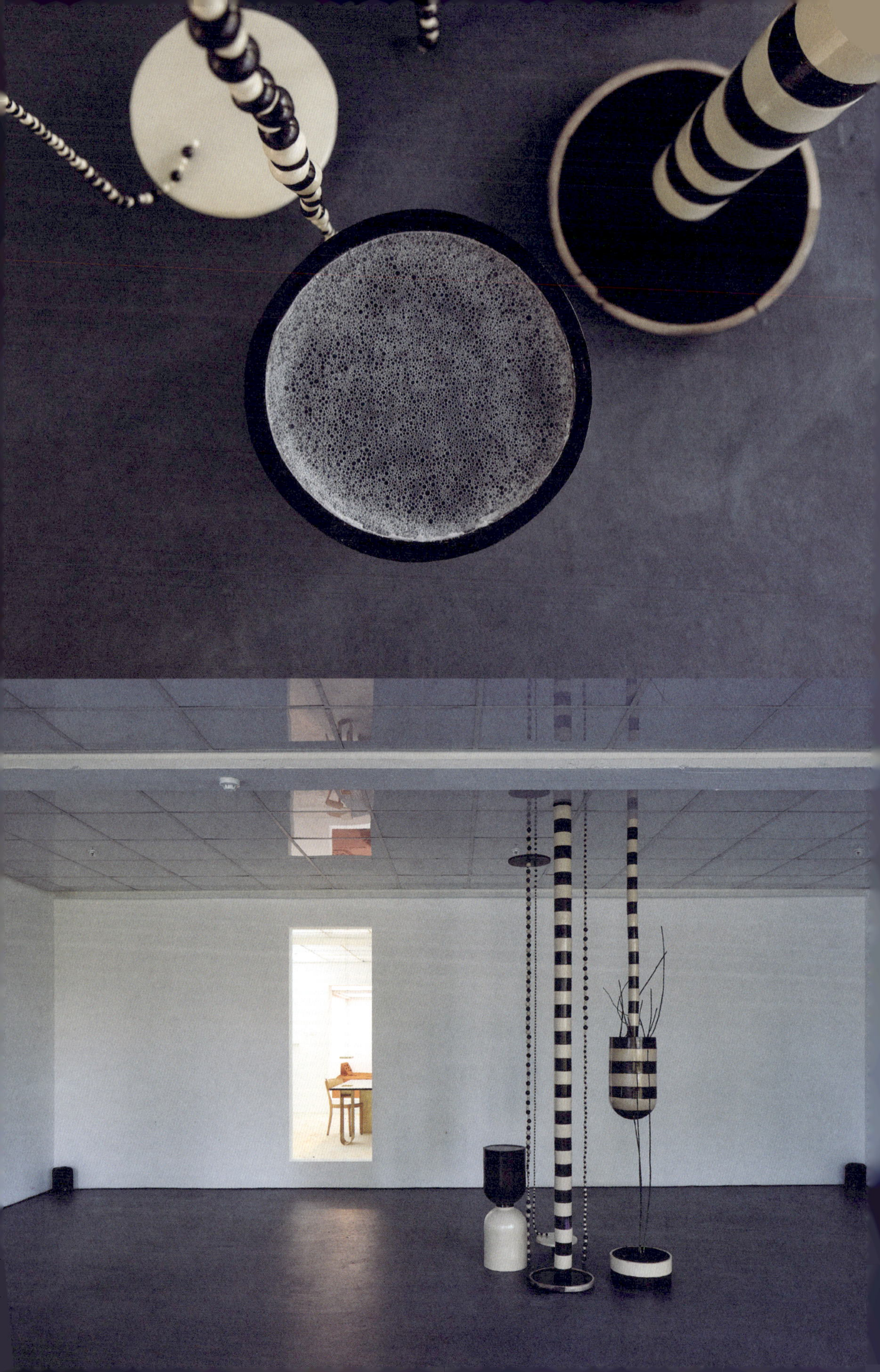

On *Digs:*
Politics of Labor and Politics of Care in Maude Léonard-Contant's Art Practice

Camilla Paolino

When Maude Léonard-Contant and I met to talk about *Digs,* I was particularly drawn to the material conditions under which the installation was envisioned, namely those of expecting a baby.[1] For a few months, conception and gestation would not only pertain to the conceptualization of the show, but also to the entire set of biochemical processes unfolding within her body simultaneously. These circumstances induced a pragmatic decision, which soon turned out to be programmatic as well. As a result, the artist proposed an exhibition in the making, a work-in-progress culminating in an installation which morphed over time. No ambition of completion would be driving the project, but rather a personal commitment: that of being regularly present and engaged in making her installation grow during the museum's opening hours. The artist would be all the while attending to the exhibition spaces and to the objects, materials, and life forms such spaces harbor. The latter would be taken care of by discrete yet vital gestures, such as watering the plants. Moreover, in her nearly clandestine incursions into the museum, the artist was often accompanied by her newborn child. The exhibition spaces and times, then, would be defined by three sorts of working activity, assuming the traits of a multifaceted construction site. A stroll through it would channel visitors to the core of the complex tangle of labor politics that generally characterizes Léonard-Contant's posture and modus operandi.

The first activity embraced the sound of pounding hammers and unfolded in a room filled with seven tons of red foundry sand. The room was accessed by a sort of vestibule, where the artist kept her work uniform and some of her working tools. Every day she would perform the same set of gestures in there: put on her work uniform and leave her street clothes in the vestibule, first ritual of the workday routine; enter the main room, where the sand was pressed to obtain a flat and compact surface; hammer wooden letter shapes to sculpt sand casts of textual fragments according to predetermined layout prints; extract the shapes from the sand by means of a screwdriver and a fair degree of physical strength; start the imprinting process all over again and continue writing. To some extent, these operations evoked tasks performed by metalworkers engaged in sand casting, a technique in which the sand is used as a mold. The exhibition visitors who encountered the artist at work could catch a glimpse of the materials and procedures pertaining to foundry production processes, with their vivid colors and their bas-relief chiaroscuros, their pounding rhythms and their muffled silences. The analogy between metalworking and Léonard-Contant's artistic operation recalls a famous precedent. The act of bringing the foundry's means of production within an institutional framework devoted to art is indeed reminiscent of the strategies devised by radical artist groups some fifty years before, at a time that saw the polemic redefinition of art as work and the rise of the art worker against the stifling grip of capitalism.[2] Despite different circumstances, *Digs* aligns with those conceptual practices that exposed the politics of labor involved in artistic production. This leads to the second activity on display: the making of art.

Significantly, while in a foundry the molds are filled with liquified metal to obtain a final product, no metal would be melted and poured into the letter-shaped holes the artist had dug into the red sand at Kunsthaus Baselland. There, the sand-casting job was not completed, suggesting that a production process of a different kind was in progress. In the museum, the sand-filled

1 *Digs* is the title of Maude Léonard-Contant's solo show featured at Kunsthaus Baselland September 9 — November 11, 2022.

2 I am referring to artist groups and coalitions such as those that formed in New York at the turn of the 1960s and 1970s, like the AWC and Art Strike, just to name a few. By carrying the materials, procedures, and modes of production belonging to factories and construction sites within the museum's halls, the members of these groups set a precedent for conceptual practices which aimed at exposing the politics of labor involved in artmaking. This came at a time of growing awareness regarding the infiltration of the capitalist logic of labor and production into any form of labor (be it cognitive, affective or even artistic), according to which everyone and everything would be put to work. For more on this, I refer the reader to Julia Bryan-Wilson, *Art Workers: Radical Practice in the Vietnam War Era*, University of California Press, Berkeley/Los Angeles/London 2010; and Helen Molesworth, "Work Ethic," in *Work Ethic*, (exh. cat., The Baltimore Museum of Art, October 12, 2003 — January 11, 2004; Des Moines Center for the Arts, May 15 — August 1, 2004), Pennsylvania State University Press, University Park 2003.

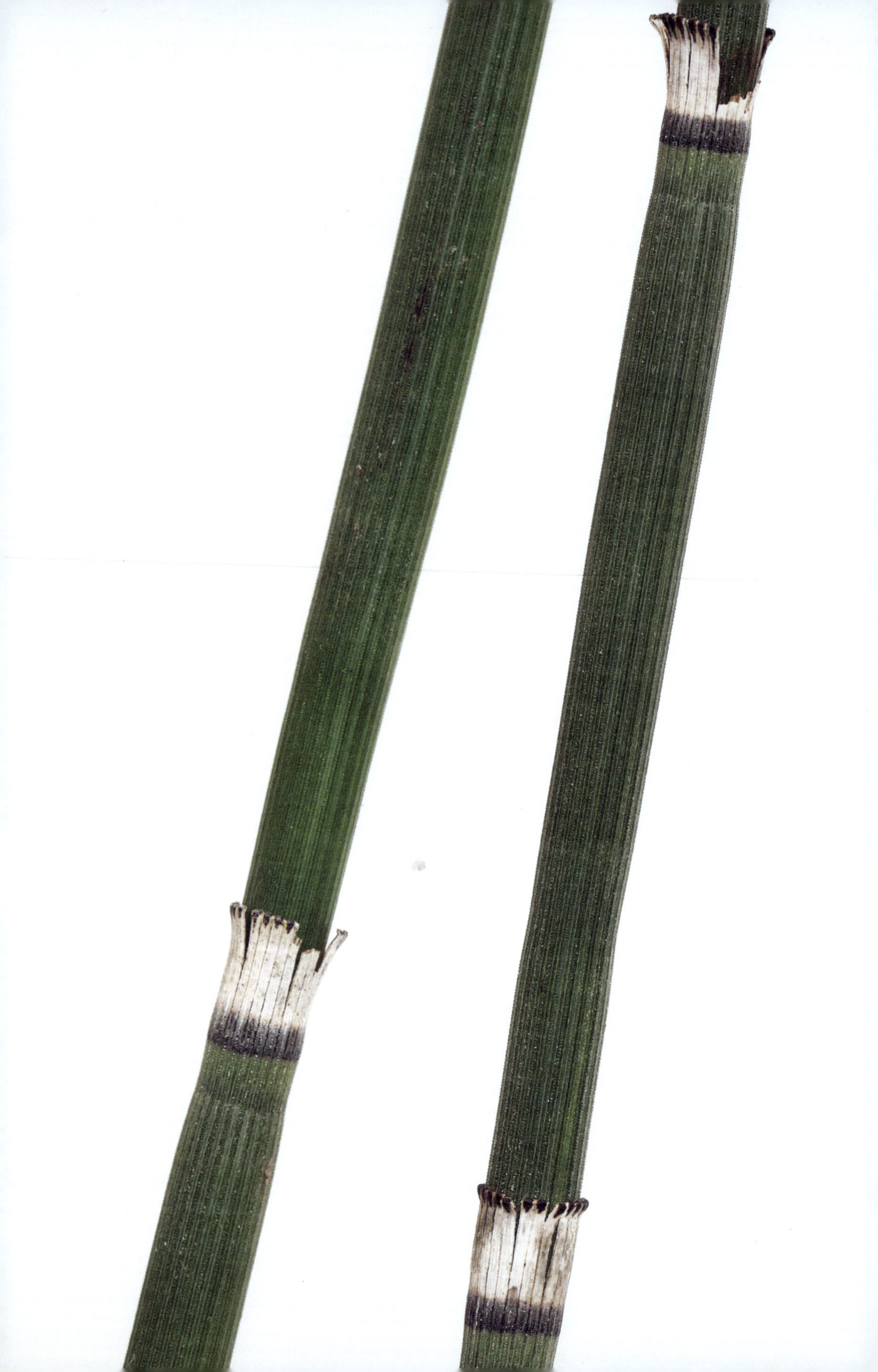

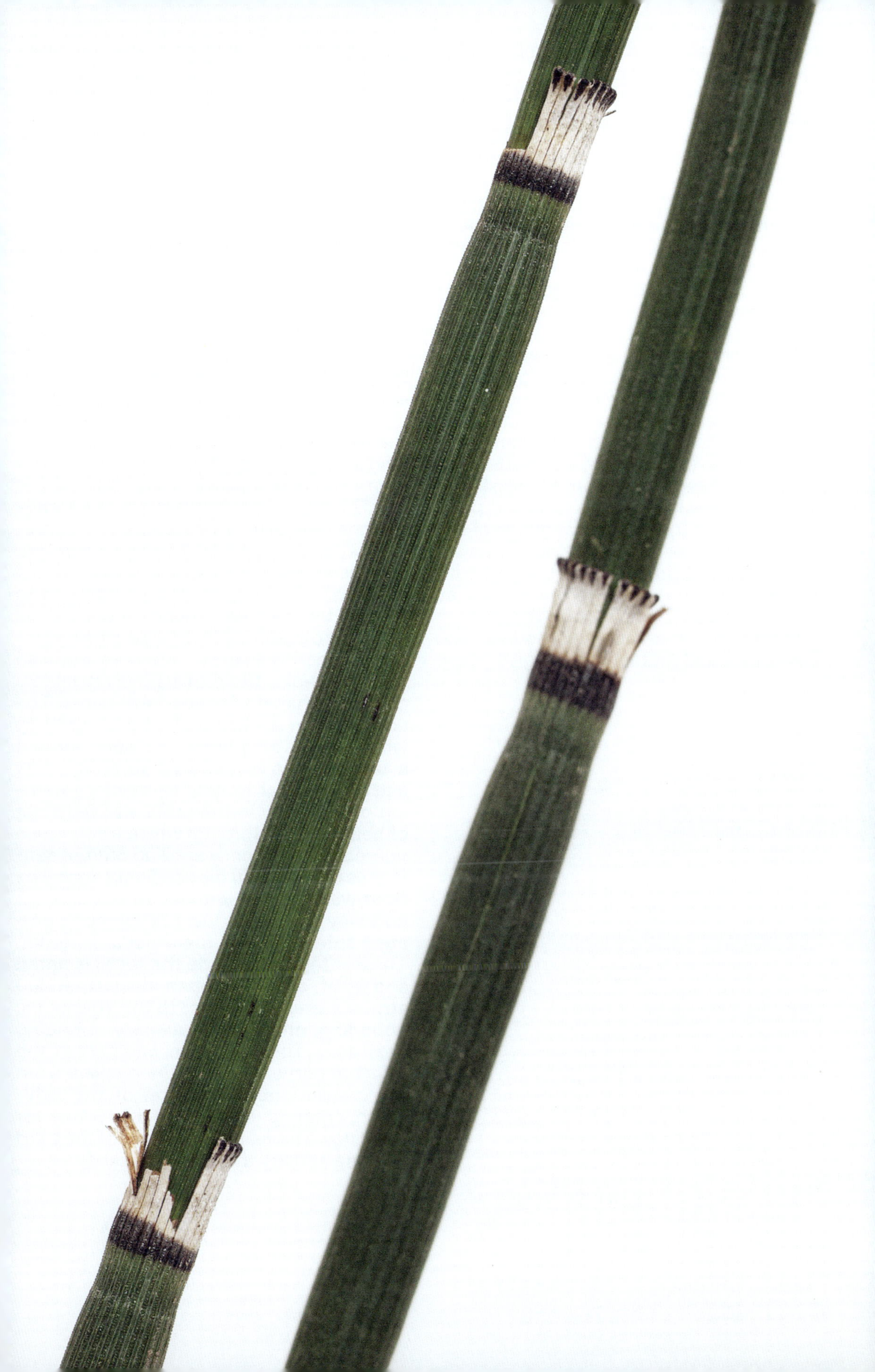

room was treated as a site of symbolic production, language and its forms resting at the very heart of it. The sand casts, rather than filled with melted metal, were laden with thoughts provoked in the silent reader, tacitly running through the sentences in her mind, or coagulated into the words softly surfacing in the murmur of her lips. In the sand matrix, obtained by means of carving, sculpture would become language and vice versa, as if by a sort of transubstantiation occurring in those negative spaces where meaning nestled. At first glance, it is tempting to inscribe Léonard-Contant within an art-historical genealogy of artists who experimented with the materialization of language, in search of a language of their own to express meanings of their own against the silencing constraints of an exclusionary culture.[3] However, Léonard-Contant undertakes a fundamentally dissimilar operation, speaking from a different position. Instead of inventing a language of her own, she digs into three existing languages (French, English, and German), whose conflictual interactions, made of mergers as much as substitutions, narrate the story of a life trajectory marked by uprooting.[4] The digs in the sand metaphorically give shape to the artist's relationship with such languages, materializing as holes in the memory of those who leave a linguistic community, or as gaps in communication of those who are becoming familiar to a new one. They represent the ellipses punctuating one's thinking processes the moment a mother tongue, under the corrosive action of a newly learned language, begins to fade. This phenomenon is also crystallized in a series of cobalt-colored salt blocks used in the vestibule as paperweights, which hold the layout prints of the textual fragments in place. The sinuous cavities sculpted in the blue lickstones are reminiscent of those left by the tongue of a cow in search of minerals: another reference to erosion, which is both an effect and a structuring agent of the tongue.[5] Léonard-Contant's act of digging also symbolizes the effort to delve into memory and recuperate the mother tongue by clinging to linguistic scraps and family sayings. The artist crafted specific instruments for doing so. In the adjacent room, reminiscent of a carpenter's workshop, the wooden letter-shaped molds employed to write in the sand were hung on the wall by plaster protrusions which infilled their negative spaces. When the letters were removed from the walls, the protrusions revealed a cryptic alphabet of shapes and forms. The composition evoked a classroom setting, with an alphabet primer on display around a table with a blackboard surface, chalk and a sponge: all tools of elementary learning processes. On the table also lay a set of headphones, through which a soft voice poured out like honey spelling out the sentences imprinted in the sand next door. The floor was covered with white felt and the doorway thresholds were reframed to create a safe space for the artist's daughter. These alterations made the room isolated and quiet, as if enveloped in a suspended atmosphere, in contrast to the strenuous, pounding, and sweaty scenery unfolding next door. This operation was part of the effort to carve out a nurturing space from the institutional dimension of the exhibition, creating yet another digs (slang for dwelling). This leads to the core of the third working activity therein performed.

3 My reflections on negativity and otherness, triggered by the ways Léonard-Contant works with negative volumes and seems to "extract" meaning from voids, are inspired by Anne-Marie Sauzeau Boetti's famous essay "Negative Capability as Practice in Women's Art." However, I see an irreducible gap between the practices Sauzeau Boetti refers to and Léonard-Contant's practice, given the different historical, geographical, and sociocultural contexts in which these artists have operated. The same can be said regarding the concept of "materialization of language," which I derive from Mirella Bentivoglio's research and, notably, from her 1978 exhibition *Materializzazione del linguaggio* (Magazzini del Sale alle Zattere, Biennale di Venezia 1978). Again, while reconnecting Léonard-Contant's work to such past experiences, sensitive differences in context and position cannot be ignored. For more on the abovementioned concepts, I refer the reader to Anne Marie Sauzeau Boetti, "Negative Capability as Practice in Women's Art," *Studio International*, vol. 191, no. 979 (1976): 24–25; Mirella Bentivoglio, *Materializzazione del linguaggio* (ex. cat., La Biennale di Venezia B78, Magazzini del Sale alle Zattere, September 20 – October 15, 1978), Edizioni: La Biennale di Venezia, Venice 1978; Barbara Casavecchia, "1966 and Thereabouts: Call Girls, Riot Grrrls in Evolution, Poetry and 'Missing Language.' Ketty La Rocca, Lucia Marcucci, Giulia Niccolai," in *Ennesima: The Image of Writing. Gruppo 70, Visual Poetry and Verbal-Visual Investigations*, Mousse / La Triennale, Milan 2015; and Barbara Casavecchia, "Taci, anzi parla," *South as a state of mind* 7, dOCUMENTA14, no. 2 (spring/summer 2016). Source: https://www.documenta14.de/en/south/463_taci_anzi_parla (consulted on March 15, 2023).

4 As is Maude Léonard-Contant's life trajectory, having the artist moved from Quebec to German-speaking Switzerland, hence shifting to a new linguistic community as well.

5 Yet another reference to Maude Léonard-Contant's lived experience in Quebec. While the sculptures on display at Kunsthaus Baselland were made by modelling the salt blocks with water, they evoked memories of the holes dug by the tongues of the two cows who lived at the family farm, where they had cobalt lickstones to provide the mineral supplements they needed.

When asked to imagine how such a space would feel, one might picture a nursery. A nursery is, by definition, a room set apart for infants or very young children. That is to say, a place designated for reproductive and care work. While the previously evoked frameworks—those of a carpenter's workshop and a foundry—might have eclipsed the circumstances in which Maude Léonard-Contant conceptualized and processed her show, here those very conditions reemerged.By taking her child to work during the exhibition's opening hours, she indeed performed an act of displacement, transposing a set of related reproductive activities to the museum's galleries. This operation calls to mind feminist conceptual practices of the late 1960s and 1970s, such as Mary Kelly's or Lea Lublin's, exposing the fact that those practices were never exclusively conceptual.[6] They were also the result of pragmatic choices, indexical of specific life experiences and working conditions, which turned into programmatic statements after consciousness raising and political awakening. Echoes of that social and symbolic struggle still reverberate in contemporary art practices, as in the way Léonard-Contant short-circuits the ideological remnants of the die-hard mythology of the autonomy of art.[7] She confronts, by the act of displacement, the legacies of the traditional sexual division of labor, which organized production in factories and households, museums and nurseries, as well as in culture and society at large, just as Kelly and Lublin did in their time. She differs, however, in that she does not treat the demands of social reproduction as the subject matter of her installation, but rather as contingent working conditions, reiterating that artmaking need not necessarily be incompatible with child-rearing and practices of care.

This included the practice of taking care of plants, which became a constitutive part of *Digs*. To explore the complex relational dimension on which the exhibition was built, the second definition of nursery is useful, as it designates a place where young trees or plants are cared for before being transplanted. The semantic coincidence reflects a further articulation of the exhibition, which harbored a set of ceramic vessels finely crafted by the artist in respect to the properties and colors of natural soil material. Peeking out of the vessels were some ruderal plants commonly called horsetails. The artist carefully collected them from the outskirts of Basel, where they were returned after the exhibition with equal care. Horsetails also grow on the clay banks of the river that irrigates her homeland in Quebec and are therefore constitutive of her affective geography, residing among her companion species of choice.[8] They are arboreal kindred to her, the color of their whorls feeling familiar and comforting just like the sound of a mother tongue. Their presence in the exhibition was a reminder that plants can travel and adapt to all sorts of unexpected places,[9] just like affects, relationships, and languages transplanted in new linguistic communities. In addition, the dispositive devised by the artist invites us to contemplate the possibility of forging more-than-human companionship, enriching our kinship with non-anthropocentric difference. The exhibition embraced indeed a multispecies community, telling the untold stories of becoming-with for the invention of solidary ways of dwelling on the planet. As Donna Haraway suggests, terraforming and storytelling require medium, soil, matter, mutter, and mother.[10] Maude Léonard-Contant's work seems to have all the right ingredients.

6 I am notably thinking about Lea Lublin's performance *Mon fils (my son)*, which took place in 1968 at the Musée d'Art Moderne de la Ville de Paris during the Salon de Mai, and to Mary Kelly's Post-Partum Document, first shown at the ICA in London in 1976. For more on these and similar practices, I refer the reader to Helen Molesworth, "House Work and Art Work," *October*, vol. 92 (Spring 2000): 71–97. For more on the relationship between Lea Lublin's performance and the concept of displacement, I refer the reader to Catherine Spencer, "Acts of Displacement: Lea Lublin's *Mon fils*, May '68, and Feminist Psychosocial Revolt," *Oxford Art Journal*, vol. 40, no. 1 (Spring 2017): 65–83.

7 Drawing on the theories of Marxist, feminist, and social art historians, the myth of the autonomy of art is here understood as part of the modernist ideology separating art from the social reality of those producing it. In other words, a mythology contributing to the idealization of a pantheon of individuals presumably endowed with creative genius and cut off from any social relations of production, which for centuries concurred to the exclusion of women from artmaking and its canons.

8 Regarding the concept of companion species, I refer the reader to the eco-feminist theories of Donna Haraway, and especially to Donna Haraway, *The Companion Species Manifesto: Dogs, People, and Significant Otherness*, Prickly Paradigm Press, Chicago 2003; and Donna Haraway, *Staying with the Trouble: Making Kin in the Chthulucene*, Duke University Press, Durham 2016.

9 "*Can*, not necessarily *may* or *should*," Haraway adds to this consideration. Donna Haraway, *Staying with the Trouble*, p. 120.

10 Ibid.

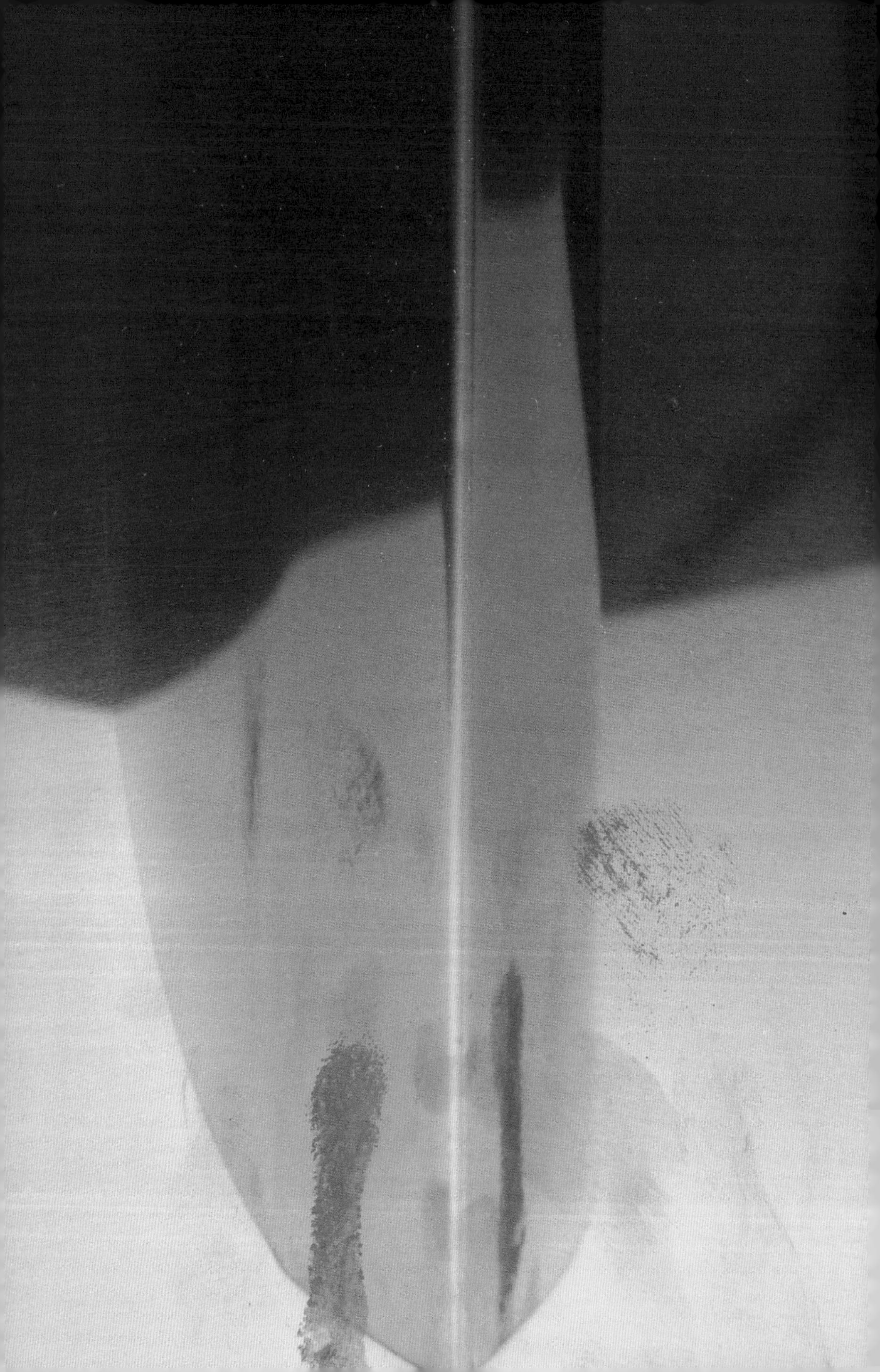

AAAAABBCCCCDDDDDEEEEEEEEEE
FFFGHHHHIIIIIIKLLLLLLLLLMMNNNNNOOOOPPP
QRRRSSSSSSSSSTTTTTUUUUUVWWXYYZ
2022
40 × 1938 × 10 cm
Plaster, shellacked wood

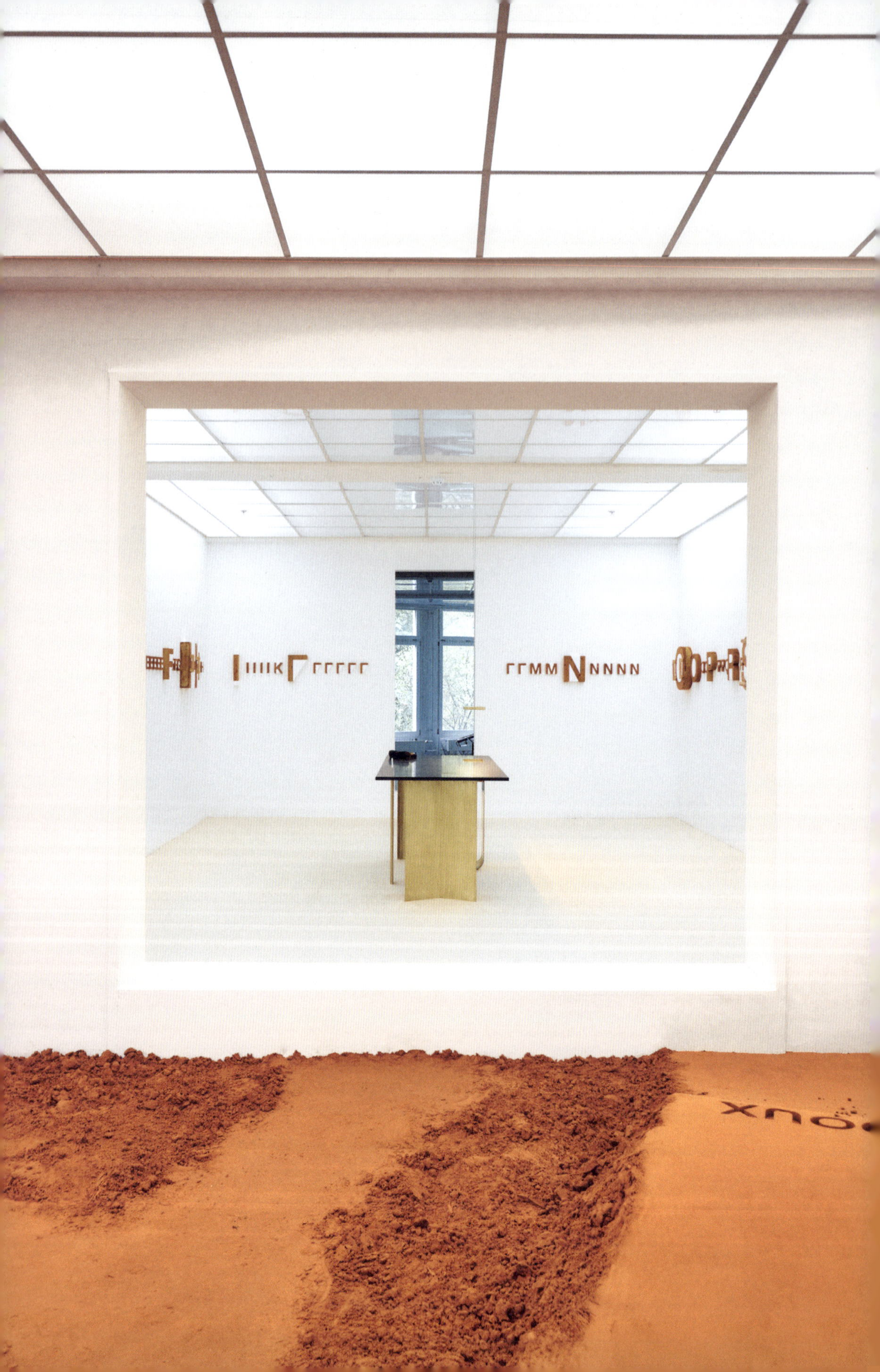

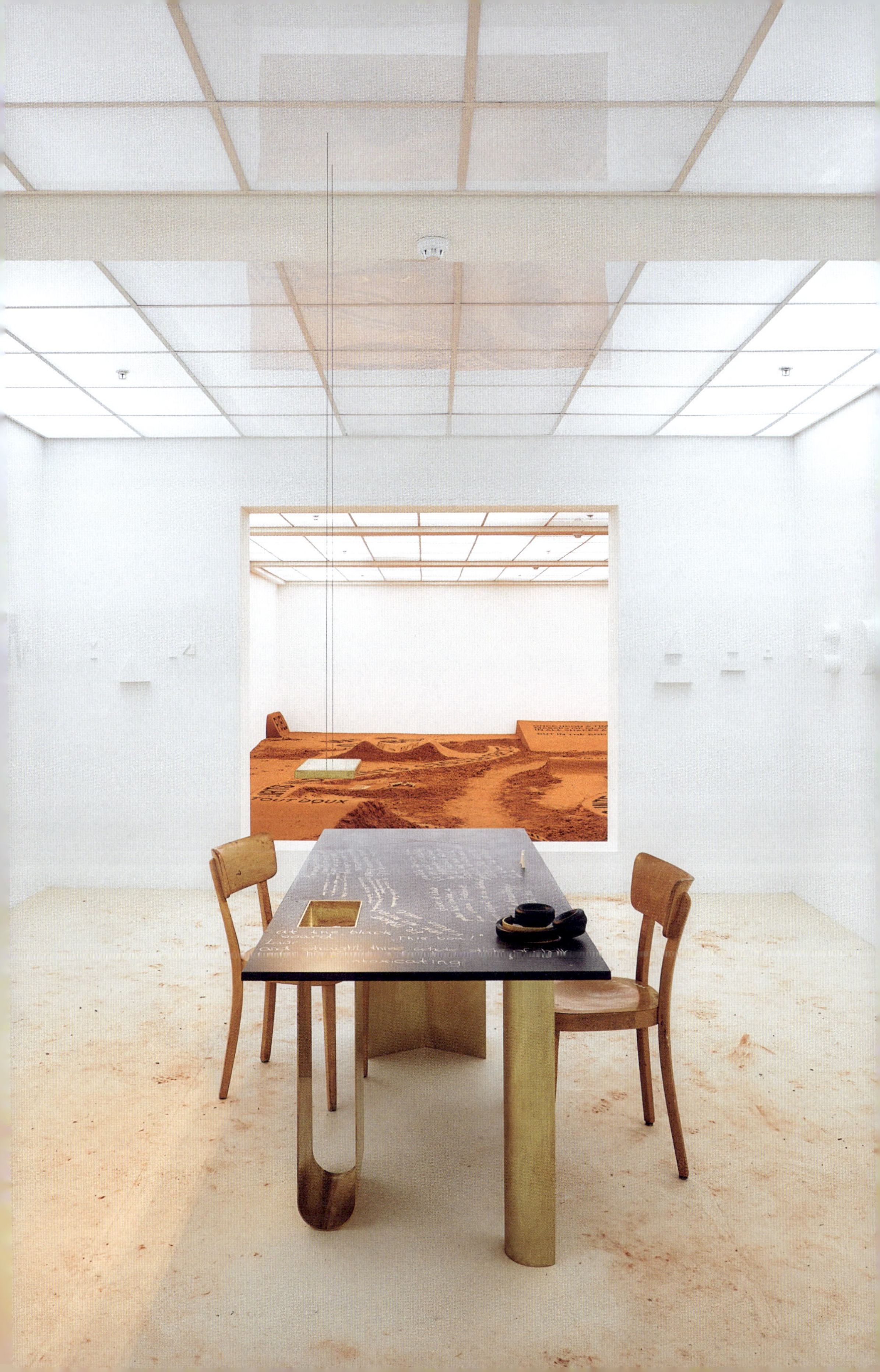

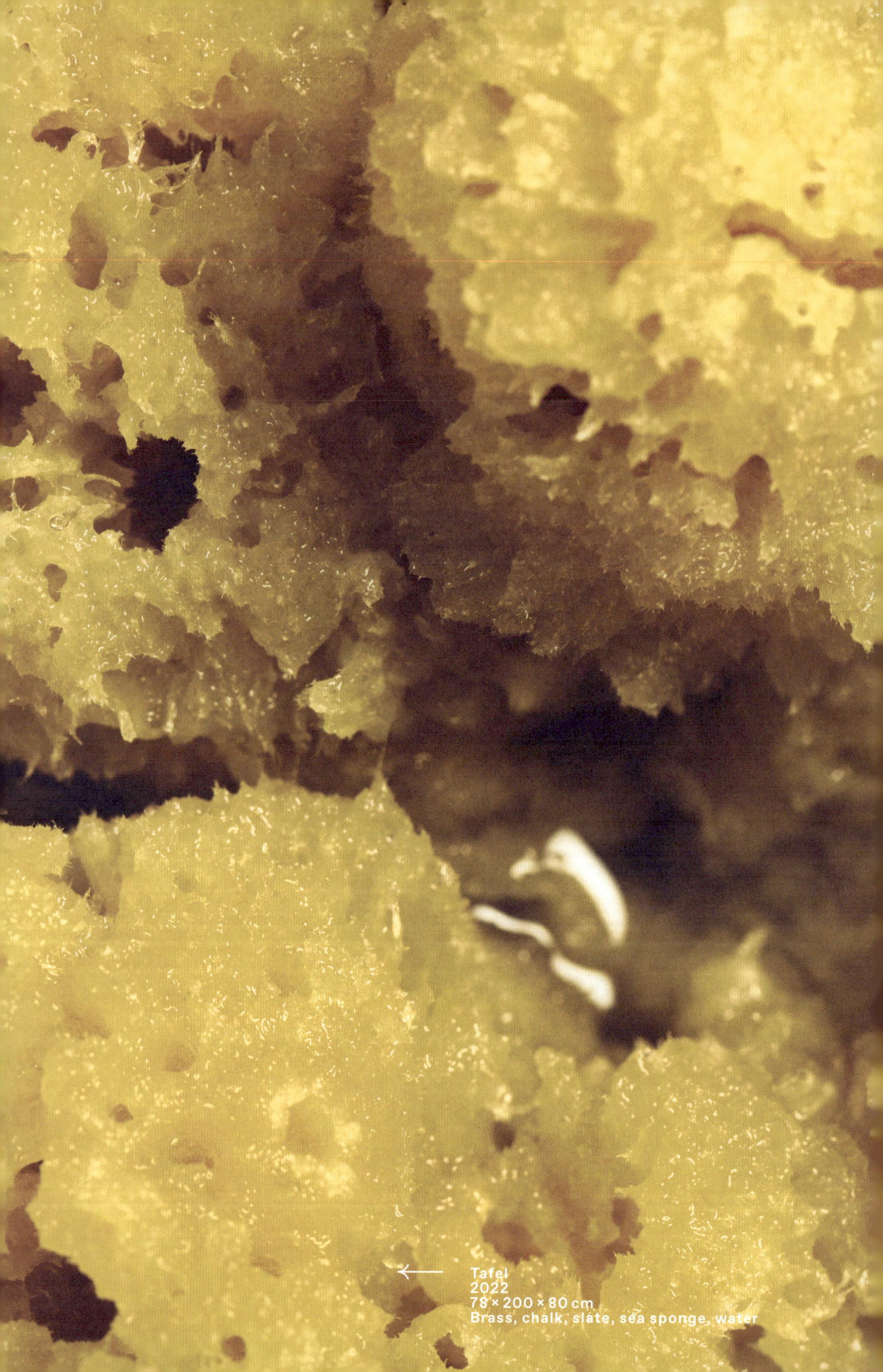

← Tafel
2022
78 × 200 × 80 cm
Brass, chalk, slate, sea sponge, water

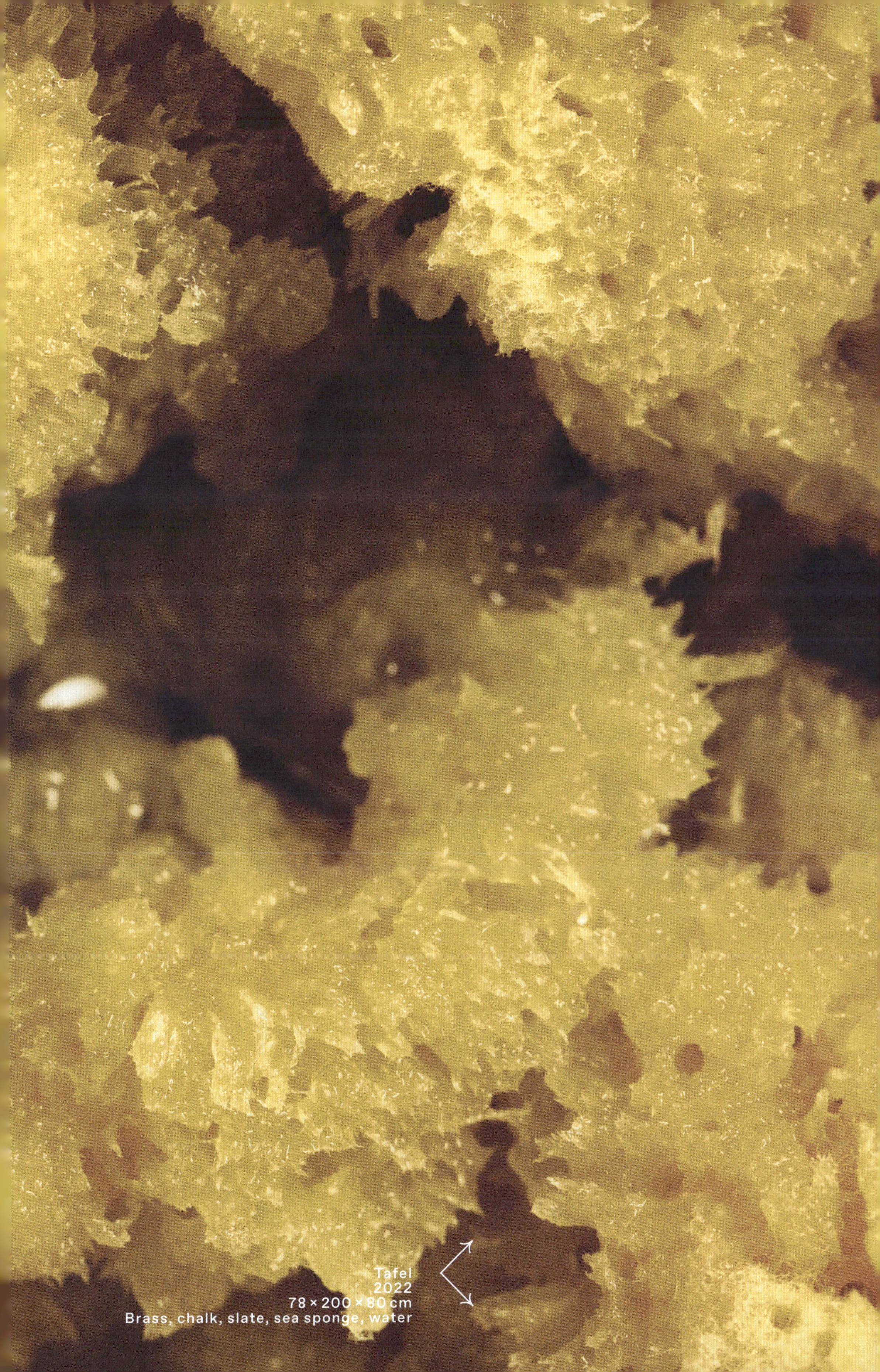

Tafel
2022
78 × 200 × 80 cm
Brass, chalk, slate, sea sponge, water

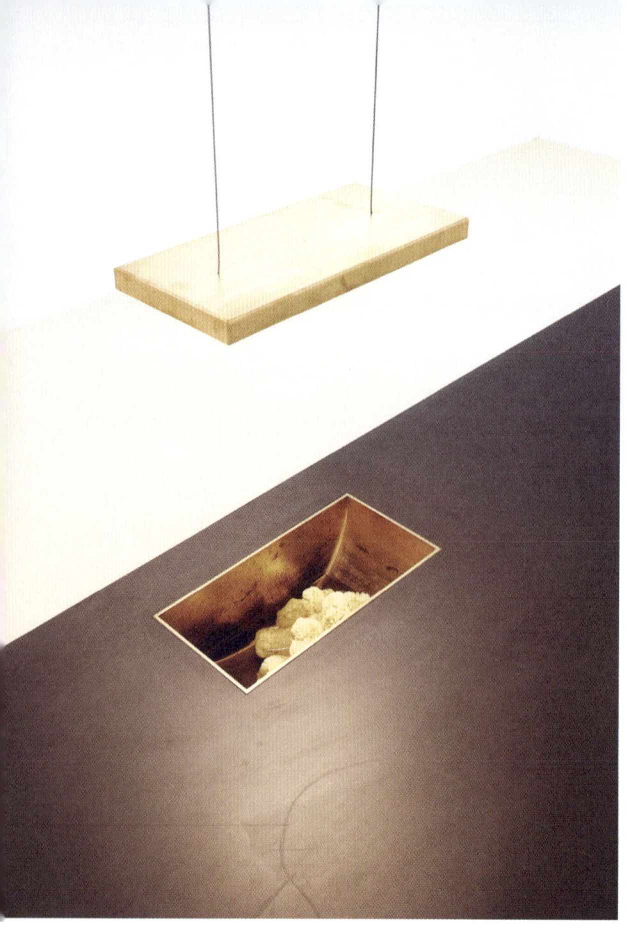

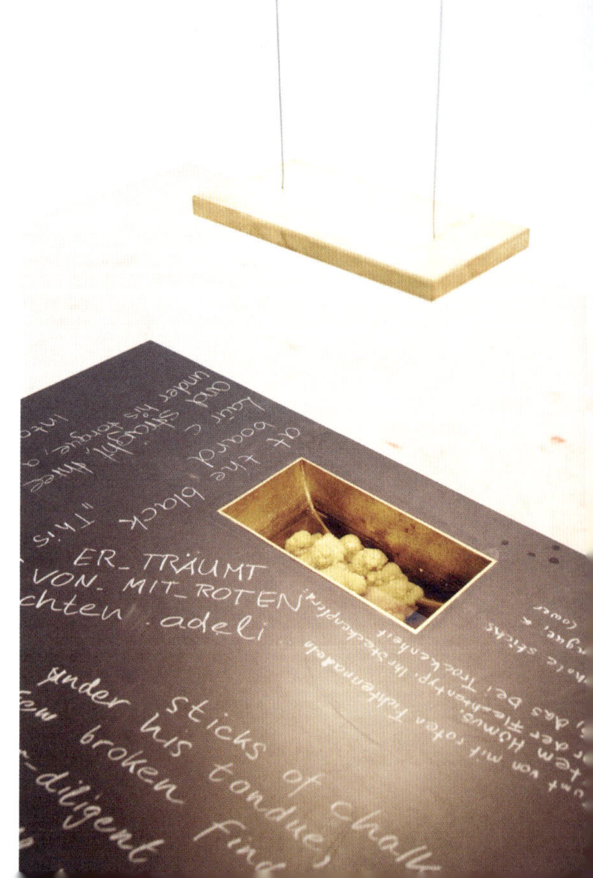
ER_TRÄUMT
VON_ MIT_ROTEN
sticks of chalk
under his tongue,
broken

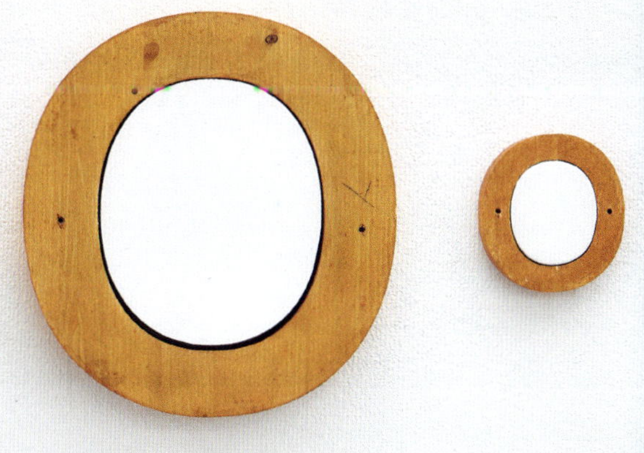

AAAAABBCCCCDDDDDEEEEEEEEEE
FFFGHHHHIIIIIIKLLLLLLLLLMMNNNNNOOOOPPP
QRRRSSSSSSSSSSTTTTTUUUUUVWWXYYZ
2022
40 × 1938 × 10 cm
Plaster, shellacked wood

Earth-moving
2022
60 × 1196 × 811 cm
Foundry sand, tools

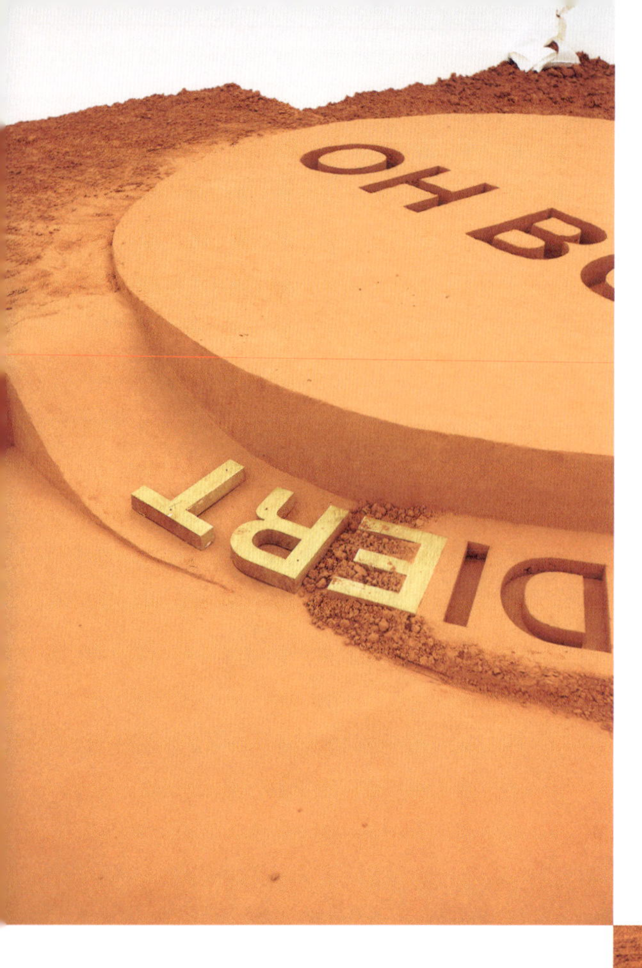

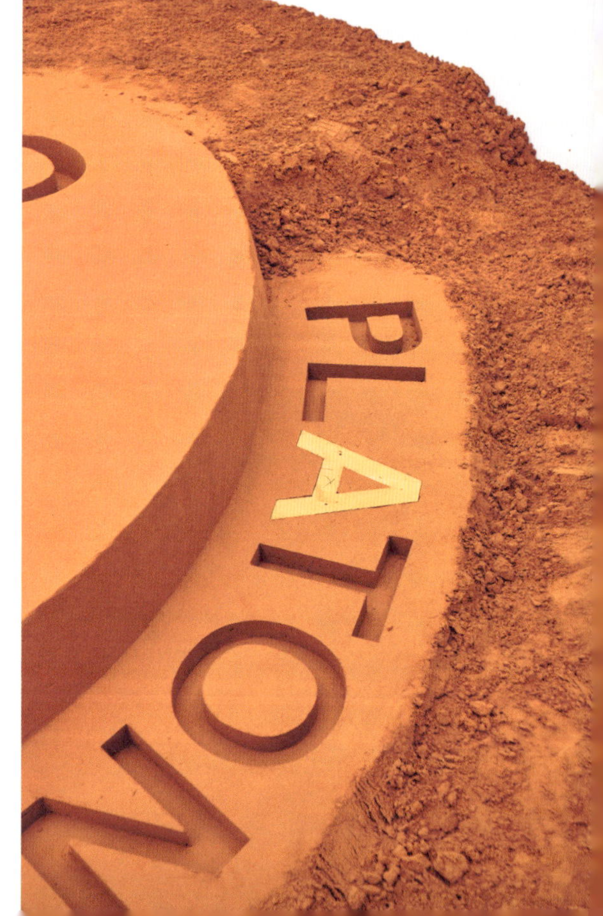
PLATON

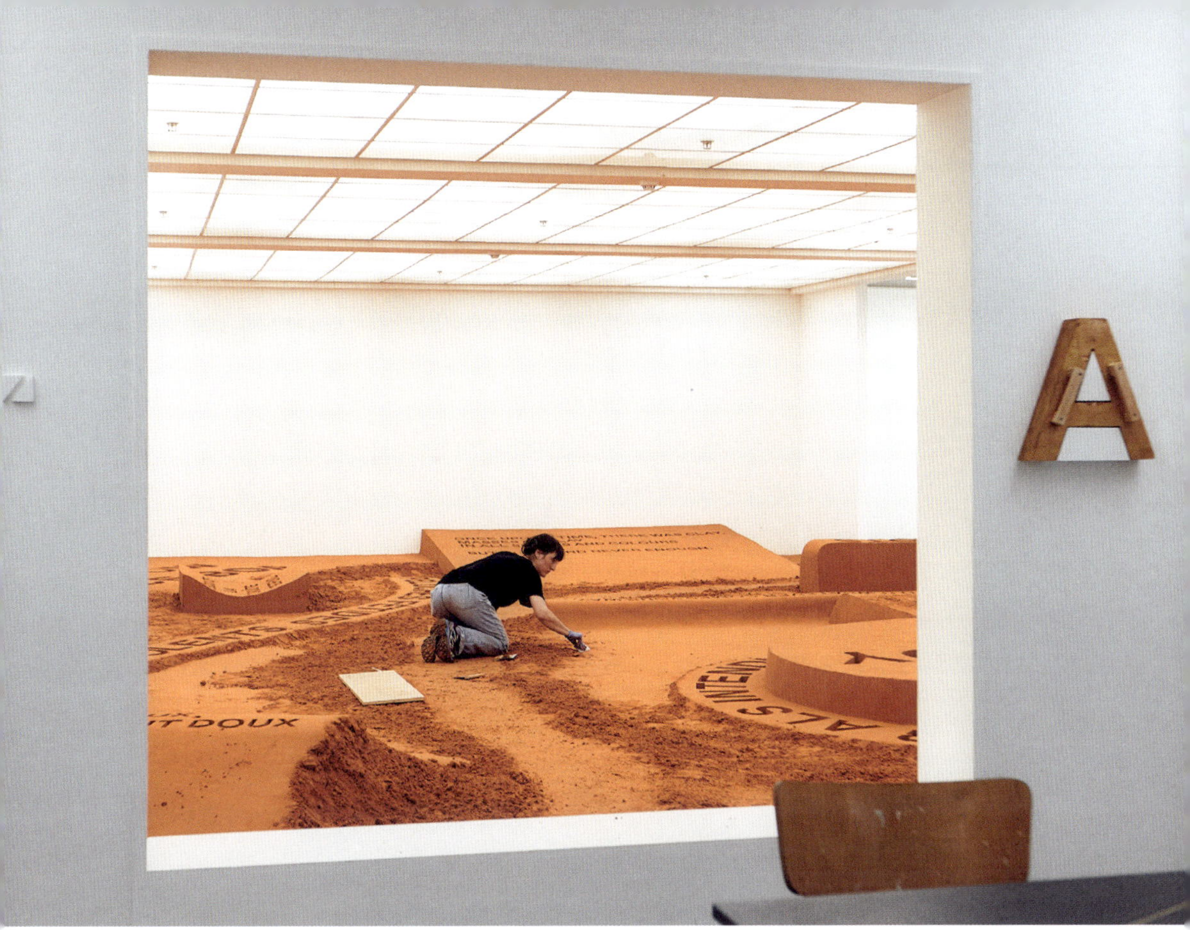

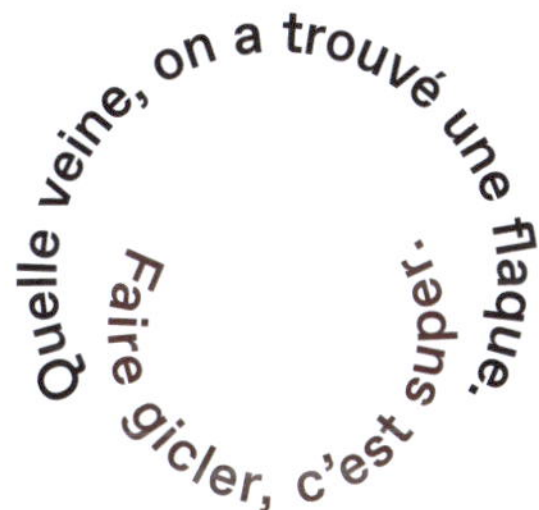

Ça met du baume au cœur et surtout, ça change les idées.

Comme nous étions restés un peu barbouillés du goûter, cette consolation nous est douce.

Et on éclabousse de plus belle !

Bientôt à court de liquide, nous nous en prenons aux coquilles d'escargots éparses entre les murets décrépis — c'est tout aussi bath. Momifiées par un été qui traîne en longueur, elles craquent sous le pied de la meilleure façon.

Nous découvrons vite qu'en s'y mettant à plusieurs, nos piaffements déclenchent une salve retentissante ; notre petite troupe exulte ! Jusqu'à ce qu'Antoine remarque que certaines carapaces sont, contre toute attente, encore habitées.

Le malaise nous reprend.

Earth-moving
2022
60 × 1196 × 811 cm
Foundry sand, tools

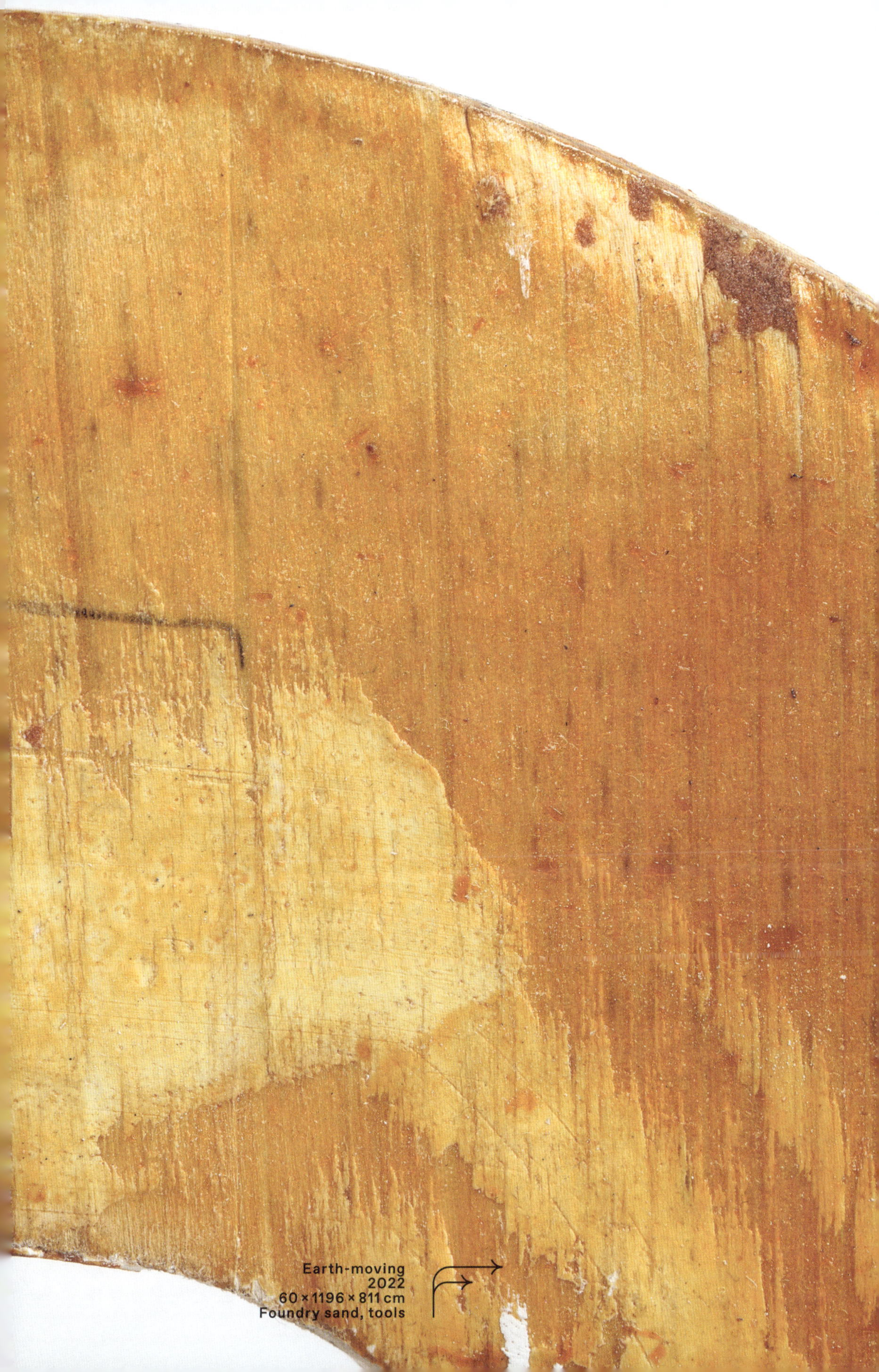

Earth-moving
2022
60 × 1196 × 811 cm
Foundry sand, tools

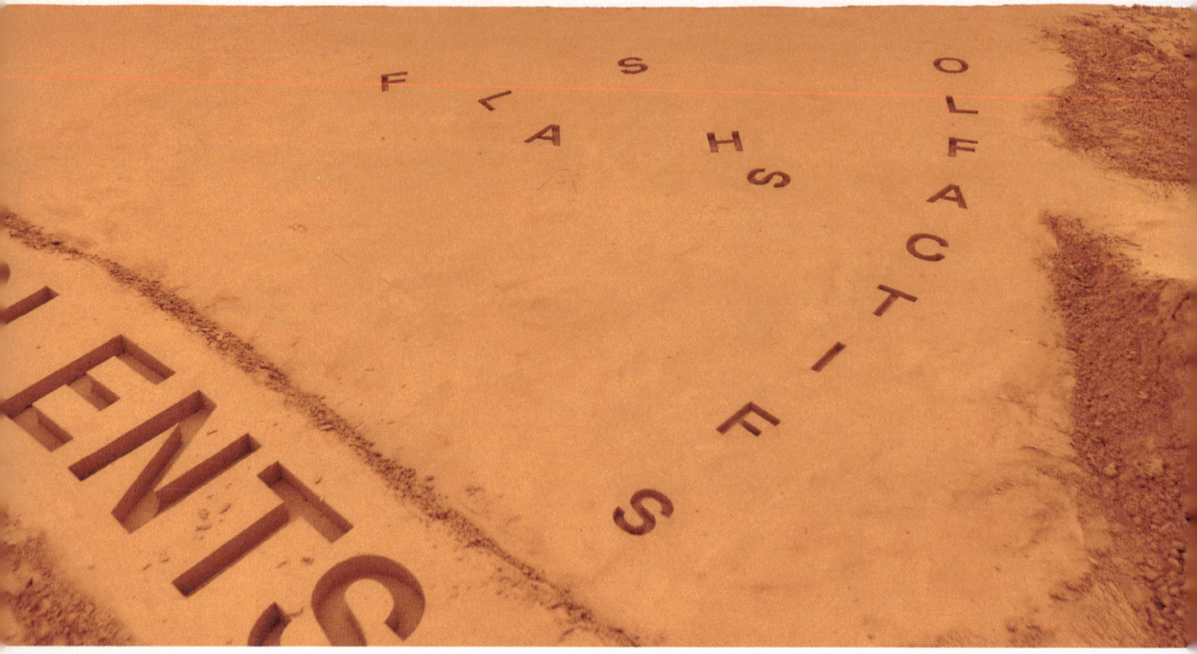

OLFACTIFS

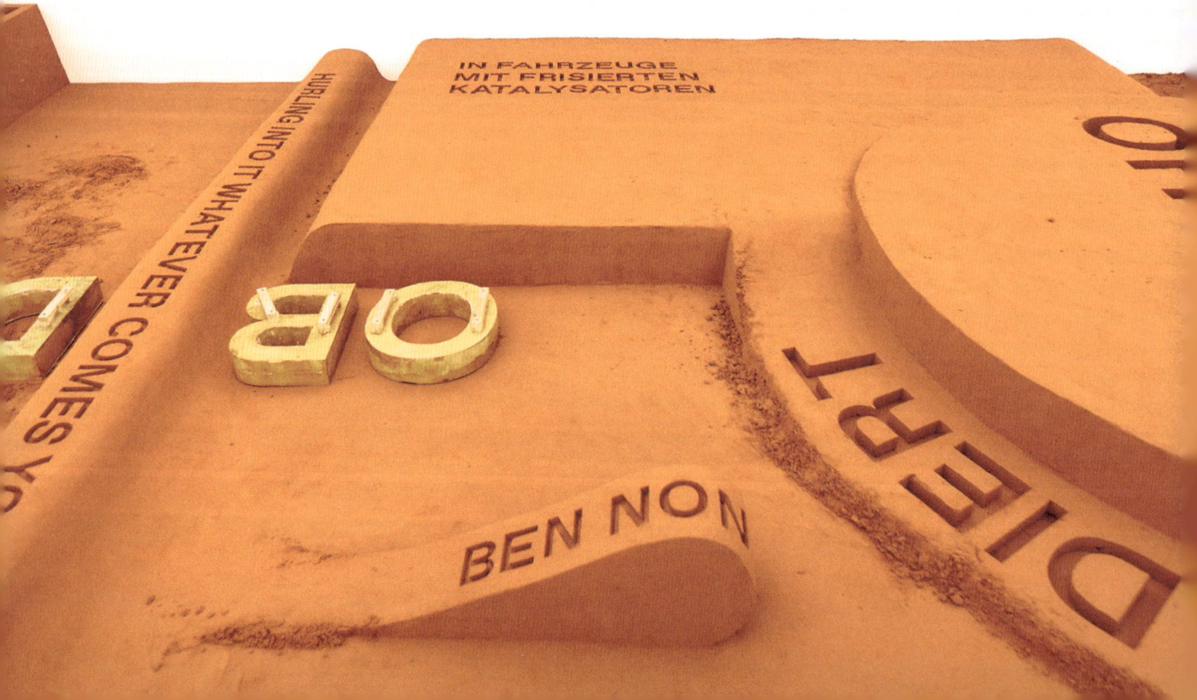

IN FAHRZEUGE
MIT FRISIERTEN
KATALYSATOREN
HURLING INTO IT WHATEVER COMES
BEN NON

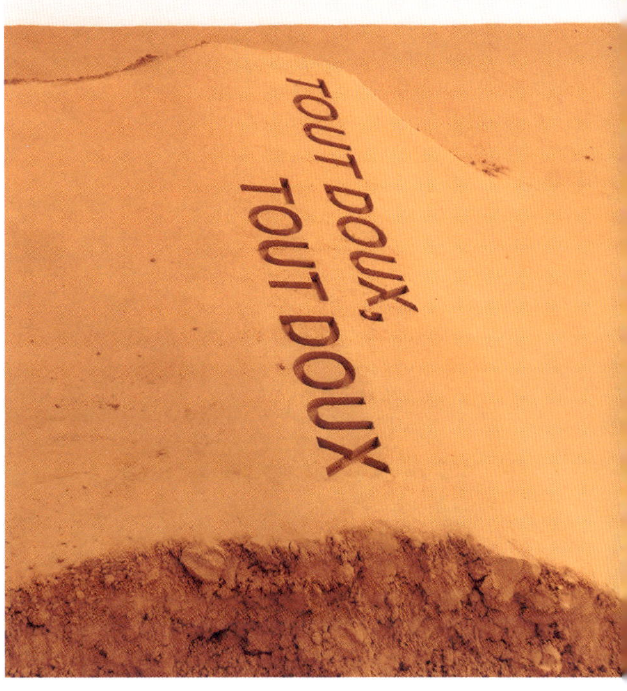

Tu le tiens bien bas,
ton museau
constellé d'aiguilles.
Safre!
Pourquoi avoir brouté
ton chemin jusqu'au
champ d'en bas?
L'herbe y est plus tendre,
mais le porc-épic y rode
à la brunante.
Te voilà servie ma pauvre.
Les épines équipées de barbillons
continueront leur chemin
dans ta chair
si on ne les retire pas.
Alors tout doux, tout doux.

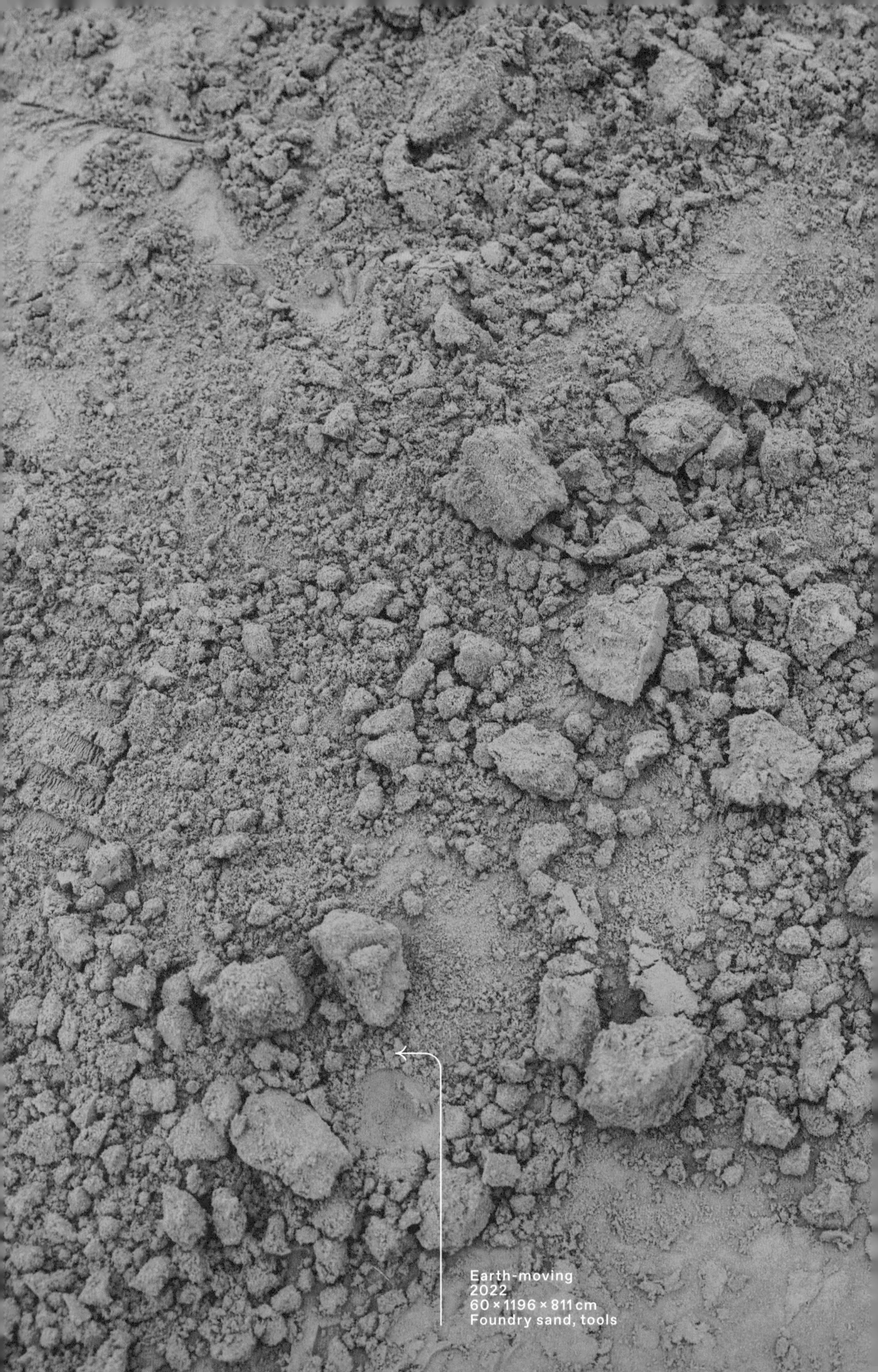

Earth-moving
2022
60 × 1196 × 811 cm
Foundry sand, tools

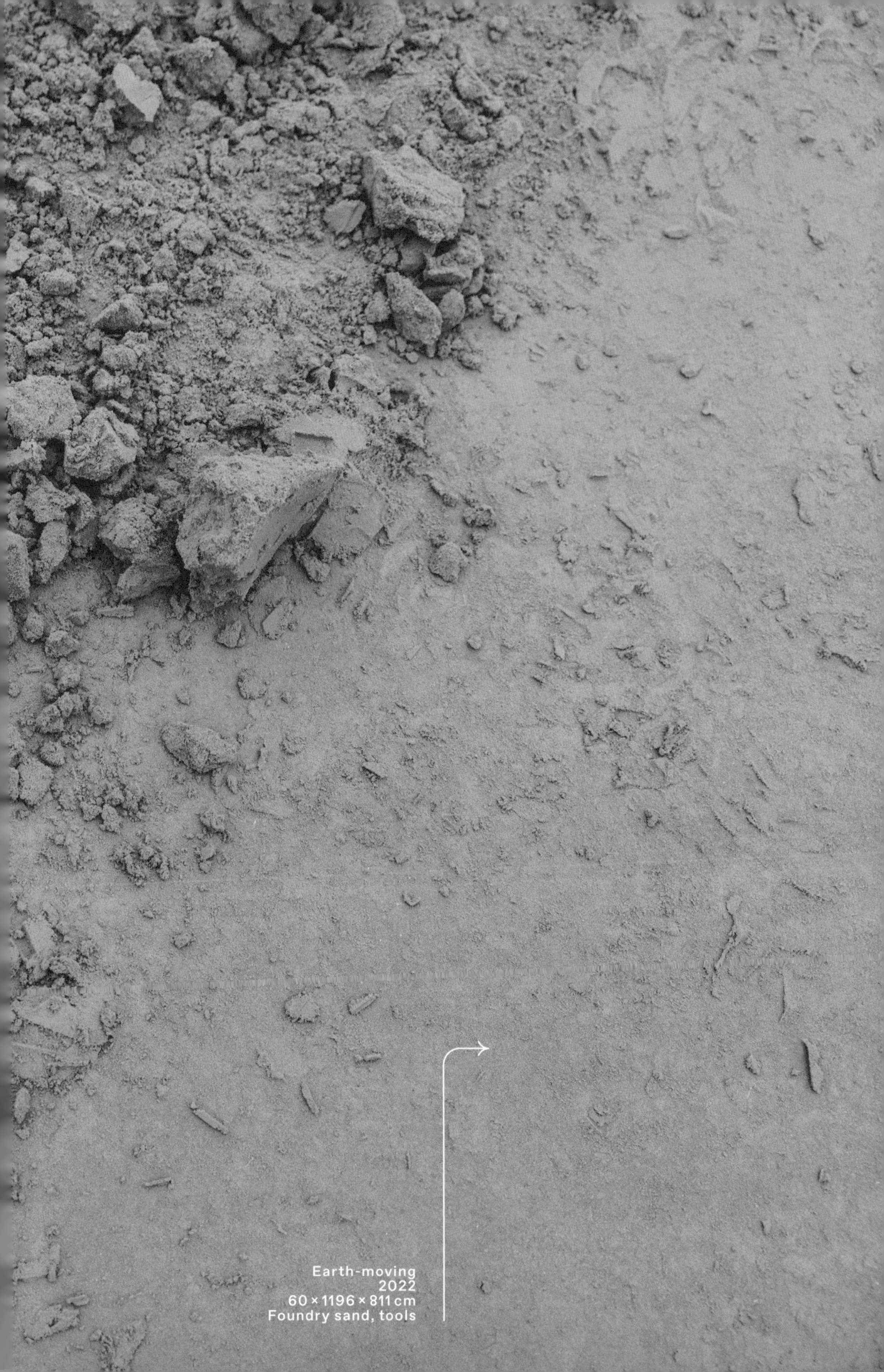

Earth-moving
2022
60 × 1196 × 811 cm
Foundry sand, tools

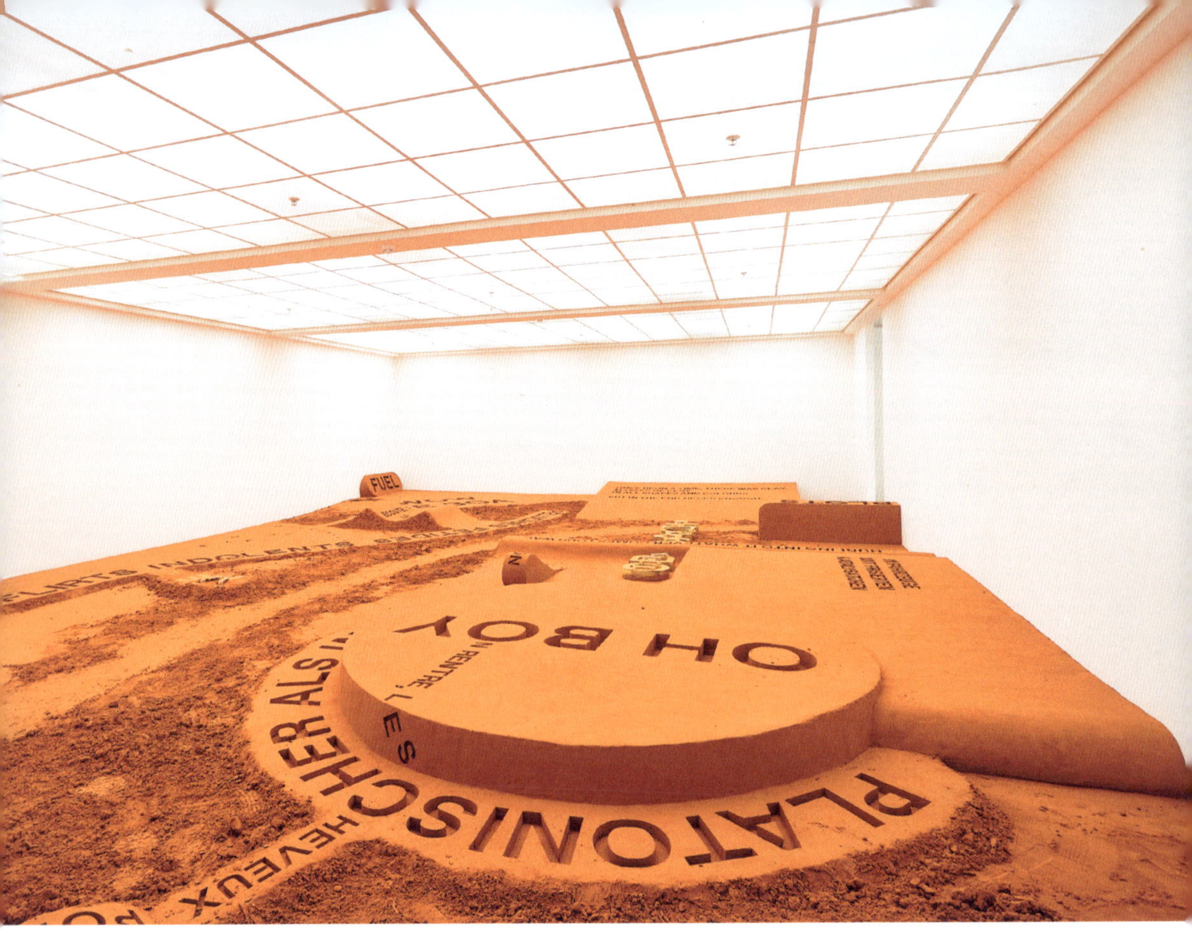
FUEL
FLIRTS INDOLENTS
OH BOY
PLATONISCHER ALS

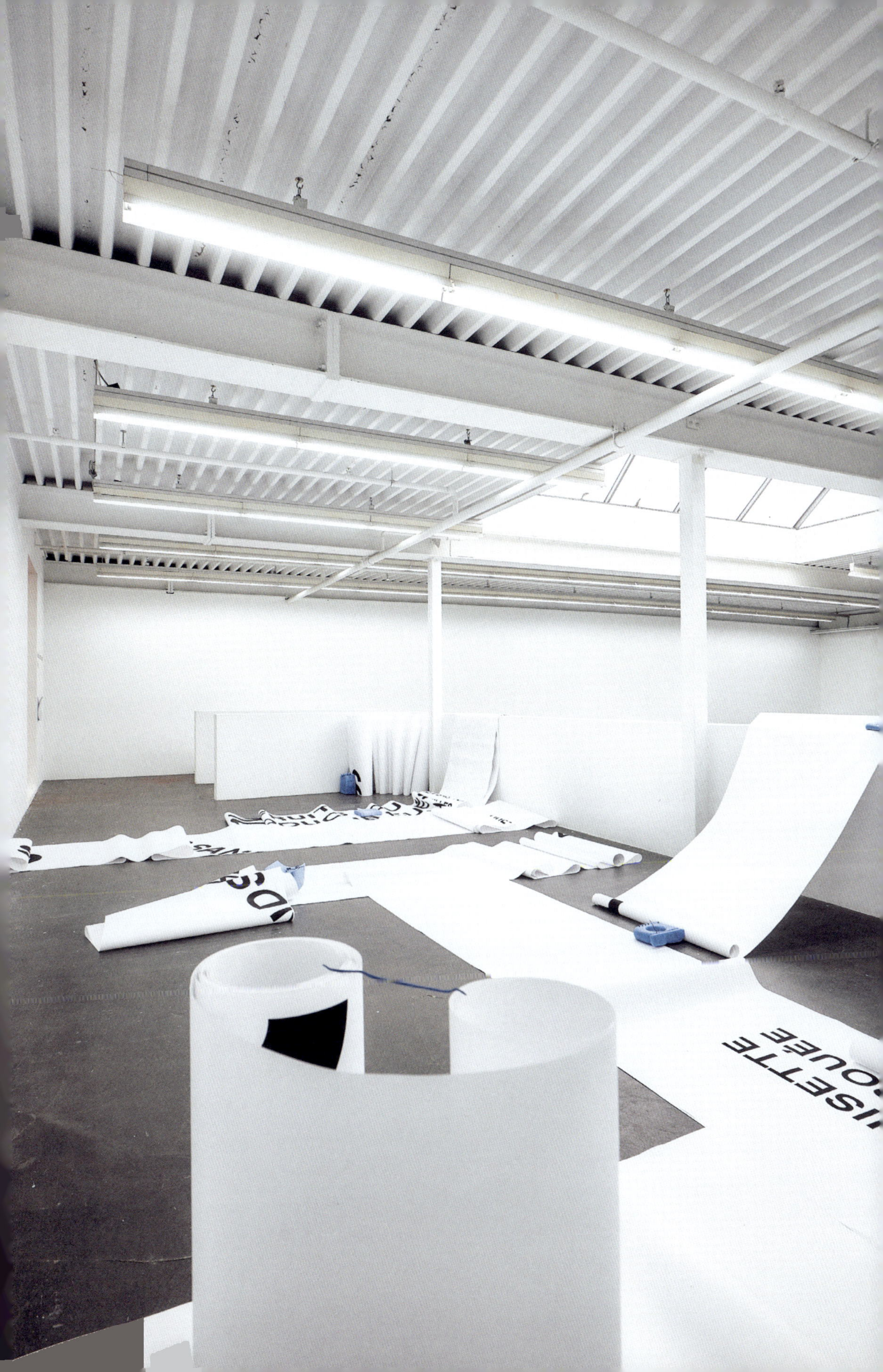

Paperweights/Layout
2022
Variable dimensions
Inkjet prints on plan paper,
cobalt mineral lick, porcelain

Paperweights/Layout
2022
Variable dimensions
Inkjet prints on plan paper,
cobalt mineral lick, porcelain

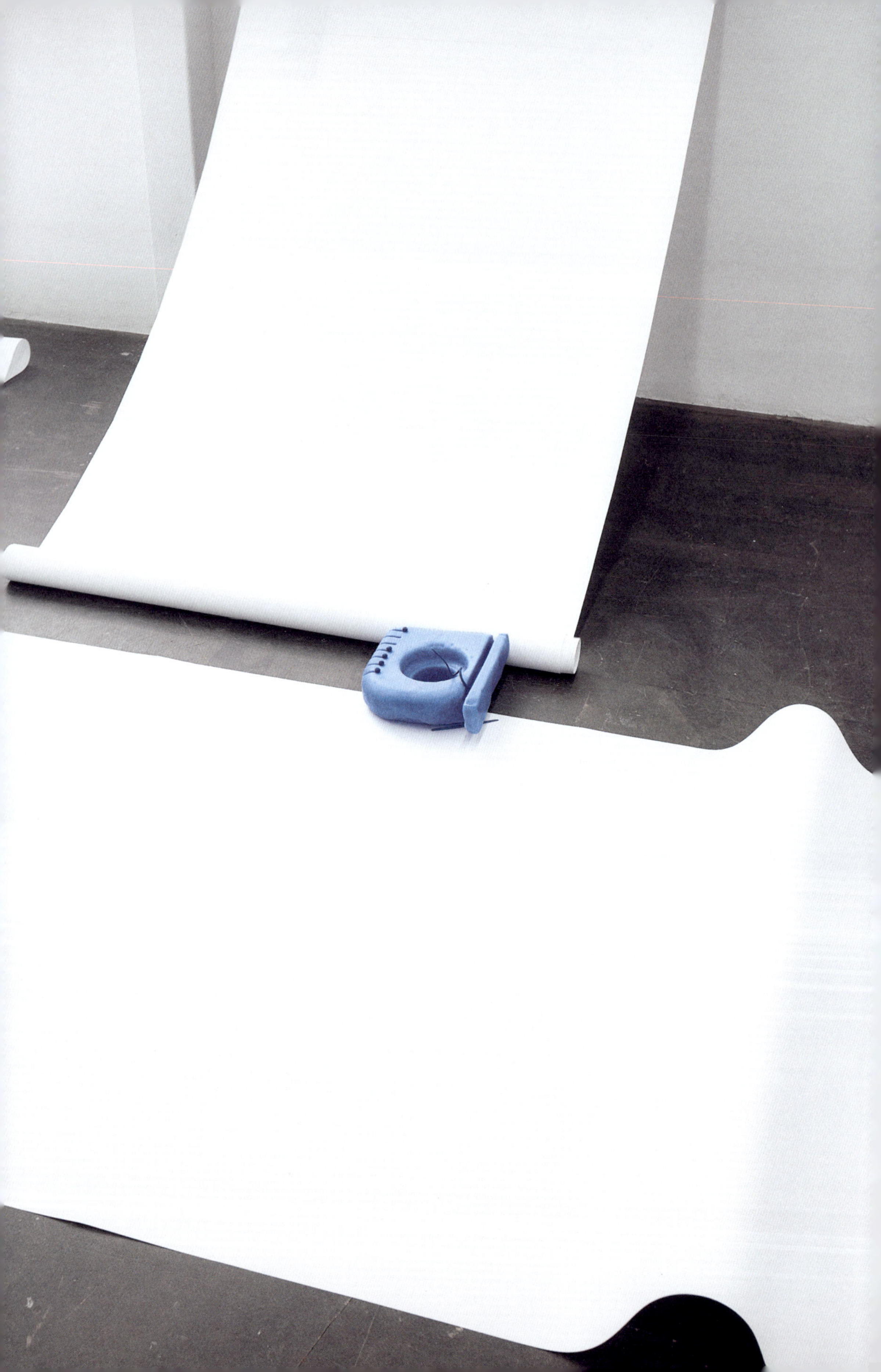

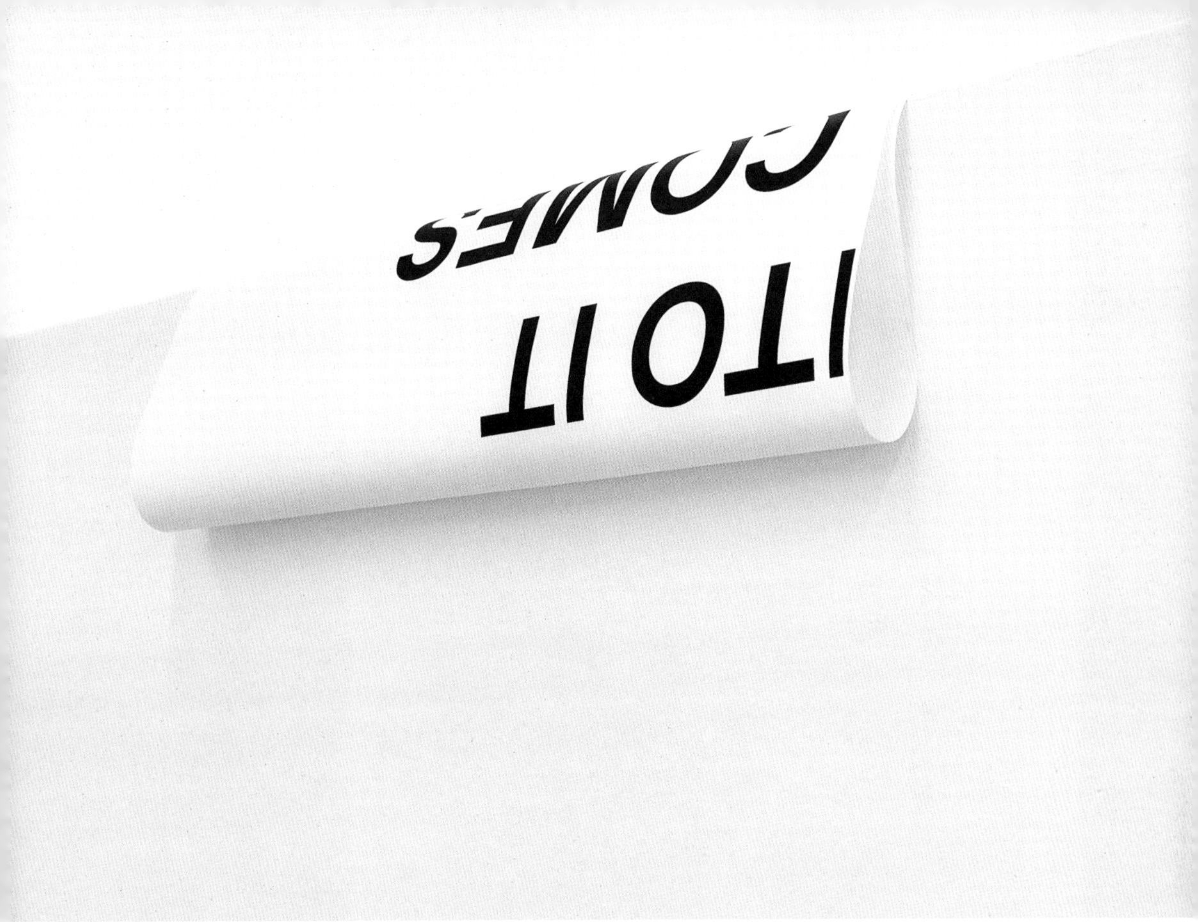

Paperweights/Layout
2022
Variable dimensions
Inkjet prints on plan paper,
cobalt mineral lick, porcelain

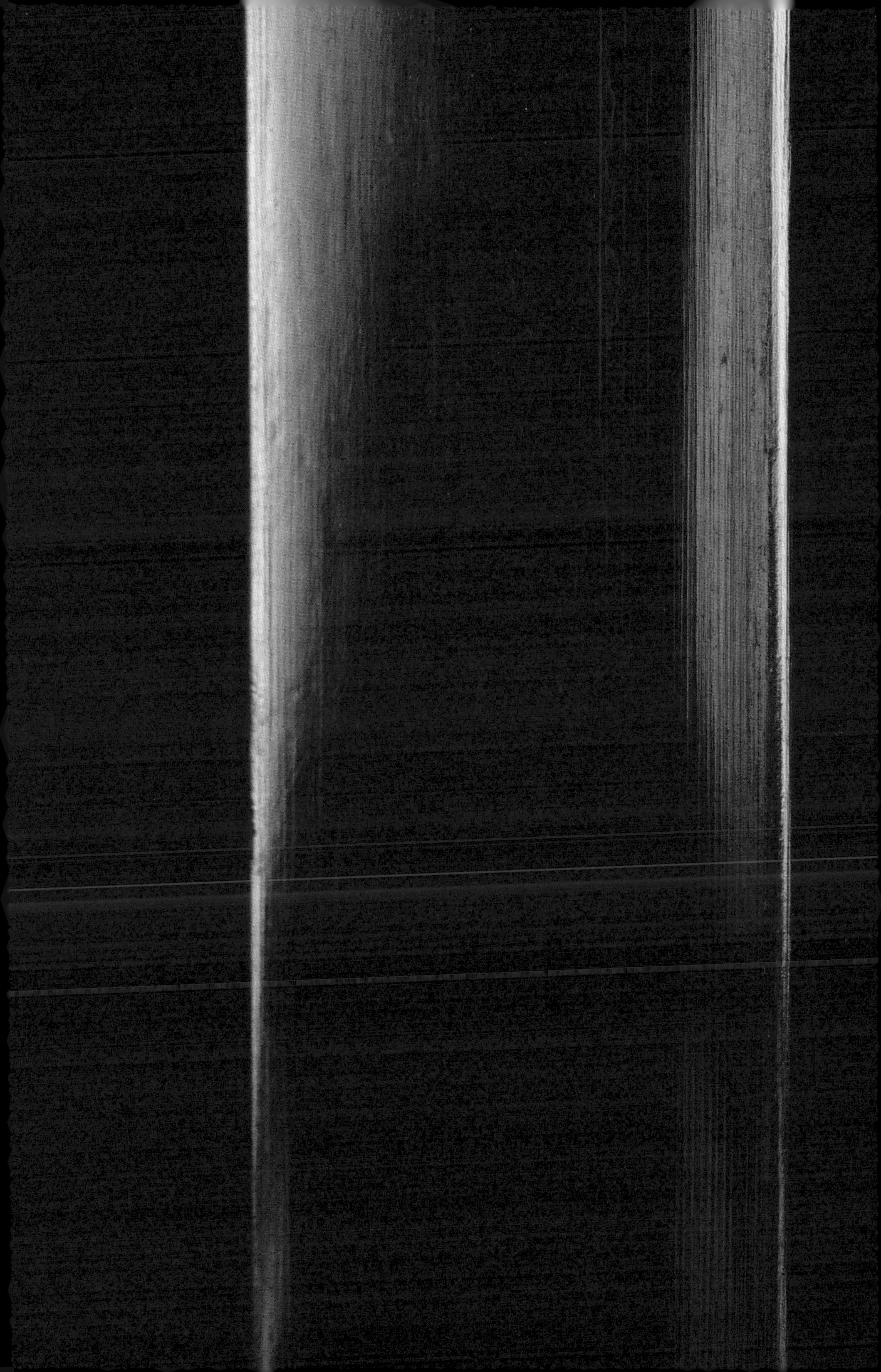

Des monceaux de coke crissant. Soupesez ses pépites, étonnez-vous de leur légèreté, sélectionnez vos morceaux favoris. Ceux-ci seront à déverser en cascade au centre du drap de lin blanc. Une fois cette tâche exécutée, qui le souhaite peut saisir les quatre coins de l'étoffe empesée pour les réunir en un nœud lâche ; on obtient de la sorte un baluchon sonnant et trébuchant.

Joli ! On jubile en douce un moment, le paquet à la main, puis on le balance au gré d'une marche hardie. Vite lassés, on le laisse à la fin choir au sol d'un geste négligent — blackboulage insensé, avoir su ...

(... que son cœur fuligineux
nous resterait en tête
des générations
durant.)

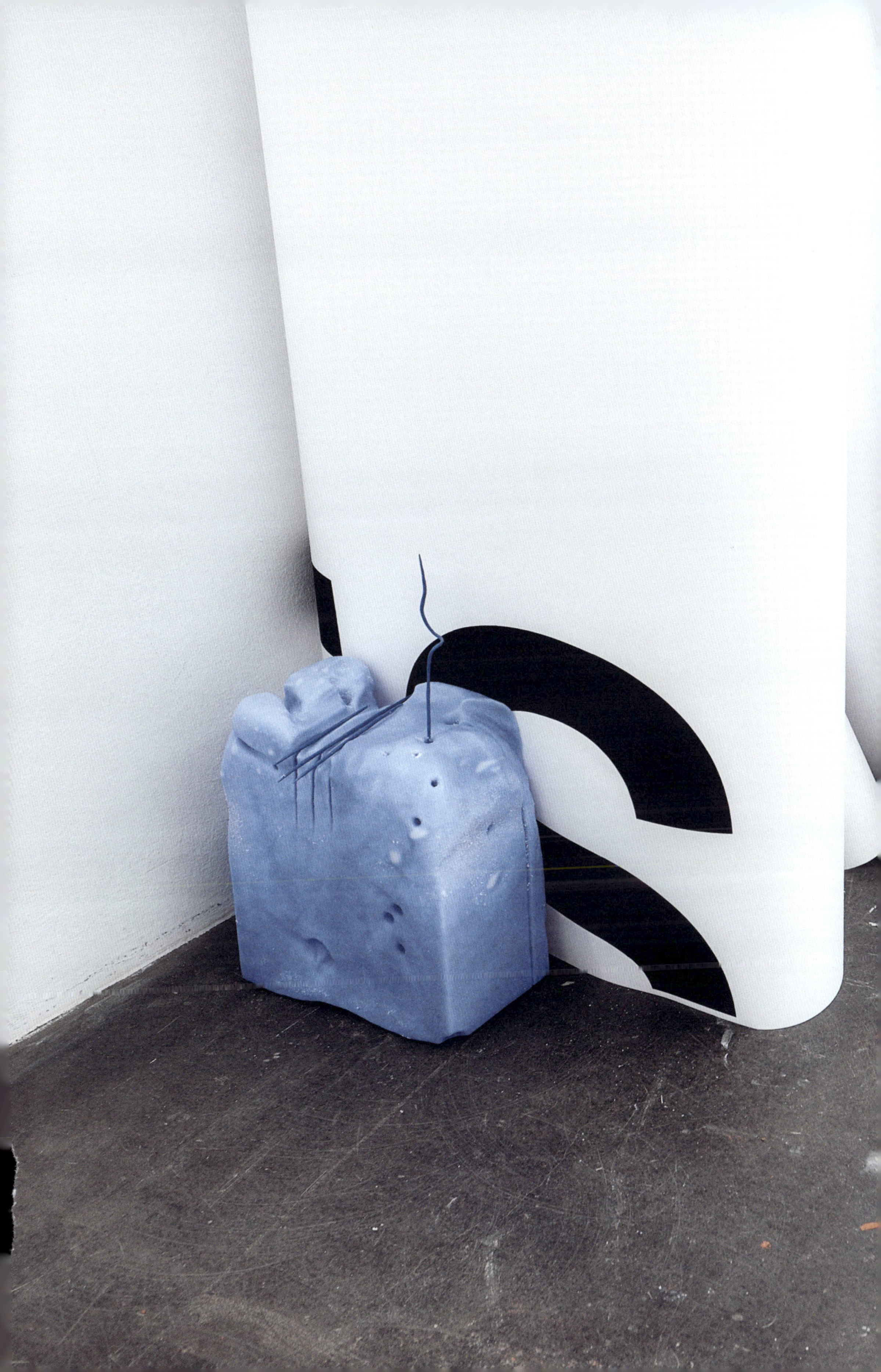

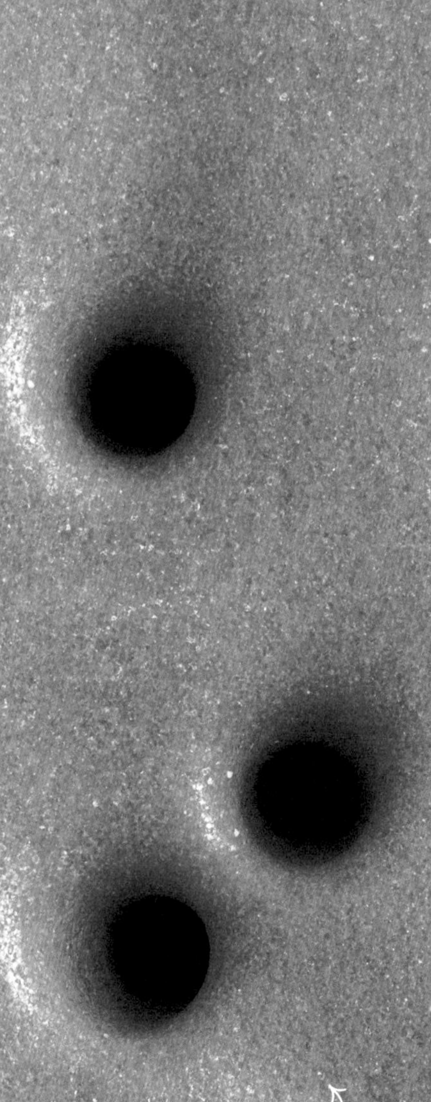

Safre
2022
30 × 15 × 20 cm
Cobalt mineral lick, porcelain

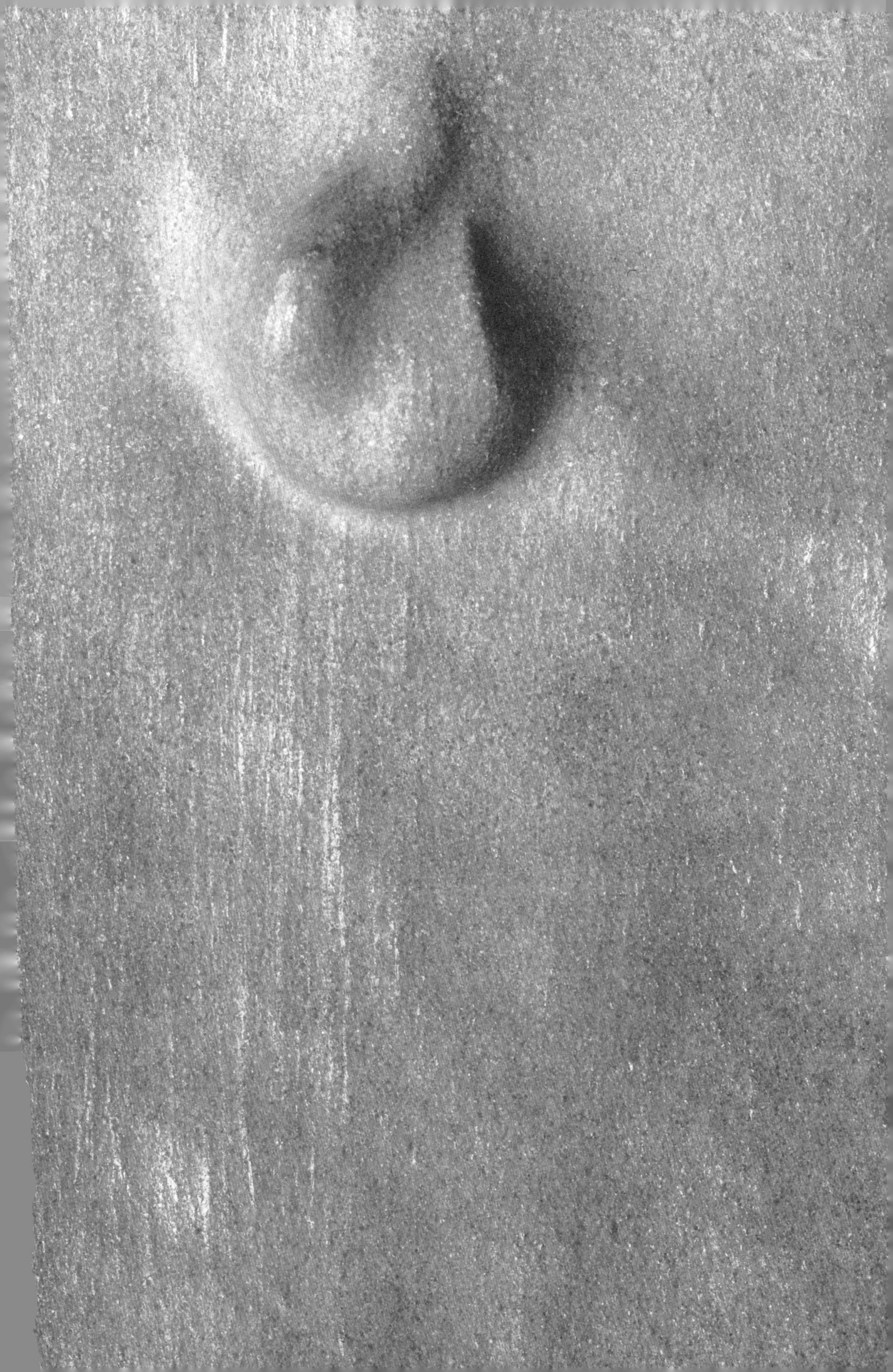

The first years were spent with feet and hands in the sand, as has been proudly recounted time and again. That was, as they say, hard work after which we would return home heads held high, loaded down with a wonderful harvest.

There is still talk of the fat years, followed by a long period under the relentless hegemony of clay, due to which the foundations of the new house became unstable, the crops suffered and buying a cultivator could no longer be postponed.

Something simply had to be done.

This second soil was subject to a huge mishmash, as the recipient of untold eggshells whose skins had to be removed before crushing them and of smelly elixirs produced by the good witch-in-charge, which were supposed to encourage the release of nitrogen and combat the Colorado beetle. The straw had to make a contribution and so did useful, left-over weeds. The devas of the plants were invoked with great urgency and the desperate need for crops finally gratified.

And today?

One single wormy tuber infested our garden with a fungus that felt so gloriously at home that the entire plot was immediately left to lie fallow. That was already three seasons ago. Since then, we've religiously checked on the soil, sniffed at it and examined it for signs of improvement.

All that remains of the former days of glory are memories of sumptuous tangles of earthworms, toads occasionally impaled on a pitchfork, lush borage ensconced in the earth, sage transformed into lace by the slugs and, last but not least, potato fruit that rolled out of our hands into the wheelbarrows. You get the picture.

Boots firmly anchored in a furrow, you dig the last crumbs of black dirt out from under your fingernails.